HISTORIC RAILWAY DISASTERS

*

Also in Arrow Books by O. S. Nock
The Railway Enthusiast's Encyclopedia

O. S. Nock

B.Sc., F.I.C.E., F.I.Mech.E.,
Past President: Institution of Railway Signal Engineers

Historic Railway Disasters

ARROW BOOKS

ARROW BOOKS LTD

178–202 Great Portland Street, London W1

AN IMPRINT OF THE HUTCHINSON GROUP

London Melbourne Sydney
Auckland Johannesburg Cape Town
and agencies throughout the world

*

First published by
Ian Allan Ltd 1966
Second edition 1969
This Arrow edition 1970

*Made and printed in Great Britain
by The Anchor Press Ltd,
Tiptree, Essex*

ISBN 0 09 003410 4

Contents

Illustrations

Shrewsbury, 1907. The high-speed wreck of the West of England night mail. The train should have taken the curved track on the right of the picture.

Shrewsbury. A close-up of the overturned 4–6–0 engine *Stephenson*.

Shrewsbury. Wholesale destruction of carriages, with a G.W.R. clerestory perched above the tender.

Aisgill, 1913. The aftermath of the fire: all that was left of one of the wrecked coaches.

Aisgill. Burnt-out wreckage by the side of the line.

Aisgill. The tragic aftermath. Scene of the disaster: the line cleared and the remains covered with tarpaulins.

Aisgill. The inquest at Kirkby Stephen station: relatives waiting to identify victims.

Between pages 128 and 129

Quintinshill, 1915. The fire almost under control: one of the rearmost coaches of the troop train, a Great Central 12-wheeler, little damaged in the collision, but gutted by fire.

Quintinshill. The mass military funeral of the dead soldiers, in Carlisle.

Abermule, 1921. The splintered wreckage of the up express.

Sevenoaks, 1927. The Pullman car *Carmen*, jammed across the piers of Shoreham Lane bridge.

Sevenoaks, 1927. The 2–6–4 tank engine *River Cray* after the derailment.

Sevenoaks. The work of salvage. The wrecked engine can be seen ahead against the cutting side. An almost demolished coach in the foreground, after lifting.

Charfield, 1928. An aerial view of the smouldering ruins, after the fire under the bridge. The express engine is just discernible amid the smoke on the left.

Charfield. The mangled wreckage of burnt-out carriages piled against the bridge. The chimney and smokebox of the G.W.R. goods engine can be seen through the arch.

Ashchurch, 1929. Rescue work by night after the collision in dense fog, between the Bristol-Nottingham night express and a goods train.

Reading, 1914. An interesting contemporary 'montage' of the accident, which the author saw shortly after it occurred.

Between pages 192 and 193

Shrivenham, 1936. The wrecked 'King' class engine No. 6007, and overturned carriage.

Shrivenham. The shattered remains of the leading coaches.

Southern Electric Collisions. Wreckage on the viaduct at Battersea after the collision on April 2, 1937. The collision in fog, near South Croydon Junction, October 1947.

Harrow, 1952. View from down electric line platform showing the wrecked engines of the down express.

Harrow. The fearful destruction of engines and stock: the locomotives of the down express smashed beyond repair, and the pile of wrecked carriages between the platforms.

Harrow. Clearing the line. Night work among the ruins.

Harrow. View looking north from the damaged footbridge.

Lewisham, 1957. Destruction of modern stock, under the heavy over-bridge that collapsed.

Preface

There is a peculiar fascination about the study of accidents of any kind. Few amongst us fail to derive some form of thrill from the situation of high drama which results in a catastrophe, even though many lives may be lost; but in the study of railway accidents there is much more than the human aspects of the problem, than the clash of personalities that often sows the seeds of trouble, or from failures of the human element, which lead to a breach of regulations, or failure in the equipment.

The fascination of the subject has in the past led to many books being written. But in adding yet another to this collection I have endeavoured to look at accidents more from the technical point of view, and from the viewpoint of the gradual evolution of regulations for the safe operation of railway traffic. Rather more than 20 years ago, that great Editor, Loughnan Pendred, for 40 years Editor-in-Chief of 'The Engineer', commissioned a series of articles in that journal dealing with historic accidents of all kinds, and in that series I was privileged to contribute three on the subject of railway accidents. These were chosen not so much from the magnitude of the catastrophes themselves as to illustrate the principles involved, and the far-reaching nature of the outcome; consequently the relatively minor accidents on the Midland Railway at Hawes Junction on Christmas Eve 1910, and the rear-end collision between two sleeping car trains not many miles away at Aisgill in September 1913, were chosen in preference to the terrible double collision at Quintinshill on Whitsun Saturday 1915.

In the present book I have expanded upon the theme underlying the choice of those articles in 'The Engineer', and with the ready agreement of the present Editor, Mr.

Benjamin Pendred, my accounts of the collision at Abbots Ripton, of the runaway train disaster at Armagh, and those two Midland collisions are reprinted with little change from the original script. I have thus also paid particular attention to the extraordinary series of incidents, ranging from minor mishaps to serious disasters, which took place at the time the great controversy over brake equipment was raging in this country. In retrospect it is astonishing to reflect upon the attitude displayed by the railway management towards such a matter as brake power. In later years, of course, the same kind of controversy centred upon the introduction of various forms of automatic train control, and again one can reflect, a little sadly perhaps, upon the reluctance of railway managements to adopt measures now considered essential to the safe working of trains.

Working on this same basis I have added a great deal more, and the story is now carried through the evolution of block working, from time-interval to space-interval, and from 'open' to 'closed' block; through the 'Battle of the Brakes'; through the upsurge in high speed running. Then having established the fundamental safety systems the pressure of increasing traffic led to the need for additional measures, such as track circuiting, starting signal control, and finally automatic train control. Concurrently, too, can be seen the gradual improvement in permanent way and rolling stock design. Nowadays a derailment, even at relatively high speed, does not involve the wholesale smashing up of carriages, or as one newspaper described the effects of the Salisbury accident of 1906—'A boat train reduced to matchwood'.

The book could almost be described as the result of a lifetime study of railway working. Anyone who has been pro-professionally engaged in signalling for more than 40 years cannot fail to become deeply aware of the way in which accidents can happen. But of course my own interest in railways has extended far beyond my professional work, and it began long before I joined the engineering staff of the Westinghouse Brake and Signal Company. Long before my public school days I was gripped and held in awed fascination by the reports of accidents as they used to appear in the newspapers of 50 and 55 years ago; and when we were on holiday at Weymouth in the autumn of 1913, I shall never forget news coming through of the collision and fire at Aisgill. The year 1913 was full of disaster, and I must admit that the accounts of the accident and of the scene during the height of the fire, made a deeper impression on me than the sinking of the *Titanic*.

In more recent years, when professional concern was added to my general interest in railway operation, association and friendship with many engineers has fostered and quickened my impression of the problems that have sometimes led to accidents. Among these friends I should like to mention Major L. H. Peter, my first chief in Westinghouse and a lifelong advocate of continuous automatic train control; the late T. S. Lascelles, engineer, and later Managing Director of the W. R. Sykes Interlocking Signal Co. Ltd.; Dr. T. W. Chalmers, of 'The Engineer', and the late Norman Doran Macdonald, Scots Advocate, and the most fiery and outspoken critic of railways in the days when the 'Battle of the Brakes' was at its height.

I am also indebted to Col. D. McMullen, C.B.E., Chief Inspecting Officer of Railways, Minister of Transport, for some very interesting information about the Railway Inspectorate and for his help in obtaining portraits of some of the most distinguished Inspecting Officers.

Lastly I am much indebted, as always, to Olivia my wife. In this book her help has gone much further than the actual typing of the manuscript. In several cases where the details were many and complicated her interest and study of the affair has led to revisions of the draft and given, I hope, a greater lucidity to circumstances that could not, in any event, be regarded as anything but a very tangled skein.

O. S. Nock
February, 1966

High Bannerdown,
Batheaston, Bath

Preface to the Second Edition

Since the first edition of this book was published three accidents having a deep significance have occurred on British Railways. Two of them are closely linked, in cause and effect with the general theme of this book, namely the high speed derailment at Didcot on September 27, 1967 and the Hither Green disaster in November 1967 caused by a broken rail. The third, the terrible collision at Hixon level crossing in January 1968 was something entirely new. Each of these accidents has so many features of interest and importance that I have added separate chapters on each.

So far as earlier chapters are concerned, as always the writing of a book brings forth new information, and I have been able to add some interesting items to my accounts of Staplehurst and Quintinshill.

As with the first edition I have had some valuable help from Colonel McMullen, until the end of 1968 Chief Inspecting Officer of Railways, and from his successor Colonel J. H. R. Robertson, to both of whom I tender my best thanks.

O. S. Nock
February, 1969

High Bannerdown,
Bath Somerset

1

The Elements of Disaster

In the earliest days of steam railways the over-riding consideration was to get the locomotive to work. On such a line as the Stockton and Darlington speed was of very little consequence at first, and the advantage of using steam at all was that it enabled much heavier loads to be worked. To make sure that no excessive speeds were run at the opening of the line the steam-hauled train was preceded by a man on horseback carrying a red flag. And that horse was not even trotting; it was walking! When the question came of extending railways there was serious controversy about the method of haulage to be used—whether it was to be cables, horses, or steam locomotives. At first speed was a minor consideration with the majority of people concerned with the promoting of railways.

But not many years passed before the question of speed began to assume a greater prominence, and the Rainhill competition of 1829, for the prize offered by the Directors of the Liverpool and Manchester Railway, set down certain definite requirements for both weight-haulage and speed. It is however highly significant that no specification whatever was laid down for the distance in which a locomotive and its train was to be stopped. The main thing was to move. How to stop the train was not considered. But the Liverpool and Manchester Railway had not progressed beyond the stage of the grand ceremonial opening before the deficiency in brake power of those pioneer locomotives had been tragically demonstrated when the ill-fated Mr. Huskisson stepped from his carriage to walk across the line to greet the Duke of

Wellington. Along an adjoining track the ever-famous *Rocket*, driven on that occasion by Joseph Locke, was hauling another train; and although Locke saw what was happening he could not stop. He ran Mr. Huskisson down and the unfortunate man died later in the day.

Although there had been this warning of the perils of inadequate brake power so early in the history of railways that warning was largely ignored, and while engineers vied with one another to increase the tractive capacity and the speed of locomotives, no one in those early days made any attempt to develop the science of braking. It seems incredible today that railways had reached mid-Victorian times, and yet the locomotives themselves had no brakes at all. The only means of stopping in most cases was a set of hand brakes on the tender wheels working through rather cumbersome wooden brake blocks. Here was a major element of disaster which recurred again and again during nineteenth century railway history in Great Britain.

Coupled with this element of disaster was undoubtedly the capacity for increased speed that locomotives came to possess very early in railway history. By the middle of the 1840's trains were travelling at 60 m.p.h., and there is no doubt that while the great majority of drivers took their responsibilities very seriously, there were others with a dare-devil spirit in their make-up who were always prepared to take risks. There was a general opinion among travellers that risks were taken when drivers were recovering lost time. Added to this was the fact that in early days there were no hard and fast rules for regulating the turns of duty of enginemen, and what was more important, the duration of time through which they worked between proper rest periods. There were many drivers and firemen who were prepared to work far longer hours than were desirable, to earn extra pay, with the result that occasions occurred when drivers and firemen became drowsy on the footplate and in that state they were naturally not as alert as they should have been, particularly during the night hours.

Today it is perhaps difficult to imagine how *dark* the

English countryside was at night in the early and mid-Victorian eras. The towns and villages themselves were much smaller than now; lighting in houses and streets was dim, and lights along the railway were virtually non-existent. One recalls the famous riposte of Brunel when he was criticised over the darkness of the interior of Box Tunnel. His comment was: 'The tunnel is no darker than the rest of the line is at night, but it is exposed to fewer casualties.' That remark has often been passed off rather lightly, as a typical piece of Brunel sarcasm, something like his comments upon the coffee in the Refreshment Rooms at Swindon. But on reflection, one feels that it was a very straightforward and quite serious remark. Out in the country in the dead of night it would have been very easy for a driver and fireman working excessive hours to fall asleep at their post.

Associated with the lamentable lack of brake power on both locomotives and carriages were the very primitive arrangements for signalling. Almost complete reliance was placed upon the diligence of individual men along the line rather than the establishment of a system which was inherently safe. This state of affairs undoubtedly arose from the fact that many of the early railways superintendents were ex-military men. At that time, before industrialisation of the country had made any appreciable headway, and factories employing large numbers of people were the enterprise of individuals rather than large corporations, the simplest way to organise a disciplined labour force such as was needed to operate the new railways was to employ the only men with experience of personnel-discipline on a large scale, namely high-ranking army officers. Such men were experienced in establishing chains of command, and the setting up of posts and outposts at which all the men concerned were required to act in a disciplined manner according to a clear cut set of rules.

Men who were originally called 'Policemen' were stationed at intervals along the line, and conveyed the 'stop', 'caution' and 'go' signals to engine drivers by means of hand signals. These men were disciplined like soldiers, and were

15

required to stand with military precision in certain positions according to the message they had to convey to the driver. One could imagine that the railway 'Policemen' in charge of a signal post would be considered closely akin to a soldier guarding some lonely outpost in a campaign. And it was an easy step from the purely human signal to provide these men with means of signalling over a greater range of sighting, either by using a primitive form of semaphore or one of the special forms of signal such as the Great Western disc and crossbar. The message to be conveyed to the driver was decided entirely upon a time basis. If the previous train had passed a certain time previously, the policeman had to give the 'caution' signal, and after a longer time had elapsed he was authorised to give the 'all clear'. It did not matter whether the train that had gone was a fast one or a slow one, or whether a slow train was following a fast one, or the other way round. The headway between successive trains was regulated entirely on the 'time' basis. On the Great Western, the 'caution' signal was given after the previous train had been gone 10 minutes, and a further 7 minutes had to elapse before the driver was given authority to proceed at full speed.

The weakness in this system was, of course, that it was a negative rather than a positive form of indication. One could imagine a case where a train had disappeared from the policeman's sight round a curve in hilly country, and then come to a stand through some defect of its engine. It would be then standing within a relatively short distance of the policeman. Yet with the systems of signalling then in vogue, the man could, after a period of 15 or 17 minutes, give the 'all clear' to the driver while there was an obstruction a very short distance ahead. Nevertheless the time interval method of working prevailed on many railways for a very long time—long after the policemen had been superseded by semaphore arms worked from signal boxes. Even when the electric telegraph had been introduced to provide continuous communication along the line, the so-called 'Open Block' or 'time interval block' was still used.

16

With the introduction of semaphore signals to replace the hand signals of the 'policeman' the negative character of the 'all-right' indication was for some time perpetuated. Following the old hand signals the semaphores were arranged to show three indications: 'stop', 'caution' and 'all-right'. The corresponding arm positions were, horizontal, inclined down, and the arm hanging vertically down. As these early semaphores worked in a slot in the post the arm became completely invisible in the 'all-right' position. The danger that precisely the same indication could have been given if the operating mechanism had broken, or the arm had broken off altogether, was overlooked. Similarly, there was the danger of the night indications, of which white signified 'all-right'. One would have thought it would have been easy enough for some light extraneous to the railway to be mistaken for the 'all-right'. But actually there were so few lights to be seen at night that no difficulty appears to have been experienced with what would now be regarded as a very dangerous practice.

The lack of communication was revealed in many other ways. With semaphore signals that were lowered after 10 minutes, or whatever other interval was decided upon, men working on the line had no advance warning of the approach of trains. All that a signal in the 'clear' position could mean to them was that no train had passed in the last ten minutes. It did not signify that the approach of another train was imminent. One reads stories of pilot engines being sent out into the blue, as it were, to look for a train that was missing. It could have left a certain station, been cleared by the 'time interval' signal, and nothing more heard of it. Obviously its engine, or some other part of the equipment, had got into trouble down the line, and when it became so grossly overdue as to cause alarm there was nothing for it in those days but to send out a search party! Some of these searches were carried out in a highly dangerous manner, as when an engine was sent out to look for a missing train and proceeded to meet it on the same line on which the missing train was supposed to be travelling!

In the early days of railways there must have been many hair-breadth escapes from disaster through the lack of communication, and the lack of a proper system of regulating the traffic. Sometimes however several factors combined to turn the scale, and change a hair-breadth escape into a catastrophe. This was the case in June 9, 1865 on the South Eastern Railway, when the 'Tidal' boat train from Folkestone was wrecked in a most dramatic manner. At that time the harbour at Folkestone used by the cross-Channel Packet Steamers was a very primitive one, in which the ships could berth only at certain states of the tide. Consequently the running times of the boat trains in connection with these steamer services varied every day. By one of those curiosities of railway tradition also, the name 'Tidal' persisted on the South Eastern, and later on the South Eastern and Chatham Railway almost to the end of steam haulage. Boat trains that ran to and from Folkestone were always known as the 'Tidals', and this name was sufficiently official for it to be used on the train describers installed on the South Eastern Railway at the turn of the century.

Timetables were prepared showing the running of the Tidal boat train from Folkestone for every day in the month, and these were issued to stations, signal boxes, and other people concerned with the running of the trains so that they knew when the train was expected; and on this particular day one person vitally concerned was the foreman of a gang of platelayers who were working on the line near Staplehurst.

The regulations concerning repairs to the line were scanty to say the least of it. In more recent times, before the civil engineer could do anything in the way of repair other than the most simple routine adjustments, agreement has to be obtained with the operating authorities, and the exact times of the repair operation have to be fixed beforehand. Then notices are required to be issued to everyone concerned giving ample warning of speed restrictions, or any other incidentals concerning the work. Copies of these notices are required to be issued to drivers, and every possible precaution is now taken to ensure that repair work of any kind does not catch anyone unawares. What happened near Staplehurst on that day in June 1865 no doubt led to the imposition of much stricter regulations for track repair work. Near Staplehurst the line crosses a small stream called the Beult on a bridge so low that a traveller of today would hardly realise there was a bridge at all. But in June 1865 this bridge was the precise site of a track repair which involved renewing some of the bridge timbers. With present-day regulations and present-day traffic such a job as resleepering is done only on Sundays. In this early case it involved taking out the rails, and replacing the longitudinal timber baulks by new ones. There were 32 of these baulks to be replaced, and the bridge foreman and his leading carpenter had systematically replaced one baulk after another between the passage of trains.

In this earlier stage of railway development the permanent way foreman was permitted, apparently, to decide for himself when to carry out the job, and on the fatal day only one of the baulks remained to be replaced. The whole operation had so far proceeded very smoothly. No mention of it had been made in any working notices, and not the slightest delay to traffic had occurred. That it was a very risky thing to do was not fully appreciated. But worse than this, familiarity with the job led to some slackness in carrying out such safety regulations as were required.

Of course, as men who were working on the line every day of their lives, the foreman and his gang knew all about the Tidal boat train and its variation in times from day to day; but on the very last day, when one more baulk replaced would have seen the job completed, the foreman unfortunately looked up the wrong date. There was nothing in the system of communication then available that could warn him of the approach of a train, and so after the previous train had gone according to schedule, and the signals he could see from the bridge had been replaced to the 'clear' position, under the usual 'open block' then operating, he and his men got to work, removed the rails, and set about

19

replacing the timbers beneath. Unfortunately in addition to his initial mistake of reading the wrong day, and so getting a completely wrong idea of when the Tidal boat train would be expected, he posted his flagman much nearer to the bridge than the regulations required.

Very soon after they had commenced work and the rails were removed, up came the Tidal boat train at full speed. The driver got the warning from the look-out man, but it was not enough. The man was much too close to the bridge and with the very ineffective brakes then in use there was not a hope of the train being able to stop. The train came to the gap in the rails, crashed down on to the iron girders of the bridge and ploughed its way along. By the greatest of good fortune the engine and the first two carriages got across to the far side and came to rest on the ballast on the firm embankment with one of the carriages still perched in a most precarious position on the end of the bridge. But the couplings broke between the second and third carriages. The impact fractured the cast iron bridge girder; the third carriage swerved to the left, and once it was detached from the portion of the train still coupled to the engine it was completely devoid of brakes. Everything happened so suddenly that the guard at the rear end had no prior warning and had no time to get any sort of brake force on to the rear end of the train, and five coaches of the detached train went over the bridge and crashed into the swampy fields and the river Beult itself.

The carriages were of flimsy wooden construction; all were four-wheelers, and with the force of the fall they shattered themselves to pieces in the field and in the river itself. In this shocking accident 10 persons were killed and 49 injured. The fact that the accident happened to an important and well-known express passenger train emphasised the sense of shock which news of the affair created generally; but it so happened that Charles Dickens was a passenger, and naturally he wrote a vivid account of his experience.

'I was in the only carriage that did not go over into the stream. It was caught upon the turn by some of the ruins of the bridge and hung suspended and balanced in an impossible manner. Two ladies were my fellow passengers . . . suddenly we were off the rail and beating the ground as the car of a half-emptied balloon might . . . We were then all tilted down together in a corner of the carriage (which was locked) and stopped . . . I got out through the window without the least notion what had happened . . . with great caution and stood upon the step . . . looking down I saw the bridge gone and nothing below me but the line of rail . . . there was an open swampy field 15 feet below them and nothing else . . . I saw all the rest of the train except the two baggage vans, down in the stream . . . No imagination can conceive the ruin of the carriages.'

Dramatic as were the circumstances of this accident, the lack of railway operating principles which the accident revealed was even more significant. The fact that a permanent way man could decide entirely on his own when he was going to start taking rails out of a main line on a week-day leaves one in amazement today. No less astonishing to us today is the fact that the regulations then prevailing could permit an express train to come upon such an obstruction as a piece of the line removed without the driver being forewarned that any repair operations were in hand. If the flag man had been posted at the correct distance there is every possibility that the train would have been safely stopped. This accident emphasises the danger that can be inherent in working methods that are just tolerable when everybody works strictly to the rules, but which can be dangerous, and indeed catastrophic, if there is any slight deviation. Several more serious accidents were however to be suffered in this country before the danger of the open block and of the time interval system of signalling were eventually condemned.

Since the publication of the first edition of the book I have received an interesting letter from Mrs. Ethel P. Mann, now aged 86, of Sevenoaks, in which she writes that she was 'more or less brought up on stories about that Staplehurst accident'. She enclosed an extract from a letter written by

21

her great grandfather William Jull, on August 17, 1865, to his son-in-law then recently emigrated to Australia:

'I post you a paper by this mail (which should have been sent before) giving you an account of the sad railway accident on the line on June 9, when 10 persons were killed and many wounded and disabled. The scene of the accident you will well remember as it was on the farm which your father occupied. It was indeed a fearful affair. I was on the spot soon after the crash, and saw six bodies taken out dead and others severely mangled. The sufferers have been lying at different houses in this village; they were chiefly persons in good circumstances returning in the boat train from the Continent and every care was taken of them. The last sufferer Major (. . . .) has only just left us.'

2

Four Mid-Victorian Tragedies

While one can be surprised at the primitive nature of the regulations applied to railway working in the early days, by and large those concerned with running the trains were imbued with a high sense of responsibility, and the failures that in certain cases led to disaster were due as much to lack of experience as to where failure might occur as to the failure itself. One can almost hear the same comment being made time after time: 'I could not imagine *that* could ever happen.' Yet bitter experience showed that it could, and gradually the regulations and railway engineering practice were elaborated to provide many additional safeguards.

From a very early stage in railway history, nevertheless, tunnels were looked upon with a certain amount of dread by the travelling public, however much certain prominent railwaymen might make light of their incidence. In the early days of the Great Western Railway urgent representations were made for Box Tunnel to be lighted and Brunel's caustic comment on this request has already been mentioned in the previous chapter. All the same it was to provide additional safety in working through tunnels that the first divergence from the original methods of train regulation was devised. The 'time-interval' system was adequate enough for the relatively slow moving traffic of early days, out in the open, where a driver had some chance of seeing an obstruction ahead. But inside a tunnel, which might at any time be filled with smoke from other trains, it was another matter; and it was to provide additional safeguards that the first steps were taken, as early as 1841, towards the great principle of the space-interval block system, in which a second train was not allowed to proceed until the previous one had reached a certain fixed point ahead—rather than had passed the regulating point a certain fixed time previously.

The electric telegraph was used for communicating between the two ends of a block section, and in that momentous year of 1841 space-interval block working was introduced through two long tunnels. The first installation was at Clay Cross on the North Midland Railway, and the second through Clayton Tunnel, by which the Brighton railway passed under the South Downs. For 20 years the installation protected train working on these two lines, on both of which traffic developed enormously; but then, on a Sunday morning in August 1861, the very primitive safeguards provided by this early apparatus broke down under the strain of heavy traffic, and a disaster occurred in the middle of the Clayton Tunnel. Over the rest of the Brighton line the time-interval system was in operation and the regulations allowed the dispatch of trains at five-minute intervals.

On this particular Sunday morning three trains were involved, advertised to leave Brighton at 8.5, 8.15, and 8.30 a.m. But with the working arrangements prevailing, and having regard to the physical coditions on the line, the elements of disaster were already present before any of those trains reached Clayton Tunnel. From Brighton yard to the mouth of the tunnel the gradient is continuously at 1 in 264: not a heavy gradient in itself, but trying enough to a heavily-loaded engine starting cold. Even in the last days of steam, on the Brighton line, with such competent engines as the 'King Arthur' class 4-6-0's, the speed of up expresses had rarely reached as much as 45 m.p.h. by the time Clayton Tunnel was reached. A 100 years ago, with the little single-wheelers of John Chester Craven the acceleration would have been much slower, and with a five-minute interval permitted successive trains could well have been less than two miles apart. Added to that, the intervening distance of $4\frac{1}{2}$ miles, from Clayton Tunnel south end to the picturesquely named 'Lovers Walk Junction', included the obstruction of

Patcham Tunnel. Although this is only 700 yards long visibility was quite often gravely impaired by smoke.

The block signalling arrangements at Clayton Tunnel were primitive in the extreme. There was a small cabin at each end, each equipped with a single needle telegraph instrument for each line. On the approach sides of the tunnel there were warning signals located about 350 yards in rear of the portal and worked by a hand wheel in the respective cabin. The idea was that a train could be warned of the state of the line through the tunnel; but if the previous train had not cleared the only means of telling a driver to stop was by the signalman displaying a red flag from his cabin, or a red lamp after dark. The 'distant' or warning signal was a crude affair, which was automatically returned to danger by a treadle when the train passed. There was a means of indicating to the signalman that the semaphore had worked properly, or otherwise. If it did not, an alarm bell was rung in the cabin.

The three trains concerned were an excursion from Portsmouth to London, an excursion from Brighton, and the regular 8.30 a.m. express, and on this particular morning all three were running late. The stationmaster at Brighton afterwards alleged that they had been dispatched at the minimum intervals stipulated in the regulations; but actually the departure times from Brighton were 8.28, 8.31, and 8.35 a.m. with only *three minutes* between the first and second train. The respective drivers would have been aware of the very close interval between them, and in climbing the long adverse gradient from Lovers Walk Junction that interval could well have become less by the time they reached the south end of Clayton Tunnel. Even so, with the primitive form of block working in force through the tunnel itself the trains should have been protected by the important safety feature of the space-interval block. The tunnel is $1\frac{1}{2}$ miles long, and if the trains already running at such close intervals had closed in on one another the signalling arrangements through the tunnel itself should have spaced them out safely.

Unfortunately two other factors supervened to increase the risk of a disaster.

The signalman at Clayton Tunnel south cabin, incredible though it may seem, was working a continuous 24-hour turn of duty. His normal turn of 18 hours was long enough in all conscience; but there was an arrangement by which he worked a still longer turn in order to get one clear day off during the week. He was thus very tired, and although he was clearly a man with a high sense of responsibility his reactions to unusual circumstances were not as quick as could be desired. And the first unfortunate event was that when the Portsmouth excursion passed the warning signal the automatic arrangement for restoring that signal to danger did not work. It is thought that the alarm bell rang to warn the signalman of the failure; but in half-a-minute the train passed his cabin, and he duly sent the 'Train in tunnel' signal on the telegraph to his colleague at the north end. It was only then that this tired man realised the danger of the situation. It was made worse by the second train having gained somewhat on the first during the climbing of the gradient from Lovers Walk, and before the unfortunate signalman could do anything the Brighton excursion was approaching, having passed the defective signal, still showing a false clear aspect.

He had time to do no more than dash to the outside of his cabin and show the red flag as the engine of the second train passed and entered the tunnel. The situation was now doubly dangerous. No signal had come from the north end to indicate the first train was clear, and for the second time he sent the signal 'Train in tunnel' to the other man. He had no means of holding any conversation with the man in the north cabin, and telling him what had happened. All he could do was to signal on the telegraph, 'Is tunnel clear?' The man at the north end was puzzled, having twice received the telegraphic code 'Train in tunnel', and then the query 'Is tunnel clear'. At that moment however the Portsmouth train emerged, and the north end man, still concerned only with one train, signalled back 'Tunnel clear'. Far from it! The circumstances were now infinitely worse than anyone could then have imagined, and disaster was inevitable.

When the second train entered the tunnel its engine was steaming hard, but the driver had, for a fraction of a second, seen the red flag unfurled by the signalman at the south cabin, and belated though it was it was enough to signify danger ahead. Actually that belated signal was the crowning misfortune of the whole affair, for if the driver had not seen it and continued at full speed he would probably have got through the tunnel safely, even though closing in further on the Portsmouth excursion. As it was he shut off steam, while his fireman screwed down the handbrakes. With the primitive methods of braking at his disposal, although his speed was not much above 30 m.p.h. the train travelled about half a mile into the tunnel before he could stop. It was while the second train was stopping in the tunnel, and its driver was wondering what was the meaning of that flicker of red he had seen, that the unfortunate and tired signalman in the south cabin took the final step to ensure an absolutely certain catastrophe.

When he received the signal 'Tunnel clear' from the north end he assumed that *both* trains had safely emerged, though a second's reflection would have told him that the Brighton excursion could not possibly have got through in so short a time. In his relief at getting the signal 'Tunnel clear' he put away his red flag, and waved a confident 'White' for 'All clear' to the driver of the third train as it came steaming past his cabin. In the meantime, in the darkness of the tunnel, the driver of the second train had decided *to set back* to the tunnel entrance to find out the reason for that glimpse of a red flag. The appalling result can be better imagined than described! The second train was not only blocking the line, but was being propelled backwards, and in the frightful collision that followed in the darkness of the tunnel 21 passengers were killed and 176 seriously injured.

At the time of this terrible accident the Board of Trade Inspectorate was constantly urging upon the railway companies the need to abandon the time-interval system of working, and to use a space-interval block. The majority of the railway managements then argued that space-interval working was impracticable and would slow up the traffic to such an extent as to cause extreme congestion on the lines. Others argued that the installation of more signals would tend to induce slackness among drivers, and lessen the degree of alertness that was needed in running fast trains. Clayton Tunnel was seized upon as a double argument against the principles the Board of Trade was urging, because in the first place the signal that was provided did not work, and secondly the space-interval block through the tunnel failed to protect the second train. Much, unfortunately, was yet to happen before the inherent soundness of the space-interval block was generally acknowledged.

*   *   *   *   *

The story now moves forward to the year 1867, and the scene to the Chester and Holyhead main line of the London and North Western Railway. Events centred round the running of the down day Irish Mail, which was due to leave Chester at 11.43 a.m. and run non-stop to Holyhead. Rules were laid down for the handling of local movements to ensure these were not protracted unduly before express passenger trains were due; but the signalling arrangements provided nothing in the way of safeguards if some untoward event took place, and the line happened to be blocked. On this particular day, August 20th, 1867, a heavy pick-up goods was running ahead of the Irish Mail, and it left Abergele at 12.15 p.m., 19 minutes before the mail was due to pass. The regulations required that slow trains should be shunted at least 10 minutes before an express was due, and to allow the train to go forward to Llandulas was cutting things fine, particularly as the intervening section involved the climbing of a bank inclined at 1 in 100–147 on which the speed of a 43-wagon goods train would be necessarily slow.

When the train arrived at Llandulas it was found that some wagons were already in the sidings, and the long train could not be shunted in its entirety. It was necessary to

28

divide it, and put some wagons in one siding and some in another. This itself was a cumbersome job, particularly as time was getting short before the mail was due to pass. As things were the circumstances were becoming definitely dangerous. Although there were signals at Llandulas the arrangements then in force did not provide for the stopping of the mail at Abergele if the line was occupied by some wagons of a goods train. Reliance was placed entirely upon the local signals; but in the event, the stationmaster at Llandulas—incredible to relate—decided to do some shunting on the main line. Having divided the goods, and got part of it stowed away in one of the sidings, he proceeded to shunt three timber wagons on to the remnant of the train that was still standing on the main line.

That remnant consisted of six wagons and the brake van. They were standing on a gradient of 1 in 147 descending towards Abergele. The wagon brakes were not pinned down, but the van brake was screwed hard on. The stationmaster's idea was to shunt the three timber wagons on to the seven vehicles left on the main line, couple them up, and then stow the 19 into another siding clear of the track of the Irish Mail. As the goods train only arrived at Llandulas at 12.24 and the Mail was due at 12.39 the shunting operations would have to be pretty snappy. And snappy they were—far too much so! The three timber wagons were fly-shunted towards the seven standing vehicles on the main line at a speed that was definitely excessive. The brakesman racing beside them failed to get to a brake lever and pin it down, with the result that the three heavily loaded wagons hit the standing ones with some force. It can only be inferred that this very rough shunt, and the suddenness of the impact, broke the cast iron pinions through which the van brakes were applied, because the seven vehicles started off down the 1 in 147 incline and rapidly increased speed.

At this precise moment the Irish Mail was running through Abergele. Although the overall speed demanded by the Post Office contract frequently caused some embarrassment to the locomotive department of the London and

North Western Railway the actual speeds run were not very high, even by the standard of the period, and on this particular day it was estimated that the 'Lady of the Lake' class 2-2-2 No. 291 *Prince of Wales* was not running at much more than 40 m.p.h. with its load of 13 coaches. There were, of course, no such things as continuous brakes on the train, and so, even at this relatively low speed, some distance would be needed to stop—even in an emergency. The runaway vehicles were not travelling very fast however, and the colision between seven lightly constructed wagons and an express passenger train would not, in the ordinary way, have anything very much more than a minor smash, particularly as the driver of the express had about 150 yards warning and could get his brakes on and reverse the engine. In any event his speed had fallen off considerably on the rising gradient from Abergele towards Llandulas.

But fate turned this relatively minor accident—reprehensible though its causes were—into a disaster of the first magnitude. The last two wagons of the runaway, those immediately next to the brake van, were laden with paraffin oil—nearly eight tons of it, in a number of small casks. When the collision occurred some of these casks burst. The engine, tender and first four vehicles of the Irish Mail were deluged in oil, which immediately ignited, and a terrible fire broke out with such suddenness that there was no chance of liberating any of the passengers in those leading coaches. There were 32 of them, and not one survived. The astonishing thing is that the rest of the train was quite undamaged. With the promptitude and sublime courage shown in many such an emergency men leapt to the task of separating the undamaged coaches from those involved in the fire, and on a gradient it was then easy to push these coaches out of harm's way. So slight had been the shock of the collision that all nine coaches had remained on the rails.

The prime cause of the disaster was, of course, the faulty operating methods that permitted shunting on the main line while an express train was approaching, and the disregard even of the meagre regulations by the stationmaster at

Llandulas. But once the runaway had been initiated it was the lack of brake power that made the collision inevitable, and the unlucky chance of the oil casks merely consummated the tragedy. While there are still unbraked goods wagons in existence however the dangers of a runaway are still present, even today. At the very time of proof correction there occurred the accident to 'The Northern Irishman' near Warrington, in which the driver and fireman of a modern diesel electric locomotive were killed when they ran into some runaway wagons, at night. Had some of the runaways contained oil, Warrington of 1966 might have become a second Abergele.

* * * * *

In mid-Victorian times the permanent way was in course of gradual development. Steel was beginning to supersede wrought iron as the material for the rails themselves, and the practice of ballasting and packing the sleepers was receiving constant attention to make the track more suitable for the speeds at which locomotives could, by that time, regularly run. But points and crossings were a subject of great difficulty and apprehension. As railway traffic developed some very complicated layouts stations and yards grew up. There seemed to be no co-ordinated plan in the majority of instances. Sidings and connections were added piecemeal; and although speed in such localities was slow it was not necessarily so on the main lines where points and crossings were encountered. Accidents of a minor kind were frequently occurring because of derailments at facing points, so much so that some engineers deliberately avoided the use of facing points on main lines. Any divergence, except at dead slow speed, had to be made by drawing ahead and then shunting back. When the ever-famous Settle and Carlisle main line of the Midland Railway was built in 1876, there was not a single instance of facing points between Settle Junction, and the immediate approach to Carlisle.

The abhorrence of facing points in mid-Victorian days reached its culminating point on the night of August 1st,

1873, when disaster befell the night Tourist express from Euston to Scotland as it was passing through Wigan station. Traffic was building up rapidly in readiness for the commencement of the grouse shooting season, and the 8 p.m. express was loaded to no less than 25 vehicles, many of them family saloons, and it was drawn by two engines. The exact cause of the grievous misadventure was never finally fully determined, but in fact the sixteenth coach became partly derailed as it passed over the facing points at the south end of the down main platform. At this location a loop line diverged to the left, to serve the outer side of the platform which was then—and still is, an island. The sixteenth coach was a family saloon, that had been chartered by a titled lady, and it was immediately followed by a luggage van. What happened to these last two vehicles takes some believing. The van was completely derailed, swerved to the left and demolished a shunters' cabin. But the couplings held, and the station staff had the terrifying experience of seeing this crack express go racing through the station with the sixteenth coach partly off the road, and what they at first thought was the rear van swaying and lurching about on the ballast. Still more amazing was the fact that both these vehicles were completely re-railed at a crossing at the north end of the station.

In the meantime the driver of the train, feeling an unusual jerk, had looked back and seen sparks flying from the rear of the train. He stopped some distance north of the station, and walking back found he had only 17 vehicles on. As yet he did not know of the terrifying experience the occupants of the sixteenth and seventeenth vehicles had been through during the passage through Wigan station. But their experience was nothing to what had happened further back. The couplings had broken between the seventeenth and eighteenth coach and without any brakes to check their motion the rearmost vehicles, all derailed, literally ran amok. Some piled into a heap on the loop line; another ended completely upside down on the platform, while yet another had crashed through a parapet wall and landed on the roof of a factory

Staplehurst, 1865 A sketch made on the morning after the crash

Abergele, 1867
  The scene of the disaster, looking eastwards

Abergele
  The jury visiting the scene

Abergele Searching for victims among the blazing wreck of the train, from a drawing made 1½ hours after the collision

Wigan, 1873

Scene immediately after the breakaway

Wigan

The trail of destruction left in the station itself

Norwich, 1874 The head-on collision, showing vividly the wholesale destruction of the light wooden coaches

Abbots Ripton, 1876

A sketch by one of the passengers, showing the injured being removed in all the difficulty of darkness and a snow storm

Abbots Ripton

General view of the scene after the line had been partially cleared. The Stirling 8-foot single engine No. 48 in the left foreground

Abbots Ripton

Raising the engine of the *Flying Scotsman*; the 2–2–2 'Single' No. 269

Penistone, 1884

Above General view of the wrecked carriages, with the colliery and the signal box in the distance

Left View from the signal box, looking towards Sheffield

some distance below. Only the last two vehicles remained upright on the ballast, and relatively unscathed. In the six coaches which were so thrown about and shattered 13 passengers were killed and 30 injured.

Naturally the main emphasis of the Board of Trade enquiry, which was conducted by Captain Tyler, was to try and ascertain how the sixteenth coach became derailed at the facing points. Everything else stemmed from this initial happening. The consequences were made far worse by the absence of brakes on the derailed vehicles; but at that time in British railway history this grave deficiency was not acknowledged as the peril it was, except by the Board of Trade.

The occurrence was serious enough for a Court of Enquiry to be set up, and nearly everything discussed and examined centred upon whether the facing points had been moved during the passage of the train. No fewer than 104 witnesses were examined, of whom 69 were railwaymen. There were no facing point locks on the North Western at that time, but the very exhaustive examination of the track all went to show that nothing was wrong, and that the points had remained properly closed all the time. The signalman could not have moved his lever unless he had previously put the home signal to danger; this he did not do. The permanent way was not in the best of condition, and a little rough riding and side oscillation of the six-wheeled carriages may have been momentarily aggravated on a short stretch between some trailing points from a siding, and the facing points to the loop at which the derailment took place. The stock rails were joggled to take the width of the point tongues, in each case by about 5/16in., and this joggle was continued between the two pairs of points. As the 'joggling' was a little different from what is nowadays understood by the term in regard to straight-cut switches, it should be explained that the rails were wide to gauge by about $\frac{5}{8}$in. over this distance, and if the Caledonian composite had gone hard to the right on this length, and hitting the joggle at the end bounced over to the left, it may have jumped the point tongue and borne off down the loop line. This is, however, mere conjecture.

Nothing at all was proved, but the Court of Enquiry felt that the speed was too high, having regard to the condition of the permanent way.

Of course there was then no automatic continuous brake, and after the parting of the train the rear coaches ran more or less unhindered to their destruction, but curiously enough the question of brake power does not seem to have been raised during the enquiry. The accident did bring to the fore the desirability of having facing point locks; for although all the equipment for actuating the points was in good order, and the working by the men concerned was quite correct, the terrible results of the smash showed what could happen if a pair of points was moved while a train was passing. Wigan did for the practice of facing point protection what Armagh was to do for continuous brakes some 16 years later.

*   *   *   *   *

In the days before space-interval block working became the Law of the Land for both double and single lines of railway, the usual method of working on single lines was by means of telegraphic train orders. On single line sections the various trains had their booked crossing points with trains running in the opposite direction; but difficulties arose when one or other of the opposing trains was running late and decisions had to be taken as to how long one train could be held at the appointed crossing place waiting for its belated opposite number. Then the telegraph had to be used to issue revised instructions, and the greatest care had to be taken to ensure that these were clearly understood. Considering how much depended upon these telegraphic orders the record of safe working on single lines was a very good one. On the Highland Railway, for example, it was not unusual for more than *eight hundred telegrams* to be sent out from Inverness in a single day!

The occurrence of one deplorable accident was nevertheless enough to highlight the dangers inherent in the system. It was the Great Eastern Railway that was unfortunate enough to sustain that accident, on a line that had enjoyed an enviable immunity from trouble until the fatal evening. Before the opening of the East Suffolk line through trains from London to Yarmouth travelled via Norwich, entering the terminal station, Thorpe, from the Ipswich direction, and then reversing to take the tracks of the old Norfolk Railway, which ran from both Lowestoft and Yarmouth through Norwich, and then westwards on to two routes, one north-westwards to Fakenham, and the other to Thetford and Brandon. The first section eastwards from Norwich Thorpe was single tracked, to Brundall, and this station was the booked crossing point for the 8.40 p.m. up mail from Yarmouth and the 5 p.m. down express from Liverpool Street. The evening of September 10th, 1874, was dark and raining, and the London train was running late. It was due to leave Norwich at 9.10 p.m. and it had not arrived when the night inspector, Cooper by name, came on duty at Thorpe station. His first concern was for the mail, and on calling on the stationmaster, one Sproule, he suggested ordering the mail to proceed from Brundall without waiting there for the London train. There was apparently an order which permitted the London train to be detained at Norwich until 9.35 p.m. rather than delay the mail.

The stationmaster hesitated. It seemed that while his inspector was thinking more of the mail he was more concerned with getting the London express away. After some argument he gave his reply in rather vague terms, with a rather testy 'All right', and Cooper interpreted this as giving authority for the mail to be instructed to come forward from Brundall. He went to the telegraph office and told the clerk, Robson, to order the mail up. Robson wrote out the message, but Cooper had hurried away without signing it, and at 9.22 p.m. it was transmitted to Brundall without proper authority. The mail was due at the latter station at 9.25 p.m. Acknowledgement of the instruction was telegraphed back to Norwich at precisely 9.25 p.m. In the meantime the London train had arrived at Norwich Thorpe, and the day inspector, Parker, who was about to go off duty, went up to the fresh engine which had backed on to the rear of the train

35

ready to proceed to Yarmouth. Parker had actually made out an order authorising the train to proceed to Brundall. He was unaware of its late running, and had assumed that the usual 'meet' with the mail would take place at Brundall. At that moment Cooper the night inspector came up, and Parker immediately asked him whether he had given any special instructions about the mail. It is difficult to conceive what made Cooper answer as he did because he said 'No; certainly not', and then busied himself, with Parker, in getting the express away.

One can only imagine that having told the telegraph clerk to send the instruction to Brundall, but not actually signed it, he was imagining that Robson had not sent it but was waiting for his signature. At any rate, after the departure of the London express at 9.30 p.m. he seems suddenly to have had uneasy thoughts, for he rushed to the telegraph office and asked Robson if he had ordered the mail up. One need not dwell upon the remaining verbal exchanges between the inspector and the young telegraph clerk. It is enough to say that at 9.32 p.m. a message was sent to Brundall to try and stop the mail; but it had already left, and in the blackness of the night the two trains came into head-on collision near the Yare bridge. Twenty-five persons, including all four enginemen, were killed and 73 injured. Tragedy though it was—the blame resting heavily upon Cooper for his unsigned order, and on the 18-year-old Robson equally for sending the order without obtaining the vital signature—it was the system itself that was at fault in leaving these loopholes for the human element to enter in. In the U.S.A. accidents due to the system of telegraphic train orders were at one time of quite frequent occurrence—often with the direst results. But the fact that the system was worked for so long in Great Britain with almost complete immunity from accident was a tribute to the diligence of the railwaymen concerned rather than a commendation of the system itself.

These four mid-Victorian tragedies — Clayton Tunnel, Abergele, Wigan and Norwich between them reveal some of the conditions under which the ever-increasing railway traffic of Great Britain was being operated. If there is a moral to be drawn it is the need for better signalling and better brakes; because even at Wigan, which was primarily a derailment, the effects of the breakaway afterwards would have been greatly lessened had the train been fitted with automatic continuous brakes.

3

Abbots Ripton

By the middle 'seventies' the Great Northern was the fastest
line in the world. So far as scheduled speeds were concerned
it was then a case of 'England first and the rest nowhere',
and in England the G.N.R. led the way by a considerable
margin. By the end of the year 1875 Patrick Stirling had 12
of his famous 8 ft. bogie singles at work, and there were also
12 of his earlier 7 ft. 2-2-2 express engines engaged in fast
train working. The 8-footers were designed, in 1870, to work
trains of 150 tons at start-to-stop average speeds of 51 m.p.h.
That was equivalent to running the 105½ miles from Kings
Cross to Grantham in 124 minutes. It is an astonishing
thought that when the Gresley 'Pacifics' were first introduced in 1922 the Flying Scotsman was allowed 122 minutes
for this run. Admittedly the loads were then vastly greater,
but the comparison is enough to indicate the kind of speed
that was regularly expected on the Great Northern Railway
in the mid-'seventies'. With the speed the comparison ends.

The Stirling 8-footers were specially designed to work the
fastest passenger train service in the world, and yet the first
13 of them were built *without any brakes at all* on the engine,
and it was not until July 1876 that any of these 'racers' were
fitted with engine brakes. They had a hand-screw brake on
the tender, but for the rest the driver had to rely on the
assistance of the guard when a train had to be stopped
quickly. There was a code of whistles, by which the driver
asked for the van brakes to be applied, and on long trains
there was usually more than one brake van. But it was an
archaic way of going about things! If one looked hard to try

and find any justification for it, there was a faint glimpse of an argument in that traffic was not nearly so heavy as it afterwards became. Furthermore, the high average speeds of the mid-seventies were made without resource to high maximum speeds downhill. Even in the Race of 1888, maximum speeds in excess of 70 m.p.h. were not common on the Great Northern, though in later years the 8-footers were called upon to run very much faster.

By the end of the year 1875, nevertheless, there was a slowly-growing realisation that the deficiency in brake power almost universal on British railways constituted a serious danger, and in the summer of 1875 the celebrated brake trials had been held on a level stretch of the Midland Railway near Newark. As a result the Great Northern management had decided to fit Smith's simple, non-automatic vacuum brake. Nothing had been done towards implementing that decision by the end of the year, and a new 8 ft. bogie single under construction at Doncaster was completed in February 1876, without any brakes on the engine.

In other respects however the Great Northern was moving somewhat ahead in other operating methods. The space-interval block system was in regular use on the main line, although the rules differed considerably from what is now standard practice, in that the sections were normally 'open', and closed only after the passage of a train. Procedure had been developed from the time-interval method of working used before the block system was invented. The signals were normally set in the clear position, and often they would remain so for quite a long time. The signalman received a bell signal, indicating, for example, 'Be ready for express passenger train', when that train passed the box in rear; the signals were put to danger behind each train, and lowered again as soon as 'Line clear' was received from the box ahead, irrespective of whether another train was expected or not. There were two different types of signal box in regular use; those controlling stations or sidings were connected by ordinary telegraph in addition to having block communication. Intermediate block posts were connected with the station signal boxes only by the block telegraph.

It is important now to see how these principles were applied to the stretch of line between Peterborough and Huntingdon. For a southbound train the line is level, or slightly favourable to a point about 68 miles from Kings Cross, after which comes a five mile bank inclined at 1 in 200 ending just to the south of Abbots Ripton station. At that time there were stations, with sidings, at both Holme and Abbots Ripton; but these two stations were roughly $6\frac{1}{2}$ miles apart, and to permit of trains being run at closer headway where necessary two intermediate block posts had been installed, at Connington and Woodwalton. There was another intermediate block post to the south of Abbots Ripton, roughly halfway between that station and Huntingdon. Its name was Stukeley. These intermediate boxes were purely regulating points in the block system. They had no function other than to stop or pass on a train.

Weather conditions in the evening of January 21st, 1876, were among the worst in living memory in this district. Driving sleet and snow impeded the working of all outdoor signalling equipment, and reliable witnesses afterwards stated that ice had formed to a diameter of 3 in. on the wires. Having due regard to the state of the weather most trains were running remarkably close to scheduled time, but the late departure from Peterborough of a coal train was the factor that first threw the working on this section of line out of gear. This train left Peterborough at 5.53 p.m. 18 minutes late; but since the southbound 'Flying Scotsman' was almost punctual and due to pass Peterborough at 6.18 p.m. arrangements were made to shunt the coal train out of the way of the express at Holme, instead of farther south, as usual. What actually happened at Holme has never been established, as all the subsequent evidence was contradictory; but the fact remains that the coal train failed to stop. There was nothing inherently dangerous in its continuing on the main line, for the road was clear at least as far south as Abbots Ripton, and after the train had passed

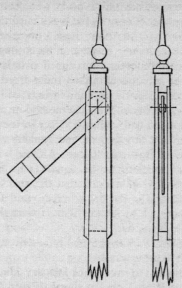

Fig. I. Type of signal in use on the G.N.R. in 1876.
[Reproduced from drawing in 'The Engineer']

signalman Osborne telegraphed to Abbots Ripton stating what had happened. The two intermediate signal boxes could take no action, save to pass on the train, since there was no means of advising them of the initial contretemps. In any case, neither block post had a siding, and no purpose would have been served by stopping the train at one place or the other.

Before describing the subsequent course of events, consideration must be given to the probable state of the signals at Holme. These, and all the others in the district, were of the type shown in the drawing. The arm worked in a slot in the post; it was not, as now usual, a counterbalanced unit, but depended for its return effect upon a balance lever at the base of the post. The wire from the signal box to the post had to be pulled, as now, to bring the arm from 'Danger' to the 'Clear' position, and when the signal-box lever was put

41

back after the passage of a train the weight of the balance lever brought the arm to danger and also tautened the wire from the signal box. At Holme the signals were working very badly owing to ice having formed on the arms and on the wires. The stationmaster had instructed platelayers to clear them, and in the subsequent inquiry some of these men admitted seeing several signals wholly or partly failing and sticking in the 'Clear' position. With the method of working then in force, arms stood considerably longer in the 'Clear' than in the 'Danger' position and the mechanism was thus more likely to become frozen at 'Clear'. Although he was aware of what was happening to the signals in his district, the Holme stationmaster maintained that the signals were against the coal train. The driver, however, said that all signals from Peterborough to Abbots Ripton were showing white—the 'Clear' indication.

On coming to Abbots Ripton the coal train driver, realising that the Scottish express was due, was quite expecting to be stopped and instructed to shunt back into the siding: and although the Abbots Ripton distant signal showed 'White' he thought that the signal might be working badly on account of the weather and slowed down preparing to stop. From his evidence it seemed clear that this distant signal was frozen in the 'Clear' position. The accompanying diagram shows the track layout and signals at Abbots Ripton. Signalman Johnson having been warned from Holme that the coal train had run past all signals was no less aware that his own signals were working badly. He was keeping a sharp look-out, despite the awful weather, and wisely used a red lamp to make doubly sure. The train was duly stopped and instructed to shunt back. In the meantime the Flying Scotsman had left Peterborough only six minutes late, at 6.24 p.m., and was proceeding south under clear signals.

'Line clear' was not allowed to be sent from a signal box to the box in rear until a train had passed into the next section, or, as in the case of the coal train at Abbots Ripton, shunted clear of the main line. The man at Woodwalton—

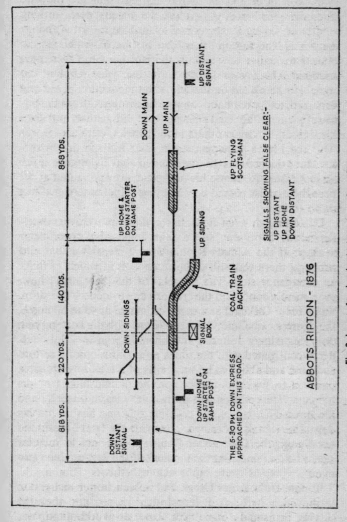

Fig. 2 Layout of track and trains just prior to first collision.

ABBOTS RIPTON - 1876

858 YDS.

140 YDS.

220 YDS.

818 YDS.

UP DISTANT SIGNAL

DOWN MAIN

UP MAIN

UP HOME & DOWN STARTER ON SAME POST

UP FLYING SCOTSMAN

DOWN SIDINGS

UP SIDING

COAL TRAIN BACKING

SIGNAL BOX

DOWN HOME & UP STARTER ON SAME POST

THE 5·30 PM DOWN EXPRESS APPROACHED ON THIS ROAD.

DOWN DISTANT SIGNAL

SIGNALS SHOWING FALSE CLEAR:-
UP DISTANT
UP HOME
DOWN DISTANT

Rose by name—had not yet received 'Line clear' from Abbots Ripton and his signal levers were at 'Danger'. Events proved however, that he was not equal to the responsibility of working a busy main line block post. Although snow was blocking up the windows of his cabin, he did not appear to realise how serious the weather conditions were becoming. In fog or falling snow the rules required fog signals to be placed on the line when the section ahead was occupied, and a red hand-lamp to be displayed from the box to supplement the fixed signals. Rose did neither, and since his signals, like most others in the district, were also frozen 'Off' the Flying Scotsman ran past at full speed. His subsequent evidence was confused and unconvincing, and at one stage he tried to excuse his negligence by saying that at the time the express passed he was using his lamp to signal to a down train.

But although even now that conditions were extremely dangerous there was still a faint hope of disaster being averted. If the Abbots Ripton distant signal was working properly there was still distance enough in which to make an emergency stop. The progress of the 'Scotsman', however, merely confirmed the coal driver's evidence. The signal was frozen 'Off', and at a speed estimated at 45 to 50 m.p.h. the express came into violent collision with the backing coal train. Signalman Johnson at Abbots Ripton was thus suddenly confronted with the shock and confusion of a serious accident, and although he was guilty of a fatal forgetfulness, one has to make allowance for the circumstances of the moment. The collision had thrown vehicles and debris on to the down line, but, while realising this and having put his down line signals to 'Danger', he made the fatal omission of not sending the 'Obstruction Danger' signal back to Stukeley signal box, at once. At the moment of the first collision two more expresses were approaching Abbots Ripton, the 5.30 p.m. from Kings Cross, and a Manchester to London train which had left Peterborough 15 minutes after the 'Flying Scotsman'. Signalman Rose, at Woodwalton, was naturally very much alarmed when the 'Scotsman' ran past his box and entered the occupied section. He seems at last to have realised that his signals were showing a false 'Clear' indication, and he acted promptly and effectively enough so far as the up Manchester express was concerned. The crew of this train saw his red hand-lamp signal in time, and although, like all the other passenger trains concerned, they had no continuous brake, the driver by reversing his engine, managed to stop short of the Abbots Ripton distant signal, which they saw showing the fateful white light.

The north-bound express was not so fortunate. When signalman Johnson at Abbots Ripton eventually remembered to send the 'Obstruction danger' signal back to Stukeley it was received too late by a few seconds; the 5.30 p.m. express was actually passing the signal box as the message came through. There still remained a last line of defence in the Abbots Ripton down distant signal, which, if sighted in time, would have given the driver a chance to pull up. Therein, however, lay the crowning misfortune of the whole affair, for that signal, too, was frozen, and showing a false 'Clear'. The second collision, wherein the 5.30 p.m. down Leeds express crashed into the wreckage of the 'Flying Scotsman', and the coal train, was, however, less severe than it might have been. Immediately the first smash occurred the fireman of the coal train had gone forward with detonators towards Stukeley. He got as far as the down distant signal and fixed his detonators on the down line. He was followed by his own engine, which had been uncoupled from the coal train, and which, in charge of the driver and the goods guard, was going to Huntingdon for assistance.

They had just stopped to pick up the fireman when the Leeds express was heard approaching, and by prolonged whistling and the display of red hand signals, aided, of course, by the explosion of the detonators, they managed to warn Driver Wilson of the express. But he received the warning as he passed the distant signal, instead of a full 200 yards earlier, as he would have done if the signal had been working properly—and that 200 yards was fatal. Wilson, driving one of the Stirling 8-foot single express locomotives,

No. 48, did all he could to stop his train. Apart from the brakes on the tender, all the assistance he had was from the two brake vans on the train. The guards in these vans acted promptly enough in response to his emergency whistle signal, and he himself reversed the engine. But although the speed was thereby reduced considerably it was not enough, and they hit the wreckage of the first collision at a speed estimated at between 10 and 20 m.p.h. In all 13 persons were killed and 24 injured.

The Board of Trade inquiry, as in the case of Clayton Tunnel, and Wigan, was conducted by Captain H. W. Tyler. In it signalman Rose of Woodwalton was severely censured for failing to act in accordance with the rules; but the rule he omitted to observe was a second line of defence, necessary in this case to cover the breakdown in the signalling system, and on that account it was the working of the signals themselves that received chief attention. The slotted posts came in for some criticism. Although this design tended to facilitate the packing in of snow between the arm and the two sides, experienced engineers held that it was not so much the slotted posts as the ice which formed on the rods and wires that prevented the balance weights from restoring the arms to the 'Danger' position. Captain Tyler expressed the view that it would be safer to have double wires to each signal, and pull the arms back to 'Danger'. As regards the actual form of the semaphore arm, there was at the time of the accident a growing realisation that better counterbalancing was necessary, and the failure of so many signals on that night served to hasten the change. It was, however, some years before the famous 'somersault' type of arm was introduced on the Great Northern Railway. Therein lay a story in itself.

But apart from the eventful change in the type of semaphore another change in signalling practice on the Great Northern Railway is sometimes considered to be a direct result of the Abbots Ripton disaster, as it was made in the same year, 1876. This was the change from white to green for the 'Clear' signal at night. Although all the signals concerned in the accident showed only two colours, red or white, it had been common practice elsewhere to use green as a caution signal. The disadvantages of a white light were by then fairly generally realised although such changes could not be made at once owing to other circumstances. The question of the actual lights displayed on the night of the accident would perhaps never have entered into the investigation—apart from the fact that several false 'Clears' were being shown—but for a remark made by one of the guards of the 5.30 p.m. down Leeds express. In his evidence this man said that the Abbots Ripton up distant had a white look due to snow, a statement that tended to give the impression that snow was making a red light look white! It is, indeed, one of the most curious features of the whole case that so much nonsense was written both at the time and subsequently, around this one chance remark.

The outstanding and fundamental change brought about directly as a result of the accident was in the block working system, which was altered to have the signals normally at 'Danger'. The risk of an arm freezing so as to give a false 'Clear' was thus reduced to a minimum, since the arm would be pulled off only for a short time. If freezing took place in the 'Danger' position, the ice would probably not have time to consolidate sufficiently to prevent its being broken up when the signalman came to pull off to the 'Clear' position, and in any case if failure did occur it would be on the side of safety. In recommending this change in practice, Captain Tyler made an important contribution to the safe working of railway traffic. So deeply were the lessons of Abbots Ripton impressed upon the minds of British signal engineers that the first introduction of automatic semaphore signalling in America was greeted with the most profound opposition —because the arms stood normally in the 'Clear' position. The other feature of equipment shown by the collision to be wholly inadequate was the braking of the trains. Here, again, as in the case of the signal arm balancing, the shortcomings had already been realised, and in the previous summer trials

47

had been held at Newark with various types of continuous brakes.

It was not however until May 1876 that drawings were made for the brake gear on one of the 8-foot single express locomotives, and the first of these engines to be built new with Smith's simple vacuum brake was No. 221, completed at Doncaster in July 1876. The 'simple' vacuum brake was a good deal better than no brakes at all, but it had grave disadvantages of its own that were revealed and emphasised many times during the 13 years that followed immediately after the tragedy of Abbots Ripton.

Nevertheless it was the state of the signals rather than the inadequacy of the brakes that received most attention at the time. It was considered that nothing short of double-wire working would have been effective in the very bad weather conditions that existed on the night of January 21st, 1876. Apart from that however a signal arm that was not counterbalanced in itself was inherently dangerous, and engineers on various railways began to work out new designs. Ideas were not confined to the design offices. On the Great Northern Railway a signal inspector at Hitchin, Edward French by name, proposed the use of a centre-balanced arm, and in September 1877 he took out a provisional patent for it. In those days the idea of any individual in the service of a railway company taking out a patent for an idea was anathema to the higher management, and French instead of getting any credit for ingenuity got instead a sharp 'rap over the knuckles'. The situation was made so unpleasant that an outsider who was prepared to help French financially withdrew his support, rather than be further involved.

Before long French was saddened to see semaphores of the kind he had proposed being adopted as standard on the Great Northern Railway. This is the unhappy origin of the very celebrated 'somersault' arm that became so characteristic a feature of the line for more than 50 years. The principle of French's semaphore was the placing of the spindle, itself carried on a bracket casting extending to the left of the post, on the vertical centre line of the arm but above its horizontal

48

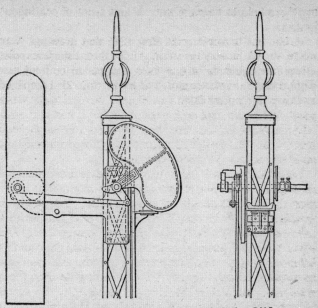

Fig. 3. Drawing of somersault signal as later standardised on G.N.R.
[Reproduced from drawing in 'The Engineer'.

centre line, so that it was balanced completely when horizontal and when vertical had the maximum return effect
without any counterbalance being required. The arm was
intended to move to the vertical for 'all-right' but in practice
often did not travel quite so far. It was driven by a rod from
a crank on the post actuated by the down rod, the spectacle
originally being carried separately a short distance below, a
practice favoured by several lines at one time but lasting
longer on the G.N.R. than on any other. In later years that
railway itself placed the spectacle level with the arm. The
G.N.R. was noted for its large numbers of very high signals,
no expense being spared to get a sky background whenever
possible, especially for the distant and home signals; and for
some years 'splitting' distants were provided for every possible movement including crossover junctions. The 'somer-

sault' semaphore gave a very clear and distinctive 'all-right' indication, but was expensive to install and maintain and it is doubtful whether any advantage it may have had was worth the extra cost involved. Although it may well have come into existence in any case, the accident at Abbots Ripton may fairly be regarded as having provided the chief incentive to its production.

4

The Battle of the Brakes: the Casualty List

For some years before the double collision at Abbots Ripton
in January 1876 the provision of better brakes was becoming
something of an issue in Great Britain. The time was certainly overdue. Seeing that trains were then occasionally
making speeds approaching 80 m.p.h., the fact that powerful
new locomotives were being built without any brakes on the
locomotives themselves, and that reliance was continuing to
be placed on hand-applied brakes on the tender and the
co-operation of guards was, to put it bluntly, quite ludicrous.
Then, in the year 1871, the American inventor, George
Westinghouse, paid his first visit to England. Despite his
ability to show how fast the American railways were equipping their trains with his newly designed air brake, he found
it exceedingly difficult to make any impression upon the
railway managements of Great Britain. This is not altogether
surprising. The Inspecting Officers of our own Board of
Trade were already doing all they could to influence the
British railway managements towards the introduction of
better brakes, and were having very little success. An
American inventor was not likely to succeed at that period
in history, when our own Government officials were failing
also.

The attitude of British railway management in general
was at that time extraordinarily parochial. Not only did they
resent the intrusion of any device invented or developed outside the country, but many of them were exceedingly re-
luctant to use good ideas that had been developed on
another railway in this country. The air of self sufficiency
generated among some administrations certainly takes some

51

believing in these days. Westinghouse found this attitude very puzzling. He had every justification in believing that his own air brake was vastly superior to anything that was being used in Great Britain at that time, and in an attempt to get some publicity for his inventions he approached the technical journal 'Engineering'. His reception there was very favourable, but one of the two Joint Editors, John Dredge by name, in propounding what he believed to be the fundamentals of a really satisfactory continuous brake for railways, went considerably further than Westinghouse had so far progressed.

Westinghouse in his first design had certainly provided the 'power to stop' in a way that it had never been provided before. He used what is now known as the 'straight air' brake. In other words, air was supplied directly from the locomotive to the brake cylinders of all the vehicles in the train, to apply the brake. Dredge felt this was not going far enough, and that the original Westinghouse brake did not contain one essential safety feature that he felt was vital. Dredge propounded this view: 'If a part of the train broke loose from the rest, the brakes must come automatically into play; the failure of the brake apparatus on one or more carriages must not interfere with the action of the brakes on the rest of the train.' The Westinghouse brake as it existed in 1871 did not fulfil this requirement, because if a portion of the train broke loose, only that part connected to the engine would be subject to the brake power provided from the engine. These ideas, or rather those fundamental principles, were embodied in a leading article in 'Engineering'; but while they were welcomed by the Board of Trade Inspectorate, they were more or less ignored by the great majority of British railway managements. Westinghouse returned to America and immediately applied himself to the designing of apparatus that would fulfil the requirements laid down by Dredge. Several new patents were taken out, but the ultimate outcome was the perfecting by 1874 of the celebrated triple valve, which for many years was to be the corner stone of the Westinghouse automatic air brake.

Two English railways, the North Eastern, and the London, Brighton and South Coast stood out from the rest in their attitude towards the application of brakes to passenger trains. Both these Companies were early in the field with trials of the full Westinghouse automatic air brake, and its superiority on all counts was demonstrated at the Newark trials in 1875. Before that, however, Westinghouse himself had made contact and a considerable impression upon the higher management of the Midland Railway and at one time that Company had nearly 100 locomotives fitted. Despite its evident efficiency however, there was in other quarters, particularly among the locomotive engineers, a very deep-seated prejudice against the Westinghouse brake, simply because it was American; and in that prejudice, and all the strained relations that stemmed from it, lay the root of a very unhappy 20 years in British railway history.

Two very unsatisfactory forms of continuous brake were developed and widely used in Great Britain from this time onwards. On the London and North Railway the old practice of the driver whistling for brakes was developed to the extent of providing a chain brake, covering sections of the train which were operated by the guards. It is true that brake power at the front end was at last increased by putting steam brake equipment on to the locomotive; but the onus of applying the brake on the train was left with the guards. This crude and ineffective form of brake was developed at Crewe and sponsored by F. W. Webb. It had the strong approval of the great chairman of the L.N.W.R., Richard Moon; but one is inclined to think he backed it on the principle that it was devised within his own organisation, rather than for any technical merits it possessed. Moon was constantly urging his senior officers to do all they could to foster the 'do-it-yourself' attitude; to minimise the use of agents and contractors, and the home-made Clark and Webb chain brake naturally appealed to him on those grounds. C. J. Bowen-Cooke, in his classic work of 1893 'British Locomotives', upheld the record of the chain brake, although it was by that time outdated and rapidly being replaced. As a good North

Western man he backed the home product. It is certainly true that no major disaster occurred through the use of chain brake; but its power to stop was very poor, and it relied more on extreme diligence on the part of the train crews than upon any inherent merits it possessed in itself. The London and North Western Railway had a very high tradition of smooth running, and of smooth stops under the action of the brakes. There is no doubt that the care taken —and indeed care then was imperative—in operating the chain brake, helped to establish what was afterwards a highly cherished tradition of the line.

The fact that the Midland Railway was giving very serious consideration to the Westinghouse brake at the same time was probably one reason why the North Western would have nothing to do with it. Anything the Midland did at that time was abhorrent to Euston and Crewe; but it so happened that Midland relations with the newly-formed Westinghouse Brake Company were not of the happiest. There were strong influences on the Midland that resented the use of an American design of brake, even though the outstanding feature of the automatic brake had been devised through the promptings of an English technical newspaper. Nevertheless, the fact that the Midland, above all companies, was giving such serious consideration to the Westinghouse brake made developments on that line watched with very great interest all over the country. If the relations between the railway company and the manufacturers had remained as cordial as they were at the start, one feels that before very long every railway in the country would have adopted the Westinghouse automatic air brake.

But friction between the two parties developed on more than one front. The Midland having got compressed air on their locomotives proposed to use it also for the sanding gear. For some reason the Westinghouse Brake Company took extreme exception to this action, and in the meantime the opponents of Westinghouse within the Midland Railway organisation were extremely active in trying to find some alternative form of brake. It was in this kind of atmosphere that Smith's Vacuum Brake Company came into its own, manufacturing the simple or non-automatic vacuum brake. This was a relatively cheap device to install and unfortunately for a time it became extremely popular. The Midland began fitting their trains with it in place of the Westinghouse; it was taken up by the Great Northern, the Manchester, Sheffield and Lincolnshire and the Great Western, though at the same time the Westinghouse was taken up by the Caledonian, the North British and the Great Eastern in addition to the Brighton and the North Eastern which were the first users of the automatic air brake. If the L.N.W.R. Clark and Webb chain brake had a series of mishaps to its discredit, Smith's simple vacuum brake eventually had a trail of death and disaster.

It is extraordinary to recall how that wretchedly dangerous device came to be a rallying point for those large and important companies which, for reasons that could hardly be conceived, decided to set the recommendations of the Board of Trade at defiance. It is worth quoting some of the remarks of important railway officers and directors at this time. In 1877, on August 30th, the Board of Trade had issued its famous circular to the railway companies, impressing upon them the necessity for fitting all their passenger locomotives and stock with continuous automatic brakes. It was perhaps to be expected that Smith's Vacuum Brake Company took exception to the Board of Trade circular and called the conditions laid down in them, 'unnecessary and inconsistent'; but three years later the chairman of the Great Northern Railway told his shareholders, 'That Smith's Vacuum Brake was held in very high esteem; it was not automatic and did not meet what the Board of Trade wished'. Other railway officers and directors expressed their strong resentment at any form of dictation by the Board of Trade, so far as mechanical equipment was concerned, but the record of Smith's vacuum brake over the years proved to be a truly terrible one.

The first two instances to be mentioned were of hair-breadth escapes rather than disasters, though the implications were there for all to see. In 1878 on the Midland Railway an express running at high speed near Bedford broke the coupling between the engine and the leading van. The brake was thus rendered useless and a very serious accident was avoided by the driver, with great skill, contriving to keep ahead of the swiftly running carriages behind him. Fortunately the line was clear and he was able eventually to bring the runaway to rest. Next there was a case of an axle breaking on the 'Flying Scotsman', when that train was running near Bawtry at a speed of 60 m.p.h. Many of the carriages were derailed; but in the mishap the vacuum pipe was broken and so once again the brake was useless. The train ran for nearly 1,300 yards before it could be stopped, and in the course of this run one carriage wheel came within inches of a bridge parapet. At that moment the slightest swerve in the wrong direction would have sent the carriage over the parapet and probably dragged a considerable portion of the train with it.

Yet another hair-breadth escape occurred in March 1880, once again with the 'Flying Scotsman', when one of the coupling rods of the engine broke while running at full speed, and one portion kept whirling round breaking a part of the vacuum system in the process. The driver could do nothing, and in such conditions it was little short of a miracle that the train kept to the rails. Even so it *ran for two miles* before it could be stopped. Inability to stop in case of emergency is a terrible thing, and two accidents in the 'eighties' of last century, one on the Midland and the other on the Manchester Sheffield and Lincolnshire would have had far less dire results if the trains had been fitted with continuous automatic brakes. The first of these happened in August 1880, at Wennington, a little junction in North Lancashire, where the Furness and Midland Joint line diverges from the main Midland line from Leeds to Morecambe. An express for Lancaster ran through the junction at high speed and became completely derailed. The engine itself was fitted with the Westinghouse brake, but the train was unbraked except for one hand-worked brake van. The power to stop was negligible, and the train ran for over 160 yards on the ballast, and then crashed into a bridge.

In the report on this accident prepared by Colonel Yolland, who will be ever famous in the history of railway safety appliances for the spontaneous way in which he fooled the primitive interlocking at Kentish Town Junction, hammered away for all he was worth at the need for fitting better brakes. He pointed out with some vehemence that the Board of Trade had been advocating this for 20 years, and he added: '. . . with the exception of a very few railway companies that recognised the need and acted upon it, it may be truly stated that the principal railway companies throughout the kingdom have resisted the efforts of the Board of Trade to cause them to do what was right, which the latter has no power to enforce, and even now it will be seen by the latest returns laid before Parliament that some of those companies are still doing nothing to supply this now generally acknowledged necessity.'

'Resist' was a mild word for the attitude displayed by some of the railway managements. Sir Edward Watkin, who was simultaneously Chairman of the Manchester, Sheffield and Lincolnshire, and of the South Eastern, was generally acknowledged to be one of the toughest customers in the Victorian railway firmament: as obstinate as he was ruthless and ambitious. Under his direction the M.S.L. adopted Smith's simple vacuum brake, in keeping with the policy of its partner in the fast London-Manchester service, the Great Northern. So, in July 1884, there came the first and more serious of two accidents near Penistone. The train concerned was the 12.40 p.m. from Manchester, coasting downhill from Woodhead Tunnel, and hauled by one of Charles Sacre's very handsome outside-framed 4-4-0 engines of the '423' class. The train in question was always known as the 'Boat Train', because in addition to its through portion for Kings Cross it conveyed through carriages on certain days of the week for Grimsby Docks, to connect with steamers for Hamburg and Rotterdam.

On the day in question, while rounding the curve at Bullhouse Bridge, the driver suddenly began to feel an uneasy motion; the next moment there was a report and the crank axle was broken. The jolt caused a defective coupling between the tender and the leading vehicle to break and this immediately severed the vacuum pipe and left the entire train without any brake power. So while the engine and tender remained on the embankment, upright and scarcely damaged, the rest of the train, devoid of any restraining influence, went down the bank and was completely wrecked, with a casualty list of 24 killed and over 60 injured. Much of the discussion following this grievous accident centred round the prime cause, the breaking of the crank axle. Many were still constructed in wrought iron, but controversy ranged around the use of inside, as against outside cylinders. With the latter a straight crank axle could be used, yet statistics in the previous year, 1883, showed that breakages were then just as frequent with outside, as with inside cylinders.

Quite apart from the prime cause of the accident, it could have been little more than a minor incident if the train had been fitted with continuous automatic brakes of one kind or another. Major Marindin reported for the Board of Trade, and he said: 'The value of a brake having, above all, automatic action can hardly be contested; and although the Board of Trade has, as yet, no power to insist upon the adoption of a continuous brake possessing these qualities, yet I would remind the Manchester, Sheffield and Lincolnshire Railway that this is the second emphatic warning which has been given to them.' Yet despite this, a certain manager, whose identity may be readily guessed, said shortly afterwards that: 'He would prefer an occasional Penistone to being compelled by Government to put on something which he did not want!'

Three years later the records of the Manchester, Sheffield and Lincolnshire Railway were stained by yet another serious accident, in which the ineffectiveness of the simple vacuum brake played a very considerable part. This time, however, the operating circumstances that led up to the collision were much more complex than the breaking of a locomotive crank axle. It was the St. Leger week at Doncaster, and race specials from many parts of the North of England were converging upon the town. These special trains were run into sidings cleared of all other traffic for this one hectic week, and those coming from the west were stopped at a platform some 1½ miles short of Doncaster itself, for ticket examination. This ticket platform, named Hexthorpe, was in the middle of the ordinary block section between Hexthorpe Junction and Cherry Tree Lane signal boxes, and there were no fixed signals at the ticket platform itself.

During St. Leger week the practice had grown up of suspending block working over the 1½ mile section between Hexthorpe Junction and Cherry Tree Lane. The race specials came in so thick and fast that the time taken in clearing the section, with ticket examination intermediately would have led to congestion, and so permissive working was adopted, with two flag signalmen stationed between Hexthorpe Junction box and the ticket platform. The special regulations concerning this method of working, with which all enginemen working over the route should have been made clearly familiar, were contained in a book covering regulations for working over all parts of the M.S.L. line—a bulky document. Any driver seeking information would have to plough through an enormous amount of matter which did not concern him before he came to the vital points. It is to be feared that many enginemen working race specials into Doncaster that week were not at all familiar with the arrangements, but were guided by the indications given by the fixed signals and the instructions of the flag men.

On this fatal day two Midland excursions had followed each other into Hexthorpe very closely. The driver of the second had received no special instructions by printed notice or otherwise. But he had worked into Doncaster in St. Leger week in the previous year; and assuming the arrangements were the same he ran very cautiously from Hexthorpe Junction, and stopped short of the previous train while the latter was at the ticket platform. Then his turn came to go in, and he drew up at the platform. Immediately following came an ordinary M.S.L.R. express from Liverpool. One would have thought that the regular men, working over their usual route would have exercised some caution in the neighbourhood of Doncaster. But while this man admitted to knowledge of the special notice he had not attempted to go through this massive document in any detail.

When he approached Hexthorpe Junction, first the distant signal and then the home were at danger. He slowed down, and when his speed was down to about 10 m.p.h. the 'home' was lowered. As there was no other fixed signal affecting his route at Hexthorpe Junction he assumed, quite wrongly, that he was 'right away' to Cherry Tree Lane, and put on steam vigorously. The first flag man gave him no indication, and the second made a somewhat ambiguous signal which the fireman saw but did not understand. They were travelling at between 35 and 40 m.p.h. when they rounded a curve and came in sight of the Midland train standing at the ticket platform. There was then between 200 and 250 yards between them and the obstruction; but although the driver applied the 'simple' vacuum brake fully, and went to the extreme of reversing his engine, he could not stop in time.

Quite apart from its ineffectiveness as a stopping agent, even when all was well, the perils of the simple vacuum brake in emergency were vividly illustrated in this bad accident. The speed of the M.S.L.R. train at the moment of collision was estimated at between 10 and 15 m.p.h. Of course all the carriages were of wood, and quite light construction; but in the driver's own words: 'We seemed to do more damage after we had stopped, with the train pushing us on.' In other words, once again the impact of collision had broken the vacuum pipe and immediately released the brakes on the rest of the train, which all came thrusting forward. The Midland driver said in evidence: '. . . the second shock of the collision drove my engine 20 yards further on.' The casualty list included 25 killed and no less than 94 seriously injured.

Coming on the Manchester, Sheffield and Lincolnshire Railway, which already had such a bad record, this accident caused a tremendous sensation. The immediate verdict was that it was due, almost entirely, to the lack of care shown by the driver of the Liverpool train; and he and his fireman were arrested, and committed to trial for manslaughter. But as the Board of Trade enquiry proceeded other factors began to become apparent. Major Marindin conducted the enquiry, and he was highly critical of the somewhat casual way in which ordinary block working had been suspended. He agreed that there were occasions when this was permissible, but he laid down: 'The only conditions under which block signalling could be safely suspended would be that every train should be *stopped*, not merely "brought up" or "checked" at the block signal cabin at the entrance to the portion of line on which suspension is in force, and the driver verbally informed of the state of the affairs.'

Then there was the simple vacuum brake. Sir Edward Watkin made this classic remark: 'He had always protested against automatic brakes, and the Hexthorpe accident very much strengthened his reasons for doing so.' Did ever a responsible railway officer talk such irresponsible nonsense! Seeing that the train in question was not fitted with automatic brakes, where was the logic—or was it that Sir Edward preferred to go on having accidents of the Hexthorpe magnitude, which the automatic brake would have prevented! Feeling against the contemporary railway managements ran high at the time, and 'Punch' published a cartoon in which a policeman arrests the driver, while the director walks off. 'Punch's' comment was: 'Yes, you've got one of them! But you ought to have both!'

The trial of the driver and fireman at York Assizes before the Lord Chief Justice of England excited great interest, and intense sympathy for the enginemen. It was of historic interest in that it was the first big legal case in which the newly founded Associated Society of Locomotive Engineers and Firemen—today known as 'A.S.L.E.F.'—engaged eminent counsel to defend the driver and fireman. It was a long drawn out battle, but after hearing all the evidence the jury brought in a verdict of 'not guilty'. The Lord Chief Justice included this remark in his summing up: 'He could not but think that the railway company was seriously to blame for having had in use a brake which not only was not the best in existence, but which was known to be insufficient and liable to break down.' The odium heaped upon the Manchester, Sheffield and Lincolnshire Railway over this affair was evidently more even than the thick-skinned management could stand, and very shortly afterwards a decision was taken to change to the automatic vacuum brake. This however was not before Sir Edward Watkin had made another of his outrageous utterances. At the next meeting of the company after the result of the trial he had the effrontery to tell the shareholders: 'it was a misfortune that the Lord Chief Justice should have exonerated the driver and fireman.'

So far as England was concerned Hexthorpe and its sensational sequel really sounded the death knell of the simple vacuum brake. Yet it was not until two years later that the catastrophe occurred that stirred Parliament to insisting on automatic continuous brakes. In the meantime the casualty list for that phase of the 'Battle of the Brakes' when various types of non-automatic brake were in use gave these grim statistics, for five leading railways:

Railway	Type of Brake	Number of Accidents	Casualties	
			Killed	Injured
L.N.W.R.	Clark & Webb Chain	11	9	137
L.N.W.R.	Webb simple vacuum	7	1	36
Midland	No brake at all	1	8	23
Great Northern	Simple vacuum	15	3	32
M.S.L.	Simple vacuum	8	54	195
G.N.R. (Ireland)	Simple vacuum	4*	85*	289*

* Includes Armagh (See Chapter 5)

5

The Armagh Runaway Train Collision

In the previous chapter reference was made to a series of accidents all of which could have been avoided, or their effects greatly lessened by the use of better brakes. At this distance in time it is very difficult to understand why so many of the leading railways of this country put up such a fight against the introduction of continuous automatic brakes. With some administrations one can appreciate that they were looking to the cost of the equipment; but on the contrary some of the largest and richest companies were among the most stubborn in their attitude, while the leading Scottish companies whose finances were not nearly so favourable, were among the first to use continuous automatic brakes. There is no doubt there was much diehard opposition to the pleadings of the Board of Trade inspectorate. One can only conclude that much of that opposition was opposition for its own sake—a sentiment that refused to be advised by the Government. In the end there was a catastrophe in Ireland, that so shocked public opinion that both Houses of Parliament were ready enough to pass legislation compelling the use of continuous automatic brakes.

Even so, the frightful accident near Armagh on June 12th, 1889, was due in the first place neither to a failure of the brake nor to an error in train working. One of the most tragic features of many railway accidents is that, once the initial blunder has been made, by some operator of humble rank, opportunity after opportunity of saving the situation has been lost and one after another has, on the impulse of the moment, acted unwisely and added his quota to the disastrous sequence of events. Of this there is no more terrible example than the chain of events leading up to the wrecking of the 10 a.m. excursion train from Armagh to Warrenpoint Great Northern Railway of Ireland, on the morning of June 12th, 1889. There was no actual failure of apparatus and although the system of signalling and the train brakes were far from perfect, judged by present standards, the general conditions were not inherently dangerous until mis-judgment and hasty action made them so.

The affair had its origin on June 11th, when the locomotive department at Dundalk was asked to provide an engine and carriages for a party of 800 excursionists travelling from Armagh to Warrenpoint on the following morning. The traffic manager decided that the train was to consist of 13 vehicles, including two brake vans, but otherwise the rest of the arrangements were made by the running shed foreman, William Fenton, who was acting for the locomotive superintendent in his absence. Only one driver, McGrath by name, was available for the duty and he was told to take the train. The seeds of trouble had already been sown. In the inquiry after the accident Fenton admitted he did not know the road from Armagh to Warrenpoint, yet, having selected the usual locomotive allocated to such jobs, he had, to quote his own words, 'no doubt whatever about its being able to take the train of 13 vehicles over the Newry and Armagh line'. Unfortunately the section of line between Armagh and Newry is heavily graded, as will be seen from the accompanying profile. The locomotive chosen was No. 86, a small 2-4-0 of a class built by Beyer, Peacock & Co. in 1881, and normally used on the Belfast-Dublin expresses. They had 6 ft. diameter coupled wheels, and cylinders 16 in. diameter by 22 in. stroke. They were handsome little things but their modest proportions do not, even at a first glance, seem adequate for the working of a load of at least 160 tons behind the tender over a lengthy rising gradient of 1 in 75. The circumstances were made infinitely worse by the inexperience of the driver. Here again, Fenton left things very much to chance; for when McGrath made no objection to

64

Armagh, 1889 The 0–4–2 engine of the ordinary train, and shattered coaches of the excursion

Armagh View on the other side of the embankment showing how the wreckage was scattered

Shrewsbury, 1907 The high-speed wreck of the West of England night mail. The train should have taken the curved track on the right of the picture

Shrewsbury A close-up of the overturned 4–6–0 engine *Stephenson*

Shrewsbury Wholesale destruction of carriages, with a G.W.R. clerestory
perched above the tender

Aisgill, 1913

The aftermath of the fire: all that was left of one of the wrecked coaches

Aisgill   Burnt-out wreckage by the side of the line

Aisgill

The tragic aftermath. Scene of the disaster: the line
cleared and the remains covered with tarpaulins

Aisgill The inquest at Kirkby Stephen station: relatives waiting to identify victims

taking the train, he assumed that the driver knew the road well. Actually McGrath had never worked between Armagh and Newry as a driver; his only previous experience of that portion of the line had been as a fireman of excursion trains in 1884, 1885 and 1886, and before that as a fireman on ballast trains.

Engine No. 86 with the empty coaches that afterwards formed the excursion train, arrived at Armagh at 8.35 a.m. on the morning of June 12th, having travelled via Portadown. The excursion was heavily patronised, so much so that the station-master, John Foster, proposed to add two more coaches to the train, even though the load had already been increased from 13 to 15 coaches at Portadown. This further increase now proposed by Foster led to an altercation between him and Driver McGrath. McGrath first of all refused to take the 15 coaches that engine No. 86 had brought from Dundalk, saying that his instructions from Dundalk gave the load as 13. At that Foster seems to have taunted him, suggesting that no other excursion train drivers grumbled about their loads, whereupon McGrath replied that if the load had been properly advised to Dundalk, a six-coupled engine would have been sent to do the job. The frayed tempers resulting from this dispute led to some unfortunate actions. Foster came back down the platform and met James Elliott, chief clerk in the general manager's office, and immediately told him of McGrath's protests. Elliott then suggested that the train should be banked in rear, using the engine of the 10.35 a.m. ordinary train for the purpose.

Instructions to get ready were immediately sent to the driver of that train, Patrick Murphy, but in the meantime someone seems to have realised that if the 10.35 engine was used to assist the excursion train up the bank, a distance of about $3\frac{1}{2}$ miles, that engine would not get back to Armagh in time to make a punctual start with its own train. There also seems to have been a suggestion that some coaches of the excursion train should be transferred to the 10.35 which was loaded to only six vehicles; but eventually Elliott, apparently undecided, went to McGrath and asked whether he wanted

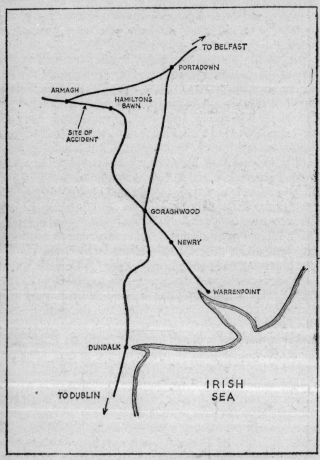

Fig. 4. Sketch map showing site of accident.

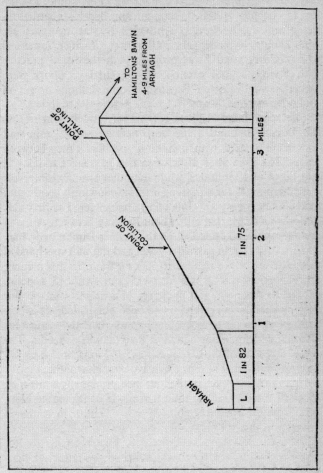

Fig. 5. Gradient profile between Armagh and Hamilton's Bawn.

assistance. Foster's taunt had evidently gone deep, for the driver now expressed great confidence in his ability to take the 15 coaches. Elliott thereupon cancelled his instructions that a bank engine should be provided. By starting time there were about 940 passengers on the train, of which some 600 were children; and in accordance with the usual practice with Sunday-school excursions, the carriage doors were locked before it started. Because of some shunting, to get on to the Newry line, it was 10.15 a.m. before the train left.

The space-interval block system was not then in use on this branch line and traffic was operated on the train staff and ticket system with minimum specified times between trains. The time interval between two passenger trains was laid down at 10 minutes, while the other specified intervals were 20 minutes for a passenger train following a goods, and five minutes for a goods following a passenger. The first staff station was at Market Hill, about halfway between Armagh and Goraghwood Junction, on the Belfast-Dublin main line. The excursion train carried a ticket and the staff was handed to the driver of the regular 10.35 a.m. train. In this manner the excursion started off at 10.15 a.m. with 15 coaches packed to repletion, and in charge of a driver who was not only inexperienced, but who had been persuaded—it is perhaps going too far to assert that he was taunted—against his instructions into taking a heavier load than he expected. The actual tare load of the carriages was $145\frac{3}{4}$ tons, and the gross load estimated at 187 tons exclusive of engine and tender.

Up to this time each of the four men principally concerned with the working of the train had made considerable blunders, from the operating point of view: Fenton, in sending a driver who did not know the road; McGrath, in agreeing to take 15 coaches without assistance; Foster, in his foolish argument with the driver, which led to the latter taking a serious risk; and lastly Elliot, the senior official concerned, for not insisting on the train being banked in rear when there was obviously some doubt as to whether the one engine could take the load. But even so, the conditions had not yet become dangerous, and as the train was fitted throughout with Smith's simple vacuum brake the worst that might apparently happen was that the engine might stall on the incline. Elliott rode on the footplate of the engine, No. 86, and told in his evidence, that they made a good start; but the statements of various witnesses differed somewhat as to the actual progress up the bank. McGrath said that once they entered upon the 1 in 82·75 gradient they were losing speed all the way; but both Elliot and the fireman stated that they got on well for the first two miles, after which deceleration began, and led eventually to the engine stalling.

Elliott in his evidence said: 'The engine did very well till it passed Derry's crossing (near the nineteenth milepost), where it began to lose speed, without any apparent cause, and continued to do pretty well till it had got to within 300 or 400 yards of where it stopped, and then the speed gradually diminished till the engine stopped about 200 yards from Dobbins Bridge. The words 'without apparent cause' cannot be lightly dismissed, for despite the hard steaming the boiler pressure had fallen only from 130 lb. to 125 lb. per square inch. The Inspecting Officer, Major-General C. S. Hutchinson, R.E., estimated that the particular locomotive ought to have been able to make a steady speed of 15 m.p.h. on the gradient, with a load of 186 tons, and Elliott's remarks hardly suggest that the driver eased the steaming at all. There was no reason for him to do so, with the boiler pressure being well maintained.

It must, however, be noted that passengers were travelling in both brake vans, and it may be that some tampering with the hand-brake wheels took place, and caused those brakes to be partly applied in one or other of the two brake vans. This might easily have led to the stalling of the engine. In any case, during General Hutchinson's inquiry a test was made on engine No. 86 with a load exactly equal to that of the excursion train, and with an experienced driver in charge there was no difficulty in climbing the bank, a steady speed of 15 m.p.h. being maintained. This would seem to justify Driver McGrath's belated confidence in his engine, so far as this particular incline was concerned; but on both the outward and return journey the train would have to negotiate in addition gradients of 1 in 70, on which curves of 33 and 30 chains radius occurred. Hence, even supposing the Armagh-Hamilton's Bawn incline had been successfully mounted, there would most likely have been trouble later on.

The train stalled, ironically enough, only about 210 yards from the summit, at 10.33 a.m. Admittedly the situation was awkward, for there was no hope of restarting on the gradient. Although he was in charge of the train, Elliott consulted McGrath as to what was the best thing to do; and when the driver suggested dividing the train he readily agreed. This, of course, was the height of folly, for with Smith's brake vacuum had to be created in order to apply the brake, and any severance of the train pipe put the brakes out of action on that part of the train disconnected from the engine. Matters were made infinitely worse in the Armagh case by the manner in which the train was divided. The intention was to convey the front portion to Hamilton's Bawn, about a mile further on, and stow it in the siding there; this siding was not a long one, and as it was believed to be already partly occupied, Elliott gave instructions for the train to be divided between the fifth and sixth coaches from the engine. This meant that the whole weight of 10 heavily laden coaches resting on a gradient of 1 in 75, had to be taken by the hand-brake of the rear van. That was bad enough, but on top of it two crowning blunders were committed.

Elliott, in his apparent anxiety to carry on with the minimum of delay, went to the van at the rear of the train and told Guard Henry what he had decided to do; and after ascertaining that the hand-brake was hard on he told the guard to put some stones behind the wheels. Without waiting to see that this was done properly and that the guard was back in his van in charge of the brake, Elliott ran back and told the front guard to uncouple. Before doing so, however, this man put one small stone behind the left-hand leading wheel of the sixth carriage—a totally inadequate precaution, yet one which Elliott admits he did not observe him to make. When the train stopped the couplings were all drawn out to their fullest extent, and the front guard, Moorhead, seems to have realised more so than Elliott, that after uncoupling the unbraked carriages of the rear portion would slack back on to the rear van unless scotched in some way.

The actual uncoupling seems to have been done carefully enough, and having observed that both portions of the train remained at rest, Elliott sent Moorhead forward to tell the driver to go ahead, while he himself went toward the rear van. It is easy to be wise after the event, but one would have thought that a railwayman of Elliott's long experience would have been alive to the difficulty, with any substantial load, of making a clean start on a 1 in 75 gradient; there must inevitably be some slight setback between the release of the brakes and the time when the steam began to move the train forward. What exactly happened was not witnessed by anyone interrogated by Major-General Hutchinson, but Moorhead, the front guard, related that he felt his van 'coming back 12 or 18 in.' which he thought was due to the engine setting back. This movement, however, was enough to overcome the one small stone scotching the sixth coach, and the unbraked coaches of the rear portion began to run back. In the meantime Henry, the rear guard, evidently had some difficulty in finding stones suitable for scotching, as he was still out of his van when the runaway began. 'As I was putting down the last stone,' he told the Inspecting Officer afterwards, 'I felt the carriages coming back.'

Panic now seized Elliott. Realising at last the peril in which his folly had placed over 600 passengers, he jumped on to the footboard of the rear van, shouting to Henry to get the brake on harder; but then, as the speed increased he jumped off crying: 'Oh my God, we will all be killed.' At sometime after the runaway began he seems to have waved the driver back, with the idea of coupling up again, but the front guard, Moorhead, in racing back to try and carry out this measure of despair, fell over some rails that were lying alongside the track, and never got as far as the sixth carriage. The rear part of the train was by this time quite out of control, and accelerating steadily on the steep gradient. The guard, after telling in his evidence of Elliott's last frantic words, said 'The speed then gradually increased, till it became so fast we could not see the hedges as we passed.' A study of the gradient profile makes it fairly evident that such a runaway could only end in disaster; for even if the line was clear the level stretch at the foot of the incline was scarcely long enough to have very much effect upon the speed.

The rear portion of the excursion train began to run back at just about the same time as the regular passenger train left Armagh at 10.39 a.m. That train with its moderate load was making light work of the severe gradient and travelling at between 25 and 30 m.p.h. when the fireman sighted the runaway. Driver Murphy made a full application of the vacuum brake, while his fireman reversed the engine and applied back steam. Although between them they managed to reduce their speed to 5 m.p.h. or less, the carriages of the excursion train were travelling at over 40 m.p.h., and the results of the violent collision which ensued were appalling. The engine of the 10.35 a.m. train stopped dead, quivered, but did not run back at all before turning over, and against this veritably immovable obstruction the wooden coaches of the excursion train shattered themselves to pieces. Remembering that the train was packed, it does not need much imagination to picture something of the carnage that ensued; there were about 600 passengers, and in those 10 coaches 78 were killed and about 250 injured.

Even now that the runaway had been halted, albeit in so terrible a way, the danger was not yet over. In the collision the tender of the 10.35 a.m. train broke away from the engine, and while still coupled to the front vehicle of the train, a horse-box, it began to run backwards towards Armagh; the rest of the 10.35 a.m. train which had parted between the first and second vehicles, also began to run back, independently of the tender and horse-box. Again, the severance of the brake pipe from the engine meant that the vacuum brake was inoperative on the train. The heroism of the crew of this train, however, prevented any further damage. As the crash occurred, Driver Murphy was thrown on to the tender footplate, and although badly knocked about managed to apply the hand-brake, stopping the tender and the horse-box after they had run about a quarter of a mile from the point of the collision. Meanwhile the guard of this train, Daniel Graham had been knocked senseless, momentarily, and when he came to it was to find that the train was running back at about 5 m.p.h. Although dazed and badly shaken he applied the hand-brake in his van and brought his portion of the train safely to rest.

As might be imagined public opinion was deeply shocked. Quite apart from the conduct of the various men responsible for the working of the excursion train, the inadequacy of the non-automatic vacuum brake was clearly revealed. It was also probable that the results of the runaway might have been less severe had the block system been in operation, and the 10.35 a.m. train held at Armagh. Very soon after this accident the Regulation of Railways Act, 1889, was passed, which gave power to the Board of Trade to order the adoption of the space-interval block system, the provision of interlocking, and the fitting of automatic continuous brakes on all passenger-carrying lines. It should, however, be added that most railways, even before the passage of the Act, had progressed some way towards the installation of these three great safeguards, and the fact that such negligence as Elliott displayed took place on a line still outside the pale only deepens the tragedy surrounding the Armagh collision. Elliott in his evidence said he calculated that time would be saved by dividing the train instead of waiting to be assisted by the 10.35, but in this his judgment, as in so many things, was entirely at fault. In his report, Major-General Hutchinson pointed out that if everything had gone smoothly it would hardly have been possible to convey the two parts of the train, one after the other, to Hamilton's Bawn and complete the job before 10.55 a.m. and by that time the regular train would in the ordinary way have passed Hamilton's Bawn.

There is a close analogy between the change in signalling practice made after the Abbots Ripton collision and the compulsory abandonment of non-automatic continuous brakes decreed by the Act of 1889, resulting from the disaster near Armagh; as the block signals, hitherto normally at clear, were afterwards changed to be normally at danger, so with the automatic continuous brakes, the vacuum in one case, or air pressure with the Westinghouse, had to be maintained to keep the brakes off; any failure, such as leakage or severance of the train pipe, resulted in the brakes being applied. Work had to be done either to lower a signal or to release the train brakes. With the Act of 1889 the fundamental principles of present-day railway operating were attained, and subsequent technical developments have tended towards elimination of mistakes arising from the human element rather than the establishment of new principles. Although above all a great tragedy, the collision at Armagh proved later to be a momentous turning-point in British railway history.

There were many people however who felt that the Act of 1889 had not gone far enough in requiring the use of automatic continuous brakes. Responsible opinion in many quarters felt that the Act should have definitely specified the type of continuous automatic brake to be used, and so secured a standardisation of practice throughout the country. Instead the automatic vacuum and the Westinghouse were permited to remain in a state of co-existence.

6

Speed on Curves: the derailments at Preston, Salisbury, Grantham and Shrewsbury

The psychological effect of the ever-famous Race to the North in 1895 left its mark on the running of express trains in Great Britain for many years to come. Until the fever of competition broke in all its intensity upon the East and West Coast routes to Scotland, the operation of express trains in this country had been marked everywhere by extreme caution. In other parts of the world national characteristics of daring and recklessness had manifested themselves in many ways; and experienced travellers often averred that French trains always produced their highest speeds when rounding curves or negotiating difficult junctions. It was not so in Great Britain. Careful regard was paid to speed restrictions laid down by the civil engineers of the various railways, and in many cases these had been fixed on the cautious side to allow for the misjudgment of individual drivers. At that time very few locomotives were fitted with any form of speed indicating apparatus and one driver's idea of 30 m.p.h. might not necessarily be those of his colleagues in the same link. Consequently the civil engineers were inclined to fix speed restrictions lower than what the track could safely sustain, to allow for the varied interpretation of individual drivers.

During the summer of 1895, when competition between the East and West Coast routes from London to Aberdeen was gradually intensified, drivers were finding from hard practical experience that they could negotiate curves with comfort and safety at far higher speeds than the upper limits laid down by the civil engineers. I should add at once however, that at first this applied only to certain sections of the line. The men of the Great Northern for example, working the East Coast trains between London and York were most punctilious in their methods. Their colleagues of the North Eastern Railway were considerably less so, while on the London and North Western some of the running made between Crewe and Carlisle would in other circumstances have been set down as downright reckless. It must be remembered however that the locomotives of those days, with their small boilers, had a relatively low centre of gravity. The tendency to overturn was considerably less, for example, than with locomotives of the final steam days when boilers were constructed to the maximum size permitted by the loading gauge. The locomotives of the '90s' rode very steadily on the curves, and it was the coaches rather than the locomotives that had a rough ride at high speed.

As the Race neared its climax some of the running, and particularly that on the London and North Western, on the North Eastern, and on the North British became positively hair-raising in the way curves were taken at high speed. The drivers who were entrusted with the racing trains became increasingly experienced exponents of the art of saving seconds, and night after night they increased their speeds on the critical sections of the line to heights which must have closely approached the danger point. There is no doubt that in the last nights of the Race there were moments when the margin between safety and disaster on certain curves was cut to the very finest degree.

The legacy of the Race was the existence of certain very fast schedules, and none was more venturesome than that of the 8 p.m. tourist express from Euston to Scotland, which was allowed no more than 112 minutes to cover the 105.4 miles from Wigan to Carlisle. With adequate engine power and experienced drivers this schedule could be quite comfortably maintained; but once the Race was over the normal practice of the L.N.W.R. returned. With indiscriminate pooling of engines and men on to each and every express train there were sometimes strange results, and on the night of August 15th, 1896, a somewhat extraordinary situation came about in the running of this very important sleeping car express. In the height of the tourist season both locomotives and men were at a premium. The London and North Western Railway was then suffering, possibly to its most severe extent, from the policy of compound locomotive building; at the same time they were enjoying excellent passenger receipts, and running heavier and more luxurious coaches on the principal express trains. In the holiday season so many trains needed double-heading that there was an acute shortage of both engines and experienced men, and on this particular night, when the tourist express itself needed double-heading, it was worked by two drivers, neither of whom had ever been on the train before, and neither of whom had ever worked through Preston as a driver on a train that did not stop. All both men knew was that they had to run jolly hard.

Now Preston is an awkward place to negotiate in the best of circumstances. Approaching from the south the main line executes a most awkward 'wriggle' in entering the principal down main line platform, and at the northern end there is a very sharp curve to the left through a yard complicated by many points and crossings. On the particular night there was plenty of engine power for the load being conveyed. The leading engine was a 6 ft. 'Jumbo' No. 2159 *Shark*, and the train engine, a similar engine but of the 6 ft. 6 in. type No. 275 *Vulcan*. With such a combination a load of at least 300 tons could have been timed quite comfortably on that schedule. Actually the load was less than 200 tons; but both drivers were anxious to maintain the fast schedule, and in their lack of experience they approached and passed through Preston station very much too fast. The speed restriction at the northern end of the station was 10 m.p.h. and competent witnesses gave their opinion that the train passed through doing at least 45 m.p.h. The results were spectacular in more senses than one. Very soon after entering the sharp curve at the north end of the platform the leading engine jumped the rails; but instead of turning over it went straight on, leap-

77

frogging over the intervening tracks to finish still standing bolt upright within a short distance of a retaining wall over which there was a 20 ft. drop into a works yard. The second engine followed, also remaining upright. Both drivers naturally made full application of the automatic vacuum brake; but while the engine remained completely upright, although somewhat battered, the rest of the train was flung in all directions. Miraculously the damage was very slight. The coaches in the train were nearly all of modern construction and stoutly built, and although they suffered much superficial damage, casualties were small. Despite the alarming nature of the derailment, the suddenness of the stop, and the scattering of the coaches only one person was killed.

This was a case of an accident where the outcome was out of all proportion to the casualty list. Few accidents in British railway history have had a more profound effect on both public and railway opinion than this derailment in the small hours of the morning at Preston. During the Race to the North there were many people who were filled with the direst forebodings as to the danger of the accelerated service being provided. The prophets of woe were present on every hand and quite apart from those who foretold the most fearsome calamities from the increases in speed that were being manifested day by day on the main lines from Euston and Kings Cross there were others who decried the entire spirit of racing, from the effects they considered it had on the enginemen concerned. Much of this, of course, was just faint-hearted nonsense; but when the accident at Preston occurred, to one of the very trains that had been involved in the racing of the previous summer, the railway managements themselves began to take heed, and a gradual process of deceleration of the Anglo-Scottish expresses began from that time onwards.

Colonel Yorke in his report to the Board of Trade said:

'The cause of the accident is clear. A reverse curve without any intervening tangent, without a check rail, with superelevation suitable only for very low speeds, and badly distributed, and with a radius at one point of only seven chains; a train drawn by two engines each having a rigid wheelbase of 15 ft. 8 in.; and lastly a speed of 40 m.p.h. or more form a combination of circumstances which were almost certain to lead to disaster.'

Although the official speed limit round that curve was 10 m.p.h. it was the experience of regular travellers who took detailed notes, including the celebrated writer on locomotive performance, Charles Rous-Marten, that the usual speed round the curve was 20 to 25 m.p.h. The locomotive policy of the L.N.W.R. had recently come under much criticism for its championship of the compound principle. It had also come under criticism for its reluctance to build locomotives with a leading bogie. At the time there were many engineers who felt that if both engines had been fitted with leading bogies the train would have got round the curve safely, even though the speed was greatly excessive. In the eyes of railway managements Preston had sounded the warning note, and a long standing agreement between the East and West Coast routes to Scotland establishing minimum times to Edinburgh and Glasgow was subsequently concluded. So that despite all the magnificent achievement of 1895 the alarming experience of Preston, a year later, resulted in express running times between London and Scotland being slowed down and remaining stagnant for more than 35 years, until the late spring of 1932.

Whatever policies of caution may have gradually taken hold of the managements of the northern lines no similar instincts had spread to the West of England by the turn of the century. On the Great Western Railway, following the abolition of the broad gauge, there was a tremendous up-surge of enthusiasm and enterprise, and a desire on all hands to show that anything that had been achieved in the distant past with the broad gauge could be completely eclipsed under modern conditions with the splendid new equipment that was coming into service on the line from 1900 onwards. The competition that developed with the London and South Western Railway for the inward-bound ocean traffic from Plymouth was merely one manifestation of the general Great

Western attitude, to establish itself once again as the Premier Line of Great Britain in all matters concerning speed; and so from 1903 onwards a new railway race track developed in Great Britain.

Whereas in 1895 the racing tracks had led from Euston, on the one hand, and Kings Cross on the other to Kinnaber Junction, now the tracks leds from Millbay Docks to Paddington, and from Stonehouse Pool to Waterloo. While in 1895 the rival routes converged at Kinnaber, from 1903 onwards the rival routes intersected for a distance of about $1\frac{1}{4}$ miles at Exeter. As in 1895 the rival routes for the most part were well aligned and suitable for the maintenance of high speed running; but there were nevertheless some very awkward locations, such as the South Western passages through Exeter and Salisbury, and the Great Western traffic centres of Newton Abbot and Bristol. Quite apart from this however, there was the South Devon line between Plymouth and Newton Abbot which then, as now, was anything but suited to the maintenance of high speed. The gradients are severe; but far more so than the gradients the incessant curvature is a very serious handicap against the making of any high sustained average speed.

In the heat of competition, which was developed to an extraordinary extent between the two companies, consideration of safety gradually seemed to recede, and there is no doubt that in the running of some of the rival trains—Great Western taking the mails, and South Western taking the passengers—serious risks were taken on the curves. One can always recall those amusing and homely words of G. J. Churchward, Locomotive Carriage and Wagon Superintendent of the Great Western Railway, in briefing the West Country Locomotive Inspector who was given particular charge of the running of the ocean mail trains, the late G. H. Flewellyn: 'Withhold any attempt at a maximum speed until I give you the word; then you can go and break your b——— neck!' Studying details of some of the running between Plymouth and Newton Abbot, both in the light of present-day speed restriction and from the *sight* of the curves as seen from the footplate of many steam and diesel locomotives, one feels that George Flewellyn and the drivers and firemen who worked with him were a great deal nearer to breaking their necks daily than was imagined at the time! The risks were taken west of Newton Abbot. The great record of the engine *City of Truro*, made on May 9th, 1904, certainly included a maximum of at least 100 m.p.h. down the Wellington bank; but there the line was quite suitable for high speed, and that famous maximum speed was achieved in complete safety.

Yet it was not on the Great Western, but with the rival trains that disaster struck the American specials. In the early days of the service the London and South Western were making a nominal non-stop run from Stonehouse Pool to Waterloo. The main line engine was attached at Devonport Junction, where the branch from the quayside joined the main line. After that there was only one stop between Devonport and Waterloo, to change engines. The London and South Western never put down water troughs, and in order to provide an even division of the work between the western and eastern ends of the journey, arrangements were made to change engines at Templecombe and to make a non-stop run from that point to Waterloo. This involved the unusual procedure of running through Salisbury station without stopping. Until that time every train had stopped at Salisbury, and no disadvantage had been experienced with the rather awkward track layout that existed at the eastern end of the station.

Coming up from the west, once through the platforms there was quite a sharp curve to the left through the goods yards and the speed restriction was one of 30 m.p.h.; but actually the situation was really much worse than a sudden transition from the straight track to a curve. The layout east of the station was such that a train from the west had either to cross over into the northernmost platform road at the west end of the station, or run through the main up platform and then negotiate a scissors crossing to get on to the up main line beyond the station. The normal path was to follow straight from the main line west of the station through the up main platform, and take the very intricate course through the scissors crossing in the middle of that quite sharp curve.

Although the American boat trains were relatively light and were thus capable of rapid acceleration, from the very outset it would seem that they were running through Salisbury station and through those intricate junctions at the eastern end at speeds that were far higher than were expedient. This may have arisen because after Salisbury there is a long and tiring incline, and drivers were anxious to 'charge' this incline with as much impetus as they could gain from a fast run through Salisbury station. On the very first run made with one of these ocean specials, when many of the highest officials of the London and South Western Railway were travelling in the train, the passage through Salisbury, although not precisely documented was undoubtedly very fast; and this tradition seems to have persisted in the running of these special trains. It was not an easy service to work into the general organisation of the railway. Trains had to be run as and when the transatlantic liners arrived in Plymouth Sound. There could be no waiting for convenient paths in the timetable.

The Specials, whether by the Great Western or the South Western route, were despatched as soon as possible, whether the hour happened to be morning, evening, or the dead of night; and although the passengers might be landed in London at all sorts of highly inconvenient hours, it was a point of honour to run these special trains at the high speeds regularly scheduled for them. Drivers and firemen had to be provided to work at odd hours, instead of in the regular rosters of ordinary service trains; and sometimes it occurred that men who had not had any previous experience of working the trains were drafted to them. For the same reason the London and South Western Railway built special sleeping cars, for use on those occasions when the American specials ran in the middle of the night.

It was a night occasion that really put an end to the competition in speed between the Great Western and the South

82

Western on these American boat trains. On June 30th, 1906, a boat special left Stonehouse Pool shortly before midnight and as usual it was worked non-stop from Devonport Junction to Templecombe. On that occasion also the driver allocated to the job of working the train forward from Templecombe to Waterloo had never run one of these American specials before. He knew the road well enough and was a fully experienced man; but the fact remains that he had never driven an express train through Salisbury station previously without stopping. He had one of the large Drummond 4-4-0 locomotives of Class 'L.12', No. 421; a good engine in every way, but one that by reason of its larger boiler had a considerably higher centre of gravity than the previous standard 4-4-0 locomotives of the 'T.9' class. The latter belonged to the general style of 4-4-0 locomotive that had been used in the Race to the North in 1895—at any rate so far as its centre of gravity was concerned; and the Great Western engines which had performed such hair-raising feats of speed on the South Devon line lay also within the same general category. But the 'L.12' engine was of a different stamp, and it may have been this marginal difference that had permitted safe running at unsafe speeds through Salisbury in the past, and which ended so disastrously in the early hours of July 1st, 1906.

The log of the ill-fated train shows that for some reason the driver started unusually slowly from Templecombe. This was odd, seeing that he had such a fast train to work. Where he could have run very fast with safety he was losing time. But when he approached Salisbury it is evident he was running very hard indeed, and the signal box times on the western approach showed that he must have been travelling at least at 70 m.p.h. in his immediate approach to the station. The result was a frightful smash. The engine heeled over as it commenced to negotiate that very intricate piece of track immediately east of the platforms; it hit the engine of a milk train on an adjacent track, and then the entire train was wrecked. There were 43 passengers aboard together with the guard, the travelling ticket collector, and two waiters; and

83

of those 43 passengers, 24 were killed. The dead also included the fireman and guard of the milk train.

Why this driver should have approached Salisbury as he did will never be known, for both he and his fireman were killed in the accident. But one thing seems fairly certain: although he was running far harder than was safe, detailed evidence of the running of the previous journeys through Salisbury on these American boat trains does indicate that he was not running very much faster, if at all, than had been customary at this location, with the smaller boilered type of 4-4-0 locomotive. In retrospect the whole affair is remarkable, because one would have thought that an occasional very fast run through that scissors crossing and round the curve would have excited the attention of the permanent way staff. Running at speeds so much in excess of the limit laid down, even though it occurred only once in a way, must have had a disturbing effect upon the track. Whether or not this disturbance was taken as 'just one of those things', and any irregularities were put right immediately after the passing of one of the specials is a matter for conjecture. But it seems very sure that with these special boat expresses, the safety margin was regularly reduced to a very small amount, and that it only needed the employment of a different class of engine to turn the risk into tragedy. As in the case of the accident at Preston in 1896, the disaster at Salisbury 10 years later had a shocking effect upon public opinion, so much so that any speeding on railways was for a time looked upon with the gravest apprehension, whether the conditions were risky or whether the trains were running on a perfectly straight stretch of first class track.

Less than two months later there came yet another alarming accident. Although this could also be placed in the category of excessive speed round curves the circumstances were very different from those at Salisbury. On the night of September 9th, 1906, at Grantham, Great Northern Railway, it is quite true that a night mail train was derailed through excessive speed on a curve; but the whole question, which was never resolved, was how the train ever came to travel as

far as it did, and get on to the particular stretch of line. The
circumstances were these: the 8.45 p.m. from Kings Cross,
which was an Anglo-Scottish express of an intermediate
character, conveying sleeping cars, but nevertheless doing a
certain amount of intermediate duty, was due to stop at
Grantham as part of its normal schedule. On the night in
question it was worked, as usual, by Doncaster enginemen
who were following through an engine working diagram
whereby they took a train from Doncaster to York; then
worked from York to Peterborough, and finally picked up
the 8.45 from Kings Cross at Peterborough to return to their
home shed. The driver in question, Fleetwood by name, had
his regular engine, a brand-new Ivatt Atlantic, No. 276 that
was only two months out of the Works. His fireman was a
premium apprentice from Doncaster Works who was gaining footplate experience. Fleetwood was a regular express
driver of long experience, and Talbot his mate, by the very
nature of his training, was a man above the average level of
intelligence for an ordinary working fireman; and yet with
these two otherwise experienced and reliable men the inexplicable happened.

Although they were booked to stop at Grantham they ran
through the station at about 40 m.p.h. At the north end the
points were set for the Nottingham branch, because the
signalman had set the road to cross a goods train from the
branch on to the main line. Witnesses on Grantham station
all gave their opinion that as the train ran through the brakes
were not on. The runaway, for as such it can only be described, took the points on to the Nottingham branch and
then the reverse curve following the turn-out. On this second
curve the tender became derailed and hit the parapet of a
bridge; all but 10 out of the 12 coaches on the train were
wrecked and many of them went down the embankment to
crash in a disastrous fire. Those that remained on the embankment were set on fire by coal scattered from the engine
firebox.

Mr. Edwin R. Harbron, of Northampton, has written this
vivid memory of the affair. 'As a schoolboy of eight, I was in

bed when it happened; but my Mother and Father, talking to a neighbour just outside our front door heard it happen and were soon on the scene, and saw the terrible consequences, with coaches burning, and the dead and injured being got out. I did not see it until the morning following, and what a mess it all was! The tender was derailed . . . it then struck the parapet of the Harlaston Road bridge midway over Harlaston Road, and sheared off the whole of the heavy brickwork from this point to the end of the bridge . . . some of the coaches were on the bridge, precariously perched on the edge of it, ready to topple into the street below.'

Both driver and fireman were killed and Col. P. G. Von Donop, the Inspecting Officer who made a most meticulous examination of every circumstance connected with the disaster, could find no explanation whatever to account for what had happened. Coming so soon after Salisbury public opinion was both shocked and non-plussed. All sorts of wild rumours circulated as to why the driver had not only failed to stop, but ran past a succession of signals that were at danger. There was suggestions that he was ill, that he was drunk, that he and his fireman had an argument and in the course of it did not realise where they were. But the mystery was only deepened by the very clear evidence of the signalman at the south end of Grantham station who stated that as the train passed him the driver and fireman were standing one on either side of the footplate looking ahead, and apparently doing nothing except observing through the cab glasses. The casualty list was a serious one, with 14 killed including the driver and fireman and a Post Office sorter; but the accident remains one of the greatest mysteries in British railway history.

Although the Inspecting Officer could find no reason for the failure of the train to stop in Grantham Station and the cause of that failure has generally been considered to remain a mystery, some recent correspondence throws another light on the subject which I do not think was brought out at the time of the enquiry. At Doncaster Shed some strong views

were held over the fact that there was not a registered fireman on engine No. 276, and instead a premium apprentice.
It was felt that while this young man might have been a good
and promising engineer, he was not competent to carry out
the duties of working an express train by himself, and that
the driver was probably doing the fireman's work in addition
to his own. Consequently the driver's attention may have
been distracted at the critical moment, although, of course,
it is hard to reconcile this supposition with the evidence
given by the signalman at Grantham South Box. This man, it
will be recalled, said that he saw both men on the engine
standing one on either side of the footplate and apparently
doing nothing except looking ahead through the cab glasses.
I understand that the A.S.L.E.F. took up strongly the practice of putting premium apprentices on the footplate without
a registered fireman, and that it was stopped.

The mystery surrounding the accident persisted for many
years, so much so, that the engine concerned, No. 276, was
always regarded as one of ill omen. Among Great Northern
men she became looked upon in the same way that on the
high seas there are unlucky ships. In the mid-nineteen twen-
ties a friend of mine was travelling on one of the high-speed
Pullman trains between Kings Cross and Leeds and was
interested to find the engine was No. 276, or as it was in
L.N.E.R. days 3276. They made rather a poor run, and on
arrival at Kings Cross my friend walked up to have a chat
with the driver. He was an elderly man who had been in
railway service for very many years, and in response to my
friend's enquiry he said: 'She is not a good engine. Never
has been since the accident at Grantham. You know, Sir,
yesterday was the anniversary of the smash, and as I took
her down I just wondered whether she might take the wrong
turning at the north end of the station!' This may have been
a leg-pull, but certainly 276 was never looked on with any
great favour.

As many more engines were built for the L.N.E.R. in the
mid-1930's, the Atlantics were gradually displaced from
their original duties and a number were drafted to the Great

Central line. Going over the lists of engine transfer at the time I was very amused to see that the Great Northern people had taken care to get rid of 3276. Then one morning in 1936 I had an engine pass to ride the 9.35 a.m. express from Sheffield Victoria to Marylebone, and as I stood on the platform, there, backing down from the shed to take the train came none other than the Great Northern Atlantic No. 3276. She was beautifully cleaned up, and I found her in charge of a couple of cheery Great Central men from Darnall shed. I must say I was greatly intrigued to see what kind of an engine she would prove. I should imagine that her driver and fireman on that occasion knew nothing of her past history, or if they did they certainly were not in the least affected by it. At that time in history she was a grand engine, and she gave me a very fast and exciting run to Leicester.

It may be no more than a coincidence, but all the accidents described in this chapter took place at night. The Preston and Salisbury derailments occurred in the small hours of the morning, while Grantham took place in the late evening. The fourth in this series of misfortunes was also an affair of the small hours, and in this case involved the West of England night mail from Manchester, while running on the L.N.W.R. Between Crewe and Shrewsbury this train was worked by a North Western engine and, of course, a stop was scheduled at Shrewsbury. But for some utterly unexplained reason the train came tearing down the bank from Hadnall, and without any slackening preparatory to stopping took the sharp curve that leads into Shrewsbury station. The engine overturned at once, and the whole train piled up on the wrecked engine. As at Salisbury and Grantham the driver and fireman were killed, and the reasons for their approach to the station in this apparently reckless and uncontrolled way were never established. Again, as at Grantham, all sorts of wild theories were advanced to try and account for what had happened; but an examination of the wreckage and of all the factors leading up to the accident gave not the slightest clue that would lead to a real solution of the mystery.

One point gave the daily newspapers a chance to do a good deal of scare-mongering. The engine concerned was a new Whale, 4-6-0 No. 2052 *Stephenson*. As might be imagined some correspondents made great play with the fact that the engine was an 'Experiment', and felt that the railway company was very much to blame for using engines that were of an 'experimental' nature! I have likened the case to Grantham, where a train approached at greatly excessive speed a station at which it was required to stop. At Grantham the train ran right through and was wrecked afterwards; at Shrewsbury it was wrecked in the approaches. The principal difference which heightened the mystery surrounding the Shrewsbury affair, was that a signalman observed the driver and fireman on the Great Northern engine No. 276 doing nothing but standing on either side of the footplate and apparently staring ahead through the cab glasses. At Shrewsbury nobody saw the enginemen at all.

Arguments were advanced that the speed of modern travelling was having a very bad effect upon the nerves of locomotive enginemen, and that some of them were breaking down under the strain. This was a very poor argument to use in the case of both the Grantham and Shrewsbury accidents, because they occurred to trains that were certainly not in the top flight so far as speed, or importance was concerned. In both cases, although express passenger trains were involved they would be regarded as secondary services.

7

Disasters on the Settle and Carlisle Line

By the first decade of the twentieth century British railway operating had reached standards of safety that were the envy of the whole world. In speed our one-time supremacy had been surpassed, both in France and America, but the comfort of the ordinary British express train, by both day and night, was worth a good deal more than a few less minutes on the journey. From the bitter experience of many accidents, the more important and significant of which have been described in earlier chapters of this book, the rules and regulations of working had been gradually perfected, and many additional safeguards in operation introduced. At the same time other factors were entering in. It was the Golden Age of railways in Great Britain. Traffic was booming: road transport was hardly a competitor at all—let alone a serious one—and there is no doubt that individual railwaymen were kept very busy, especially at peak holiday periods. As always hitherto, the safety of working largely devolved upon two groups of men, the signalmen, and the locomotive drivers and firemen. By that time all traffic working on passenger lines was regulated by signal indication. There were no longer any lines in Great Britain worked by telegraphic train orders.

Accidents from this time onwards tended to group themselves into two categories: those in which signalmen inadvertently, or through gross carelessness contravened the block working regulations, and set up conditions that were highly dangerous; and those arising from drivers overrunning signals. Although the past history of British railways had included incidents like Grantham and Shrewsbury where the conduct of the locomotive men was seemingly inexplicable, railwaymen as a body were, and still are men with a very high sense of responsibility, and the cases of purely wanton carelessness can fortunately be counted on the fingers of one hand. Failures of the human element could usually be traced to some extraordinary circumstance, and this was no more vividly the case than the events leading to the disaster near Hawes Junction—later known as Garsdale —in the early hours of Christmas Eve, 1910.

The Midland, under the dynamic management of Guy Granet, was one of the most highly organised railways in the Kingdom. Its express train service was a model of punctuality and comfort; the revenue from its goods and mineral traffic was princely; and yet its methods were such that an act of simple forgetfulness on the part of a steady and painstaking man of humble grade was to lead to an accident that brought odium upon the company out of all proportion to the magnitude of the occurrence or of the death roll. Yet if the circumstances that led to that mistake are traced back to their basic origin they take us far away from any details of signalling at Hawes Junction, or even of train working on the Settle and Carlisle line in general, and lead to matters of high managerial policy, and the clash of personalities in high places. Matters point, in the very first place, to nothing less than the appointment of Guy Granet as General Manager, because it was his accession to power that led to changes in organisational policy, and the resignation of R. M. Deeley from the post of Chief Mechanical Engineer.

Deeley had plans for the development of top line passenger motive power on the Midland Railway that would keep it at least abreast, if not ahead of what other large English railways were doing. In the famous 3-cylinder compound 4-4-0 he had an excellent engine, and his plans included the development of this principle into a large 4-cylinder compound 4-6-0. But the top-line organisation that took responsibility for the day-to-day running of the trains out of his hands offended him deeply. His plans for

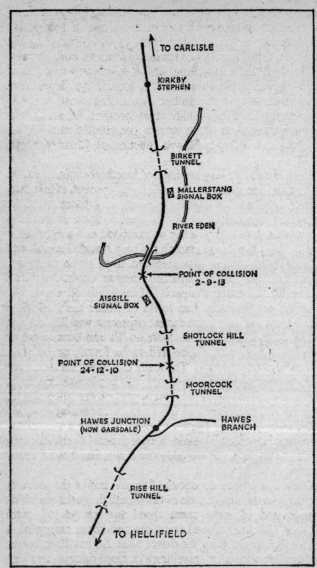

Fig. 6. Sketch map showing site of collisions in 1910 and 1913.

larger locomotives were vetoed, and finding his position intolerable he resigned. Thereafter the scope of locomotive development on the Midland Railway was dictated by the traffic department policy of running a large number of trains of relatively light formation, and a strict curb was placed upon capital expenditure in the locomotive department itself. But there was another factor that most seriously affected the working of individual locomotives, and which perhaps, more than the other two, contributed to the situation that developed at Hawes Junction on Christmas Eve, 1910.

With the day-to-day working of locomotives from end to end of the line vested in the traffic department, rather than that of the Chief Mechanical Engineer, any discretion in the allocation of engines to duties, based upon engineering knowledge, could not readily be exercised and a set of hard and fast regulations of loading for each class of engine, and booked speed of train, was prepared, from which an operating officer could decide at once whether a particular load was within the unaided capacity of the available engine. For example, on the main line south of Leeds the load for a No. 3 class engine on the fastest expresses was 205 tons. If the load was 210 tons there were no 'ifs and buts' about it; either a No. 4 class engine had to be found, or the train would be double-headed. The loads laid down for each class were on the light side, because the principle was laid down that there should be no discrimination in the allocation of engines. Any No. 3 class on the strength, for example, would work a 205-ton train south of Leeds, whether it was a first-class unit just nicely worked in after general overhaul at the works, or an engine thoroughly run down, and due for heavy repairs.

Quite apart from questions of engine power the series of accidents in the first decade of the twentieth century in which signals, and in some cases speed restrictions too, were ignored, indicated a need for some additional safeguard, a device that would warn the driver when he was disregarding the wayside signals, or travelling at a speed dangerously high

93

for the particular stretch of line. As told in the preceding chapter there had been the derailment at high speed of an American boat express on the curve east of Salisbury, L.S.W.R.: the derailment of a down Scottish express at Grantham, and again the derailment of an L.N.W.R. express, which for some unexplained reason approached Shrewsbury station at full speed. In each case the enginemen were killed, so that the reasons for these apparent lapses will never be known. Inventors were busy, and several forms of automatic train control were put on the market, including the very successful system later standard on the Great Western Railway. At that time, however, track circuiting was still in its infancy, and its potentialities were not fully realised until yet another disaster, and the harrowing circumstances in which the victims met their deaths, had deeply moved public opinion. This, the collision in wild fell country near Hawes Junction on Christmas Eve, 1910, was not, from the railway point of view, an affair of the first magnitude, but its effects were far-reaching.

During the night of December 23rd-24th, traffic over the line to and from Scotland was heavy. In addition to the ordinary trains there were many specials, and the majority of them required to be double-headed. Because of the curious locomotive policy of the Midland Railway at that time there were no engines on the system permitted to haul a load of more than 230 tons between Hellifield and Carlisle in express passenger service, and only 10 of this largest class, the '999' series were in regular use north of Leeds. The mainstay of the traffic were the No. 2 class 4-4-0s, which were limited to a maximum load of 180 tons over the mountain section. Although the practice of the Midland Railway then was to operate a series of light trains at frequent intervals, rather than a few heavy trains, the locomotive power available was generally inadequate. To save engine mileage the pilots whether working from Carlisle, Leeds or Hellifield, were detached at Aisgill summit whence they travelled the three miles southward to Hawes Junction, to turn before proceeding light to their home stations. Thus, with the pilots

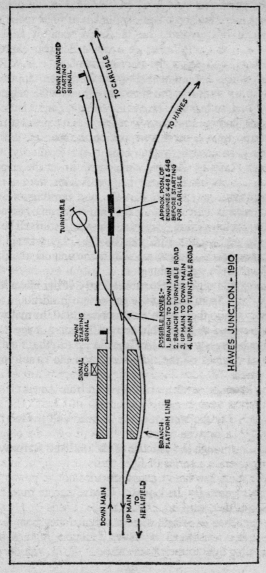

HAWES JUNCTION – 1910

DOWN ADVANCED STARTING SIGNAL

TO CARLISLE

TO HAWES

TURNTABLE

Approx. posn. of engines 448 & 548 before starting for Carlisle

DOWN STARTING SIGNAL

SIGNAL BOX

POSSIBLE MOVES:-
1. BRANCH TO DOWN MAIN
2. BRANCH TO TURNTABLE ROAD
3. UP MAIN TO DOWN MAIN
4. UP MAIN TO TURNTABLE ROAD

BRANCH PLATFORM LINE

DOWN MAIN

UP MAIN TO HELLIFIELD

Fig. 7. Track layout at Hawes Junction.

of both down and up expresses coming from Aisgill there was always a number of light engine movements going on in the neighbourhood of Hawes Junction at intervals during the day and night. The accompanying sketch map shows the railway in the vicinity of Hawes Junction.

The central mountain section of the Settle and Carlisle line contains all the elements of high drama. The wilderness of the countryside; the stupendous engineering of the railway, with its long tunnels driven through the great fells and lofty viaducts over valleys and remote ravines; the ominous lines of snow fences, and above all the frequency of incidence of wild inclement weather help to set the stage for railway working in the grand manner. Against these elemental difficulties the Midland Railway was working its Scotch express traffic with locomotives that were undersized by comparison with those of their neighbours and rivals to west and east. Train after train toiled up the 'Long Drag' from Settle Junction to Blea Moor with two engines, while from the north side to the wilderness of Aisgill expresses would not infrequently be cutting into the fury of the Helm Wind, in addition to fighting the long and severe gradients.

In the early hours of Christmas Eve, 1910, so many light engines congregated at Hawes Junction as to suggest that almost every train had been assisted up to Aisgill summit. The following is a condensed version of the signal-box log book:

4.6 a.m. engines 548 and 448 arrived from Aisgill;
4.14 a.m.: down express passed;
Engines 548 and 448 were then turned and parked in the branch platform line;
4.36 a.m. engines 247, 249, 313, and 314 arrived from Aisgill, coupled together;
4.41 a.m. down 'fitted' goods passed;
Engines 247, 249, 313, and 314 were then crossed to the turntable road;
4.47 a.m. engines 317, 312, and 42 arrived from Aisgill, coupled together, and were crossed to the turntable road;

4.49 a.m. up through goods passed;
5.20 a.m. down special express passed.

As a matter of interest the actual classes of these various light engines may here be recorded:

Engine No.	Type	Class	Description
42	2-4-0	1	Kirtley rebuilt
247	2-4-0	1	Johnson type
249	2-4-0	1	„ „
312	4-4-0	1	Johnson type unrebuilt
313	4-4-0	1	„ „ „
314	4-4-0	1	„ „ „
317	4-4-0	1	„ „ „
448	4-4-0	2	6ft. 6in. non-superheater rebuild
548	4-4-0	2	7ft. non-superheater rebuild

In the early hours of that tragic Christmas Eve, Hawes Junction would have provided a veritable 'spotters' paradise. Through the 'small-engine' policy of the Midland Railway, and the rigid restriction of train loads, Hawes Junction from being little more than a wayside signalbox became a major operating point. It is perhaps expressing things a little too strongly to suggest that on this particular night the signalman was overworked; but there is certainly some excuse for his fatal lapse of memory at a critical moment.

At this time the Hawes Junction signalman, Alfred Sutton, had no less than nine engines under his control. He was naturally anxious to return these to their various home stations as soon as possible, although the pressure of traffic was still great. An up class 'A' goods train, accepted under the warning arrangement, was approaching from Aisgill and a most important train, the midnight sleeping car express from St. Pancras to Glasgow was due shortly. After the passage at 5.20 a.m. of the down special express, Sutton crossed the two Carlisle engines, the 4-4-0s 448 and 548, on to the down main line, and these engines drew up some considerable distance short of the advance starting signal. The tracks concerned are shown in the second diagram. It was the signalman's intention to send the two Carlisle engines away as soon as he received the clearing signal from Aisgill for the special express; but it just happened that when that signal came through Sutton was very busy with other matters. Three further engines were ready to depart, southward this time; the up class 'A' goods was at hand; one of the Leeds pilot enginemen required a message concerning his relief to be sent off, and there came too, a telephone inquiry about some Hellifield engines which were at that time on the turntable road.

It will be appreciated that Signalman Sutton's attention was almost entirely taken up with the various light engines and their movements, and in his preoccupation he forgot the two Carlisle pilots. The enginemen of these two locomotives were expecting to be signalled away as soon as the special express had cleared Aisgill, and not one of the four men on engines 448 and 548 seems to have realised that they were being held much longer than would ordinarily have been necessary. Under Rule 55 one of the firemen should have been sent back to the signalbox to remind the signalman of their presence after they had been detained for five minutes; but this was not done, and neither driver whistled nor did anything to attract the signalman's attention. The latter continued to be very busy, so much so that the two Carlisle engines passed out of his mind, and when at 5.39 a.m. he was offered the midnight express from Dent he accepted it at once, and shortly afterwards offered it forward to Aisgill. It was accepted at once by the latter box, so that when the 'Train Entering Section' signal was received from Dent, Sutton merely acknowledged it, all the necessary signals having been lowered when the train was accepted by Aisgill. Of course the light engines 448 and 548 had started away when the advanced starting signal was pulled off about 5.43 a.m., but as the express passed through Hawes Junction at 5.47 a.m. travelling at 60-65 m.p.h. the Carlisle engines had very little start. In other circumstances their tail light might have been seen, but there was a heavy gale blowing, with driving mist and rain, added to which a short tunnel impeded the view ahead.

It was significant of the number of engine movements proceeding at Hawes Junction that it was not until one of the Hellifield drivers came into the box, about 5.58 a.m., and reminded him that Sutton realised that he had forgotten about the Carlisle engines, and that after an interval of eight minutes he had not received the 'out of section' signal from Aisgill for the midnight express. When the day signalman came on duty at 6 a.m. there was already a reflection of light on the low clouds driving over the fells north of Hawes Junction. That glow told its own tale, and Sutton said to the relief man: 'Will you go to Stationmaster Bunce and say that I am afraid I have wrecked the Scotch express?' That express, also double-headed, with a Kirtley 2-4-0 No. 48 piloting a 7ft. Class '2' rebuilt 4-4-0 No. 549 had overtaken the light engines at a point about $1\frac{1}{2}$ miles north of Hawes Junction, and as the speeds were approximately 30 m.p.h. and 65 m.p.h. the resulting collision was violent; even so, the effects would have not been very serious but for a disastrous outbreak of fire. Both locomotives of the express and seven out of the eight coaches were derailed; the first two coaches were telescoped and it was in these that all the fatal casualties occurred. One of the most distressing features of the accident was that some of the 12 persons who lost their lives were still conscious when the fire reached them; the gallant attempts at rescue by their fellow-passengers failed for want of suitable tools, and through the rapid spreading of the fire. The two coaches that were telescoped were lit by compressed oil gas on Pintsch's system, and the fire originated in an escape of this gas when some of the cylinders and their connections were damaged in the derailment. Owing to the locking of buffers and the derailment of wheels it was not possible to uncouple more than the last two vehicles of the train, and so the remaining six coaches were eventually destroyed by fire.

Although the immediate cause of the accident was the simple act of forgetfulness by Signalman Sutton, in letting the light engines Nos. 548 and 448 pass from his mind, it was the plain fact that he had so many light engines to deal with, in addition to the handling of ordinary traffic, that undoubtedly led to his lapse. Great attention was paid subsequently to means for safeguarding against similar lapses, but it was a case of dealing with the effects rather than the true cause of the trouble. That cause was nothing more nor less than inadequate engine power. One of the crowning misfortunes of the whole affair was that in a matter of seconds the midnight express would have been slowing down to stop at Aisgill and detach its own pilot. Had the Carlisle pilot engines left Hawes Junction more smartly they might have been sufficiently clear to have avoided the express as it drew in to stop at Aisgill.

Before considering the Inspecting Officer's conclusions, and the very extensive precautions taken by the Midland Railway Company, the essential details of the second accident may be described as there are points of similarity between the two. The collision of September 2nd, 1913, took place at a point about three-quarters of a mile north of Aisgill summit, between two southbound sleeping car expresses. As at Hawes Junction it was the mistake of an operating man that was the immediate cause of the accident. The trains concerned were the 1.35 a.m. and 1.49 a.m. from Carlisle, which on this particular morning left three and five minutes late, respectively. The first train was loaded to 243 tons tare, behind the tender and with a No. 4 class engine should have been piloted up to Aisgill; the driver asked for assistance before leaving Carlisle, but no pilot was immediately available, and on this account the enginemen would not have been blamed if a few minutes had been lost on the ascent. On the earlier part of the journey very good time was made considering that the engine was overloaded on this express schedule, and on passing Ormside signalbox, $33\frac{1}{2}$ miles from Carlisle, in 42 minutes, only one minute had been lost. Between Ormside and Aisgill summit the road is severe, and by then the engine was steaming very badly; the pressure eventually dropped to between 80 lb. and 90 lb. per square inch, and the train stalled with the engine only about half a mile from the level road at the summit.

The failure of engine No. 993 was due to unsuitable coal. With the evident intention of reducing transport of loco-motive coal the Midland Railway had placed a contract with a Cumberland firm, the Naworth Coal Company, for supply-ing Carlisle shed. This fuel had an excellent calorific value of 15,150 B.Th.U. per pound, but much of that supplied was very small, and although when efficiently screened it proved most satisfactory in service, it was unfortunately a bad con-signment that was loaded on to the tenders of the two engines concerned in the accident. Driver Nicholson told how he himself fired No. 993 for some distance south of Ormside, and between Kirkby Stephen and Mallerstang the speed averaged only 20 m.p.h. But even with pressure down to 80 lb. or 90 lb. per square inch it would have been possible to surmount the final stage of the climb had not the vacuum in the train pipe been partially destroyed, and the brakes leaked on in consequence. While most types of ejector will operate satisfactorily over a considerable range of steam pressure, on reaching the lower critical point the efficiency drops abruptly, and this evidently happened on engine No. 993 south of Mallerstang. Driver Nicholson said that the vacuum had fallen from the normal 20 in. to 15 in. before they stalled.

In the meantime the second express, having taken 45 minutes from Carlisle to Ormside, a loss of four minutes, was making considerably better speed than the first express had done between Ormside and Mallerstang. The engine concerned, however, No. 2 class 4-4-0 No. 446 had a load of only 157 tons, 23 tons inside the maximum permitted with-out assistance, although her steaming also was suffering to a lesser extent from the effects of small coal. This engine was not then fitted with a superheater; mechanical lubrication had not been applied, and Driver Caudle followed the pre-vailing custom of going round the engine, while running, to replenish the auxiliary oil boxes. In doing so, enginemen would naturally choose a stretch of line where the speed is not high and Driver Caudle went out as they were approaching Birkett tunnel. Before this the steaming had given some trouble, and he admitted feeling anxiety on that account. He was out on the running plate when they passed through the tunnel. Subsequently he said: 'I remember when we came out of Birkett tunnel I looked ahead and could see the Mallerstang distant signal, and got the impression it was in the clear position.' When, however, he returned to the cab there was no water showing in the gauge glass; the right-hand injector had failed and the left-hand injector was not functioning properly on account of low steam pressure— 140 lb. per square inch, instead of the normal 175 lb. Although he had taken so perfunctory a look at the Mallerstang distant signal Driver Caudle so busied himself in getting the right-hand injector to work that he ran past the remaining Mallerstang signals at about 30 m.p.h. without observing them at all.

Even so the Mallerstang signalman himself may have contributed in one degree towards the accident, although the men on the second express did not claim that his action in any way influenced their subsequent action. Having had his distant signal on, and the home likewise, when he saw the train approaching his first impression was that it was going to stop all right, and he lowered his home signal to allow, as he thought, the train to draw up to the starting signal. But as the train neared his box he saw to his horror that it was steaming hard, and it ran past all his signals without the slightest sign of having taken any warning. If Driver Caudle had seen the home signal change from red to green it might have misled him. But he never made the point in evidence. All his subsequent actions were based on that quick perfunctory look at the Mallerstang distant, seen when he was out on the front of his engine passing through Birkett tunnel. The train is recorded as having passed Mallerstang at 2.57 a.m., the precise moment that the first express stalled north of Aisgill.

Although the circumstances in which Caudle passed Mallerstang without properly observing the signals can be appreciated, it is difficult to understand his subsequent negligence. It would seem that he was so worried about maintaining steam pressure as to let this one point override every other consideration. According to his evidence, they were continually losing pressure, although he quoted no actual figures, so that he, too, may have foreseen a possible loss of vacuum in the train pipe. In any event he maintained his previous regulator and reverse positions, thus continuing to steam the engine hard, and watched the fireman at his work to see that the coal was put on to the best advantage. Even although he was proceeding thus blindly towards the standing train, there was still a chance that a collision might be averted. The crew of the first express saw in the distance the glare from the open fire-door as the second express climbed the bank, and later heard the heavy exhaust beat. One of the guards went back to give warning, but the enginemen of the second express were so preoccupied that when they did at last sight the tail lamps, and the hand lamp carried by this guard, there was scarcely time to apply the brake before the engine crashed into the first train. It is sad to reflect that up to the very last minute the second express might have been stopped. Driver Caudle estimated that he could have stopped from his full speed, on the 1 in 100 gradient, in 50 yards, and if the speed was actually no more than 30 m.p.h. this estimate is not far wide of the mark. As it was, the affair ended in a tragic repetition of Christmas Eve, 1910. The engine ploughed through the last vehicle of the standing train, which was fortunately a van, and buried itself in the passenger coach immediately in front. Fire broke out, but in this instance the 14 passengers whom it was not possible to extricate from the wreckage were all so severely injured in the actual collision that it is fairly certain that they were either dead or unconscious when the fire reached them. Two other passengers died later.

Taken together, these two accidents, occurring within a few miles of each other, exemplify some of the commonest forms of operating mistake: the act of simple forgetfulness by Signalman Sutton at Hawes Junction, in 1910; and Driver

Caudle's mis-reading of the Mallerstang distant signal, in 1913. At the same time, Caudle's actions after passing Mallerstang disclose a certain mentality that is induced to take serious risks for some reason that cannot be considered as other than trivial in comparison with the over-riding need to ensure the safety of passengers. The inquiry was in both cases conducted by Lieut. Col. Sir John Pringle, and in the case of the Hawes Junction accident some of his recommendations were acted upon in so comprehensive a manner by the Midland Railway as to influence subsequent practice in a way out of all proportion to the magnitude of the actual disaster, serious though it was. After reviewing all the circumstances that led to the two Carlisle light engines being forgotten by Signalman Sutton and the failure of the enginemen concerned to carry out Rule 55, Col. Pringle recommended that, 'in view of the turntable work at Hawes Junction, and the number of engine movements, this yard should be treated as a special case. The up and down lines between the advanced starting signals and the crossover roads in rear of them respectively should be track-circuited, and the levers working the starting signals thereby controlled. This block post can then be exempted from the operation of Rule 55.'

To Guy Granet, who had set such store upon the efficient operation of the Midland Railway the Hawes Junction collision was a great blow. On his recommendation the Board went much further in adopting safety measures than Col. Pringle had recommended, and in view of this the occurrence of a second accident in the same neighbourhood less than three years later was a crushing misfortune. Granet took the unusual step of asking to be permitted to make a special statement during the inquiry into the Aisgill collision. He recalled the Inspecting Officer's comments upon the 1910 accident, and described in detail the steps that had been taken in particular to implement his recommendation about track circuiting at Hawes Junction. About the gas lighting of the carriages his statement was not so reassuring.

But so far as Col. Pringle's recommendation about track circuiting was concerned, this was duly carried out at Hawes

Junction; furthermore, in the light of it a survey of the whole Midland system was made, and it was decided that in over 2,000 places the traffic conditions were such as to require apparatus for guarding against possible failures of the human element. Upwards of 900 track circuits were installed, and this work constitutes one of the most extensive early examples of the use of track circuiting in mechanically signalled territory. There is always a tendency to associate track circuiting primarily with power installation, either with large interlockings or with automatically signalled lines, and at the time of the Hawes Junction accident track circuiting was still in its infancy. Still more so was the allied art of automatic train control. While track circuiting acts as a corrective to signalmen's errors, it cannot provide a safeguard against the failure of enginemen to observe the wayside signals correctly and Driver Caudle's fatal error at Mallerstang, which resulted in the Aisgill collision, raised the question in an acute form. In his report Col. Pringle reviewed the existing systems of automatic train control and cab signalling, and in the light of subsequent development some of his remarks are of particular interest

Referring to the automatic train stops used on the tube railways of London he said: 'The arrangement is very suitable for an omnibus service at moderate speeds, especially where all the trains are fitted with the continuous brake, but there are difficulties when other conditions prevail, as on steam-worked railways. It involves special fittings to all locomotives as well as to outdoor signals. I do not think the device has been adequately tried by steam railways. Great accuracy in regard to gauge is necessary with these train stops. Whether such accuracy can be obtained when train stops are worked mechanically at considerable distances remains to be determined. Where electrical or other power is available, the maintainance of gauge should not be a difficult matter. It is certainly a device which railway companies should unite in experimenting with more fully, and should adopt, if found to be reliable and practical at high speeds. It would certainly very adequately meet the demand for additional safety.'

About the Great Western system of audible cab signalling the Inspecting Officer was not so enthusiastic. He said: 'The principle of cab signalling, in conjunction with audible signalling, has, so far as distant signals are concerned, been adopted by the Great Western at a number of important centres. The object was, primarily to meet the difficulties in connection with fog signalling at distant signals. But it cannot be said that the method has yet proved to be efficient, to the extent of meeting adequately the very complicated requirements of traffic on English Railways. It will have to be experimented with much more thoroughly and subjected to further prolonged tests under ordinary working conditions, before it will be possible to recommend it as a panacea for all difficulties.'

In Great Britain progress with automatic train control was hindered if not entirely suspended by the war of 1914-18, so that the lessons of Aisgill and Col. Pringle's recommendations in that direction had no immediate outcome. But after the cessation of hostilities the matter was revived, and one of the most important conclusions of a committee under his chairmanship, on which all the British railways were represented, was the almost unanimous acceptance in principle of the Great Western system of audible cab signalling and train control. Owing to the lapse of time, and the occurrence of other accidents from somewhat similar causes it cannot be said that Aisgill directly influenced the quest for an ideal system of automatic train control in the same way as Hawes Junction gave a fillip to track circuiting; but the shock of a second collision, and fire, in the Hawes Junction to Kirkby Stephen district, following so comparatively soon, and the widespread concern aroused did have the effect of making the public automatic train control-minded for a while. For the railway operating men Aisgill will always remain a classic example of the dire results of misreading signals.

8

Quintinshill

In the previous chapter dealing with the tragic accident near Hawes Junction one consequence of exceptional traffic was highlighted. On May 22nd, 1915, on the Saturday before Whitsun another, and far more terrible consequence arose. At that time in the progress of World War I, there were many who felt that whatever was happening on the various battlefields overseas a pretence of normality should be kept up at home. Whether or not the approach of a bank holiday did contribute to the heavy traffic that was flowing it would have been quite in the spirit of certain sections of the civilian community if it had done. But before coming to describe the almost incredible chain of events that led to such dire disaster some reference is needed to the railway topography of the area, because it had a considerable bearing on the case.

The Caledonian main line approaching Carlisle was, at certain times of the day one of the busiest stretches of double line railway in the Kingdom. Over the last $8\frac{1}{2}$ miles, from Gretna Junction into the Citadel station the Glasgow and South Western Railway exercised running powers, while from Port Carlisle Junction inwards, a distance of about $1\frac{1}{4}$ miles, the North British Railway also had running powers. Two miles out of Citadel on the east side of the line were the large Kingmoor running sheds, but there was no freight train activity in those yards. All goods traffic had to proceed further south to the Dentonholme yards, where traffic from the Scottish lines was exchanged with the North Western, the Midland, and the North Eastern.

Between Kingmoor and Gretna the line was double-tracked and there were two small intermediate stations, Rockliffe and Floriston. In years before the war the Caledonian had found it necessary to put in accommodation for berthing freight trains clear of the Gretna-Citadel bottleneck, yet still reasonably near to Carlisle, and long running loops had been put in on both down and up sides at Quintinshill a point about $1\frac{1}{2}$ miles north of Gretna. At this box also there was a trailing cross-over on the main lines. From the viaduct over the River Esk, at the head of the Solway Firth and a mile before the line passes from England into Scotland, a long rising gradient commences, first at 1 in 193 and then continuously at 1 in 200 to a summit point about halfway between Kirkpatrick and Kirtlebridge stations.

On the fateful morning of May 22nd, 1915, events centred round the time when the signalmen changed shift, that was at 6 a.m. About that time the most important regular movements were the passage of the 11.45 p.m. and midnight expresses from Euston. The former, for Edinburgh and Aberdeen was booked to leave Carlisle at 5.50 a.m., and the latter, non-stop to Glasgow, was booked to leave at 6.5 a.m. This latter train was followed at 6.10 a.m. by an all-stations local; but in addition to providing a connection from Carlisle for roadside stations to Beattock this train, always known locally as the 'Parley' had some forward connections of its own to make at Beattock. In years before the war the Caledonian Railway was assiduously trying to cultivate a long distance residential traffic from Glasgow to stations in upper Clydesdale, and the Tinto Express was put on, running non-stop between Glasgow Central and Thankerton, and then serving all stations to Moffat. The 6.10 a.m. 'Parley' from Carlisle fed into the northbound 'Tinto' which left Beattock at 7.49 a.m. Naturally much store was set upon the punctual running of the latter train, and consequently the working of the 6.10 a.m. from Carlisle had an importance considerably greater than that of a mere local train.

It is evident however that, despite the traditional speed and efficiency of train working on the L.N.W.R., and the regularity with which lost time was made up, both the

11.45 p.m. and the 'midnight' from Euston were bad time-keepers—so much so that the Caledonian had regular traffic working arrangements of its own if the London trains were more than 15 or 20 minutes late. It was considered more important not to delay the Tinto waiting for connections from south of Beattock than to sever connections to wayside stations north of Carlisle from the London 'sleepers'. So when the latter were appreciably late the 6.10 a.m. 'Parley' was dispatched ahead of them, and sidetracked at the first convenient point farther down the line. Shunting sometimes took place at Kirkpatrick, but equally often it seems to have taken place at Quintinshill where the siding accommodation was usually ample. In the six months prior to Whitsun 1915 the shunting of the 6.10 a.m. at Quintinshill had taken place on no less than 21 occasions. The frequency of a stop at Quintinshill had led the signalmen working that box into a most reprehensible practice. The box was out in the country, with no dwellings near, and the men lived in Gretna. Ordinarily it would have meant a walk, or a bicycle ride of some $1\frac{1}{2}$ miles from home to duty; but instead, an arrangement grew up by which if the 6.10 was stopping at Quintinshill the relief man rode on it from Gretna and took over his duties on arrival of the train.

It was easy enough to find out previously from the Gretna signalman if the 6.10 was stopping at Quintinshill, and as the arrangement favoured each of the signalmen working that box in turn they contrived between them a way of concealing the fact that they were changing over shift at an unauthorised time. After 6 a.m. the night man ceased to make direct entries in the train register, but made them on a separate sheet of paper. The day man, on taking over, would copy these entries into the train register book in his own hand, so that anyone examining the register would not detect by the handwriting that the change of shift had not been made at the authorised time of 6 a.m. This, of course, while a highly reprehensible breach of discipline was not inherently dangerous, except that the day man could be occupied on a task that should be done as and when events took place, and in his eagerness to cover up the deceit as soon as possible could be engaged on it when he should have been giving all his attention to immediate happenings.

Yet this practice, like everything else on that tragic morning, stemmed from that one simple fact that the two night expresses from Euston were running late. Both trains were running about half an hour late and the 6.10 a.m. 'Parley', consisting of three bogie coaches and a milk van, was despatched from Carlisle on time, hauled by the big 'Cardean' class, 4-6-0 No. 907. It ran normally out to Gretna, where the day signalman at Quintinshill was waiting to join it. For the short distance from Gretna Junction to Quintinshill he rode on the footplate of the engine, but on arrival at the box at 6.24 a.m. he was faced with the first circumstance that led to the catastrophe. The down running loop was occupied by a goods train, so the only way to sidetrack the local was to propel it through the trailing crossover on to the up main line.

There was nothing unusual or dangerous in such a manoeuvre providing certain well established safety precautions were taken, and in the six months prior to the event it had been done on four occasions. But it took a little time, and the 'train out of section' signal was not sent to Gretna until 6.33 a.m. only just in time for the first of the Euston 'sleepers' to be accepted. This train passed without incident at 6.38 a.m.; but in the meantime, in the signalbox itself events began to move rapidly towards the most fearful disaster. Just at that time a train of empty coal wagons was drawing into the up running loop. But although 'train out of section' for this goods was received at Kirkpatrick at 6.34 a.m. neither the night nor the day signalman at Quintinshill admitted to sending it. The day signalman, James Tinsley by name, on taking over was much more concerned with getting the train register up to date, and he immediately busied himself with copying the entries which Meakin, the night man, had made on a sheet of paper prior to Tinsley's arrival. At the very start his sense of responsibility was sadly lacking, because although he himself had travelled on

110

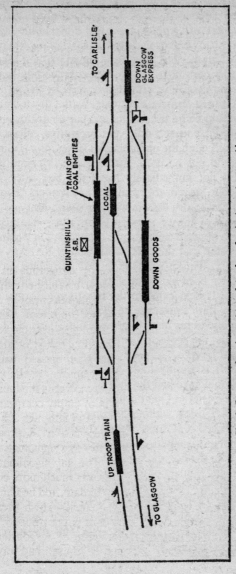

Fig. 8. Diagram of tracks, position of signals, and trains just prior to accident.

the 6.10 a.m. from Gretna, and was fully aware of how it had been shunted, he took no steps to check that the two fundamental safety precautions laid down in the regulations of the company had been carried out.

First of all the 'blocking back' signal had not been sent to Kirkpatrick, the next box to the north, to advise that box that the up main line, although cleared by the train of coal empties was nevertheless occupied by the down 'Parley' and that it would be no use asking for 'line clear' for any south-bound train; and secondly, the protective collars had not been placed upon the up line signal levers, as a reminder that they should not be used. Furthermore, Meakin, the night man, did not immediately leave the box after Tinsley's arrival, but stayed to read the newspapers Tinsley had brought and to discuss the war news with him and with the brakesmen of the two goods trains who were also in the signalbox. So what with his pre-occupation in writing up the train register, and the extraneous chatter that was going on in the box, Tinsley's attention was distracted from what should have been his prime duty. Finally, the fireman of the 6.10 a.m. 'Parley' came to the box to give formal notifica-tion of his train's presence on the up line; but in doing so he failed in one of his most important duties, namely to see for himself that the protective collars had been placed on the up line signal levers.

The rest is simply told. At 6.42 a.m. Kirkpatrick box, which should have had the 'blocking back' signal, offered an up troop special to Quintinshill. Starkly incredible though it may seem Tinsley, without pausing to look outside the win-dow, accepted it at once, and promptly pulled off all his up line signals. It is equally astonishing that the other railway-men then in the box did not realise what was happening. By that time the fireman of the 6.10 a.m. 'Parley' had gone back to his engine, or he above all must certainly have realised the danger. Then, as if this were not enough, the belated mid-night express from Euston was then offered to Quintinshill. Again Tinsley accepted it at once, and pulled off all his down line signals. To some celestial onlooker that little

112

group of sidings at Quintinshill could well have looked like the chosen scene for some deliberate, pre-ordained cataclysm. Southwards down the 1 in 200 gradient from Brackenhill summit was speeding a crowded troop train at 70 m.p.h., while across the Solway viaduct, double-headed, and trying to recover a little of its lateness was the Euston 'sleeper' also doing nearly 70 m.p.h. And at a point very near to where those two fast trains would pass each other there was a mighty obstruction!

Even at this late hour, when human frailty had set the stage for a collision without parallel, there might have been left just one chance of escape. The line south of Kirkpatrick is straight for some three miles; but just as Quintinshill is approached the line curves slightly to the right on a radius of 80 chains. At the commencement of this curve there is an overbridge. But the signalbox itself can be seen through the arch of the bridge for some considerable distance previous to this, and there was more than a slight chance that the enginemen of the troop train might have seen the standing 6.10 a.m. 'Parley' in time to pull up, save for one crowning misfortune. There was a northbound goods train standing in the down running loop, and on account of the curve in the line it obscured the 'local' from view through the bridge. So the troop train came on at full speed under clear signals. The engine was a McIntosh superheater 4-4-0 No. 121 with a load of 21 vehicles: four Great Central bogie coaches; 11 Great Central six-wheelers; five Caledonian six-wheeled vans, and one Caledonian open scenery bogie truck. The special was conveying the 1/7th battalion of the Royal Scots, who had entrained at Larbert.

This long variedly-composed train collided head on, at almost full speed, with the standing 6.10 a.m. local train, which with its brakes on was a veritably immovable obstacle. The impact was terrible and the long train which had measured 213 yards overall was reduced to a heap of wreckage only 67 yards long from end to end. The 4-4-0 engine No. 121 was virtually *destroyed* in the collision but although the 'Cardean' class 4-6-0 No. 907 was very extensively damaged, she was afterwards towed back to St. Rollox, and lay there for some time before it was decided that she was beyond repair. But immediately after that first fearful collision both engines were almost buried under a heap af shattered wooden coaches from the troop train, many of which had shot clean over their own engine. In the force of collision the tender coupling of engine No. 907 had broken and the four vehicles of that train had run backwards towards Gretna and comparative safety, though two passengers in this train were killed, presumably by the impact of the collision.

After the smash the great bogie tender of engine No. 907 was lying across the down line, to say nothing of engine No. 121 and its tender a little distance beyond. And then, less than a minute after the first collision the 'midnight' from Euston was approaching. The signalmen at Quintinshill managed to throw the signals to danger, but it was too late. This heavy express consisted of 10 bogie corridor vehicles and three 12-wheeled sleeping cars, and was drawn by two 4-4-0 engines of the 'Dunalastair' IV class. A non-superheated engine No. 140 was leading, and the train engine, of the same type as that of the troop train, was superheater 4-4-0 No. 48. At the moment of impact the speed of this train was about 60 m.p.h. It ploughed through the scattered wreckage of the wooden coaches of the troop train, and then hit the tender of No. 907 which was lying right across its track. Although the impact drove the tender forward amongst the wagons of the goods train standing in the down loop it also brought the express violently to a stop, and resulted in the first three coaches becoming telescoped.

With four large engines, two of them overturned, a mass of shattered wooden coaches, gas lighting, and live coals thrown about the line, fire was inevitable. It raged indeed for nearly 24 hours, by which time 20 out of the 21 vehicles of the troop train—or what was left of them after the two collisions!—had been consumed. Five vehicles of the express were burned out, while the fire also involved the standing goods train in the down loop. The exact death roll has never finally been established because the Battalion Roll was lost in the accident; but it was pointed out at the time that the wreckage of the troop train was so excessive that probably all those not rescued before the fire reached the coaches in which they lay were dead, or at any rate insensible, so it was confidently hoped that few, if any, were conscious when the fire reached them. The casualty report was indeed like the death roll after some major action in battle. On the troop train the ghastly figures were:

Non-commissioned officers and men killed, and identified	57
Non-commissioned officers and men since dead	26
Bodies recovered but not recognisable	82
Reported 'missing' by the Military Authorities:	
Officers	3
Other ranks	47
A total, from the 1/7th Royal Scots	215

There were also, in the troop train, no fewer than 191 injured.

The survivors were paraded in a field adjacent to the line, and out of a battalion strength of some 500 only 52 answered their names.

The driver and fireman of the troop train were killed, but apart from them there were only 10 civilian fatalities. Still a total death roll of 227 was terrible beyond words. There were 51 passengers injured in the Euston-Glasgow express, and four railway servants injured, making a total of 246. As 'The Railway Magazine' remarked at the time: 'Saturday, May 22nd, was the blackest day in British railway history!' Even with the more recent tragedies of Harrow and Lewisham in mind Quintinshill still remains without parallel. It was unusual in another respect; that the Inspecting Officer of the Board of Trade, Lieut. Col. Druitt, had virtually nothing to criticise in the equipment in the locality, in the working regulations, nor in the rolling stock of which the trains concerned were composed. He admitted that track circuiting would almost certainly have prevented the accident, but added that Quintinshill would probably have been one of the last places to be so equipped.

He thought that the means then provided by the Caledonian Railway for reminding signalmen of any vehicles standing within their control at such a place as Quintinshill should have been sufficient, if the signalmen concerned had only carried out the ordinary simple rules of block working and the regulations laid down for the purpose. The tragedy was certainly caused solely by lack of discipline on the part of the two signalmen, Meakin and Tinsley. They were duly tried and convicted for manslaughter and sentenced to lengthy terms of imprisonment.

In other circumstances Col. Druitt might have had some critical remarks to make about the composition of the troop train, seeing that it was booked to run at express speed, yet was nevertheless made up mostly of non-bogie stock, of considerable age. But it was appreciated that at that period so many additional train movements were involved due to special war traffic that any available coaching stock that was available was pressed into use. He did not suggest that the devastating fire that followed the collision was caused primarily by gas lighted coaches, and he referred appreciatively to the steady progress towards electric lighting that was being made generally on British railways.

It is nevertheless rather strange that in nearly every account of this accident, whether contemporary, or retrospective, the circumstance that touched off the entire chain of events is mentioned no more than incidentally, and that was, of course, that the 11.45 and 12 midnight expresses from Euston were each running more than half an hour late. If they had been on time there would have been no need for the shunting manoeuvre at Quintinshill. Even so, with the scant regard for discipline that seemed to have developed at that box, if trouble had been averted on that particular morning it might have developed later on.

As an afterthought to this terrible affair it might be questioned why such a large and powerful engine as 4-6-0 No. 907 was on that local train. Actually the two 'Cardean' class engines, 906 and 907 were both stationed at Kingmoor and two of their normal jobs were the 4.22 a.m. and 5.50 a.m.

'sleepers' from Carlisle northwards. But No. 907 had just recently been through the shops and she was working the recognised 'running in' turn. This involved taking the local as far as Beattock and then continuing with the 'Tinto' as far as Carstairs. From there the engine returned from Carstairs to Carlisle with the up morning Aberdeen express. No. 907 was thus in newly repaired and pristine condition at the time of the accident. Despite the great damage she sustained I gather that there was great reluctance to scrap her.

The engine of the troop train, McIntosh superheated 4-4-0 No. 121 was in charge of her regular crew, Driver F. Scott, and Fireman J. Hannah of Kingmoor. They were both killed. Scott's widow received £300 compensation from the company, and £10 annually for her two youngest children until they were sixteen. Fireman Hannah's widow received three years' earnings, equal to £270 5s. 9d., plus £10 per annum for five years for her five-year-old boy. Quite recently there was a deeply moving epilogue to this particular side of the Quintinshill tragedy. Many of the Carlisle enginemen, whether they worked for the English or the Scottish railways were Cumbrians, and Mrs. Hannah became a post-woman at Lamplugh, on the Marron Junction line. Eventually she became postmistress and continued on the job until she was well over 80 years of age. When she retired she was awarded the O.B.E. in recognition of her long and faithful service.

9

The Abermule head-on collision

The technique of operating single line railways is one which has developed in a diversity of ways in different parts of the world, largely for economic reasons. In territories where it was necessary to build railways, more for opening up the country rather than for spectacular economic and financial gains, railways were built as cheaply as possible, and long stretches of single line were laid down in remote parts of Scotland, Ireland and Wales. These pioneer single line railways formed the pattern on which many railways were built in parts of the British Colonial Empire, and indeed all over the world, and the original methods of operating were by timetable, and if necessary, telegraphic train orders, making changes to the timetable to permit of altered crossing arrangements at passing places in the event of late running. In Great Britain prior to the Regulation of Railways Act of 1889 the great majority of single lines were operated on the train order system, and through the diligence of the staff a very high degree of safety was achieved. The one serious disaster near Norwich in 1874, due to carelessness on the part of operating staff, merely highlights the record of safety that was otherwise achieved on the single line sections of railways in this country under the train order system.

Nevertheless, with the passing of the Regulation of Railways Act of 1889 absolute block working was required on all passenger lines, and on single lines additional safety measures became general with the introduction of staff or token instruments, electrically interlocked. With these, definite procedures were required to be made by the signalmen at each end of the section, and these prevented the inadvertent despatch of two trains in opposite directions into the same section. In Great Britain the overwhelming majority of railwaymen concerned with the operation of trains have always been men with the highest sense of responsibility. Any irregularity in the carrying out of regulations for block workings, particularly on single lines, would ordinarily be the result of pressure of work, a distraction by some extraneous circumstance, or an act of simple forgetfulness. The safeguards provided by the electric interlocking of the single line staff or token instruments were therefore designed in a relatively simple manner so as to provide that check, reminder, or corrective that would afford the necessary safeguard in the case of a genuine mistake on the part of men concerned.

It was not always so with the single line interlocked block instruments. British manufacturers have had to cater for railway conditions in many parts of the world, some in distinctly primitive countries where the sense of responsibility among railwaymen was not so highly developed as at home. In designing block instruments for single line railways in such conditions consideration had to be given to providing safeguards against deliberate tampering, if not actually making them 'burglar-proof'. Nevertheless I do know of one particular case in South-East Asia where the stationmasters at each end of the single line section each wanted to despatch a train to the other at approximately the same time. One of these two men secured priority over the other and extracted the single-line token from his instrument, by legitimate action, and handed it to the driver as his authority to proceed. The other man was so angry at having lost the priority, that not being able to extract a token by legitimate means he 'burgled' the instrument and got a token for the same action. He duly despatched his train, and the result, of course, was a catastrophic head-on collision.

There is, fortunately, only one case in the history of British railways of a collision on single line worked under the electric tablet system, that led to loss of life to pas-

119

sengers, but this accident, which took place in January 1921 on the Cambrian Railways, is enough to show how even the most carefully prepared schemes and regulations can break down through hasty action and careless supervision. In this respect its origin provides a parallel case to that of Quintinshill. The main line of the Cambrian Railways from its junction with the London and North Western Railway at Whitchurch through to the coast, was single tracked for the bulk of its mileage, and at the time of the accident it was equipped with Tyer's electric train tablet instruments, No. 6 pattern. It had been installed since 1890, the year after the passing of the Regulation of Railways Act that followed the disaster at Armagh. Actually Edward Tyer's system had been invented in 1878 and had first been installed in 1879. Like many notable inventors Tyer was aware of the need for safety precautions, and it was due to the foresight of men like him that when the Regulation of Railways Act was passed, apparatus necessary to meet the new requirements had been brought to a high degree of reliability. The electric tablet system was welcomed by the majority of railway administrations, for single line working because it did immediately provide a degree of flexibility in working which the old telegraphic train order system did not; and naturally the increased safety inherent in the electric tablet system was a most essential feature.

The central point in the series of events which led to the disaster on January 26th, 1921, was at Abermule Station, roughly midway between Montgomery and Newtown. At Abermule the tablet instruments were not in the signalbox but in a special tablet room leading out of the booking office. This arrangement was adopted so that the tablet working could be under the direct supervision of the stationmaster. As in the case of other single line tablet and token instrument systems, each single line section had an instrument at each end, and these were electrically connected in such a way that only one tablet, or other form of token, could be obtained from one or other of the instruments at the same time. The circuits were such that two tablets or tokens could not be out of the system at once; and a second token could not be withdrawn from an instrument at either end until the one that was already out was put back into one or other of the instruments. The safety principle is thus, that if a train is carrying a tablet that has been extracted from one of the instruments relating to a particular section of single line, that is a definite assurance of safety in traversing the section. The fact that a train has a tablet is a virtual guarantee that no other tablet will be out, and therefore, no other train will be on the line.

The Tyer's No. 6 instrument included also, electric indicators to show, at any time, the state of the line. These indicators were connected between the two instruments at each end of the section. If, by the co-operative action of the signalmen at either end of the section, a tablet had been extracted to allow a train to travel, say, from Newtown to Abermule, that is, in the 'up' direction of running, the indicators on both instruments would show 'tablet out' for the up train, while the corresponding indicator on both instruments would show 'tablet in' for the down train. Thus a glance at the instruments was enough to show the exact position of the working at any particular time.

It might be imagined that if a train arrived at Abermule from Newtown in the 'up' direction and there was a train at Abermule waiting to go through to Newtown in the 'down' direction, there would be no need to go through the procedure of inserting the tablet in the instrument, going through the motions and then handing the tablet to the driver for the down journey. As the tablet was in itself the feature of security which ensured the safe running of the train, surely all that had got to be done was to take the tablet from the driver of the train that had just arrived from Newtown, and give it to the man who was going in the reverse direction. This, of course, was inadmissable. First of all it could lead to certain slackness in working, and more important still, it would not enable the electric indicators on the tablet instruments to register the correct indications. Unless the tablet from the arriving train was placed in the instrument, and both indicators restored, so that both showed the tablets for the 'up' train were in, the second set of operations could not be carried through, so that the indicators would correctly show, for the next movements, that a tablet was out for a train running in the 'down' direction. The safety precautions were thus fully comprehensive, and for over 30 years since the installation of the system had provided complete safety in working.

To appreciate the circumstances which led to the shocking accident on January 26th, 1921, the station working at Abermule needs to be considered. The station was staffed by a stationmaster, two signalmen, a booking clerk, and a porter. It so happened that on the day of the accident the regular stationmaster was away; but his relief was an experienced man who had done duty at Abermule before. The two signalmen, who between them divided the work according to the appropriate shifts, were also experienced men and they, together with the stationmaster were the only persons authorised to participate in the tablet working. Furthermore, in 1919, special instructions had been sent out to all stationmasters on the Cambrian Railways to the effect that they must personally supervise the signalling and be present at the station when express trains were crossing on single line sections. Apart from the stationmaster and the two signalmen, the booking clerk was a lad of 15, and the porter a lad of 17.

At about 11.45 a.m. on the day in question all was quiet at Abermule station. The porter and the clerk were eating their lunch in the booking office; the stationmaster was away at his lunch, and the signalman was in charge and sitting in the tablet room. At 11.52 a.m. Montgomery station asked for 'line clear' for the 10.5 a.m. stopping train from Whitchurch to Aberystwyth. The signalman gave acceptance, and by going through the recognised procedure and co-operation with the signalman at Montgomery enabled a tablet to be withdrawn from the instrument at the latter station, and authority was thus given for the train to proceed from Montgomery to Abermule. As a result of this action the Tyer's tablet instrument at Abermule now showed 'tablet out' for the down train. This stopping train was booked to cross the 10.25 a.m. up express from Aberystwyth to Abermule, and having given authority for the stopping train to be accepted the signalman telephoned to Moat Lane Junction, 8½ miles to the west, to find out the whereabouts of the up express. He then learned that the latter train was roughly on time and it was anticipated that the crossing would take place at Abermule as usual. He then told the two lads that the down train had left Montgomery and the up express had left Moat Lane, and he himself then left the station buildings, presumably to go to the signalbox. Just about the time the signalman left, the stationmaster returned from his lunch, but neither the signalman nor either of the two lads passed on to the stationmaster any information concerning the whereabouts of either of the two trains which were then approaching Abermule.

Immediately afterwards Newtown rang requesting 'line clear' for the up express. As there was no one else near, the 17-year-old porter went to the instrument and gave permission, by appropriate action, for a tablet to be withdrawn at Newtown for the express to proceed towards Abermule. His action caused the indicator on the Abermule Newtown instrument to show 'tablet out' for the up line. Everything so far was perfectly correct, except, of course, that the young porter had no authorirty to operate the tablet instrument, and should have called the stationmaster instead of attempting to do the job himself. At this stage it should be explained that the signalling arrangements at Abermule, in common with many stations on the Cambrian Railways at that time, were rather more complicated than would be usual today. The points and signals at the east end of the station, that is the Montgomery end, were operated direct from a signal box which also controlled a level crossing; but at the west end of the station the points were too far from the signal box to be worked direct and they were worked from a separate ground frame. Thus the signalman could not attend to all traffic movements from his own box, and it was customary for the porter to operate the points and signals at the west end by means of the ground frame.

Having accepted the train from Newtown, yet saying nothing either to the stationmaster or to the signalman, this 17-year-old lad then went off, presumably, to the ground frame to set the road for the up express. In the meantime the signalman had gone to the level crossing to close the gates against road traffic. There was no hand wheel for doing this, so the gates had to be pushed over by hand. But as soon as the gates were locked against the road traffic the signalman lowered his home signal for the down train to enter the station, even though the points at the west end did not correspond. The very slip-shod working that was already apparent from the chain of events thus far described now became even more so.

The 15-year-old booking clerk was waiting on the up line platform when the down train arrived, but jumped down into the six-foot way to receive the tablet in its pouch from the driver of the stopping train as the latter drew to a stand in the station. In the enquiry following the ensuing disaster the boy admitted that it was not his duty to do this; but as the stationmaster was not there and the signalman was in the box he took it upon himself to do the job, as he had done many times in the past. There is no doubt that for all the slip-shod methods that were obviously prevalent at Abermule, the intentions of the two youths were keen enough, to keep the traffic going. Like all single line railways there were on the Cambrian main line long periods of calm followed intense activity for a few minutes, after which everything lapsed into calm. And the crossing of the 10.5 down from Whitchurch and the 10.25 from Aberystwyth was a period of intense activity. With nobody else about the boy had taken it upon himself to collect the tablet from the driver, and he then intended to run back to the office, place the tablet in the instrument quickly so as to leave himself free to collect tickets from passengers who were getting out of the train at Abermule. However, on his way to the office he met the stationmaster who was arriving rather belatedly on the scene and the boy said to his superior 'Change this tablet while I go and get the tickets'.

When the stationmaster had arrived back from his lunch he became involved with a permanent way sub-inspector who had some enquiries to make about a wagon, and in any case no one told him in so many words what the situation was regarding the two approaching passenger trains, although he could quite clearly have seen it for himself by referring to the indicators on the Tyer's instruments. What words actually passed between the booking clerk and the stationmaster in that brief encounter on the platform will never finally be established, for the evidence of both was in flat contradiction. Whereas the lad said he told the station-master: 'Change this tablet while I go and get the tickets', the stationmaster maintained that what the clerk said was 'Take this tablet for the down train; he is going on', the two statements are, of course, entirely at variance one with another and the tragedy was that the stationmaster should have acted on what he *thought* the lad said—a lad moreover, with an impediment in his speech—instead of checking himself to see what the actual traffic situation was.

In the stationmaster's words it was implied that the crossing of the two trains was not going to take place at Aber-mule, but that the stopping train was going on to Newtown because the express was apparently running late. If, instead of taking this word of a boy of 15 the stationmaster had looked at his instruments, and moreover looked at the tablet that the boy had given him, he would have seen, first of all, that the instruments for the section Newtown-Abermule had a tablet out for an up train, and that the tablet he was hold-ing was for the section Montgomery-Abermule. He appar-ently asked the clerk where the up express was and got the reply, 'about Moat Lane'. If this reply was actually what was said it was most misleading, because the train had actually passed Moat Lane about eight minutes earlier and was at that moment leaving Newtown under clear signals with a tablet authorising it to proceed to Abermule. The station-master having received the boy's word hurried along the platform and gave the tablet to the driver of the stopping train, and the signals were lowered for him to go.

Both this train and the express that was coming westwards were hauled by the standard type of Cambrian 4-4-0 passenger locomotive. Engine No. 82 was on the down stopping train and had a load of six 8-wheeled coaches. The express was hauled by engine No. 95 and consisted of six 8-wheeled coaches and a six-wheeled van. Although the circumstances were now extremely dangerous there was still one last hope that disaster would be averted. Normally, in single line working, a driver or his fireman always take the greatest care to see that the tablet they have been given is the correct one for the section; but in this case the driver and fireman accepted the tablet from the stationmaster and did not look at it. If they had they would have seen that it was the very tablet they themselves had brought from Montgomery. Similarly, if anyone had chosen to look at the indicators on the Tyer's instrument in the tablet room of the station house they would have seen that the indicators were quite contrary to what was happening outside. Thus the instruments would have shown that there was a tablet out for a down train between Montgomery and Abermule, and a tablet out for an up train between Newtown and Abermule. And here was a down train about to leave Abermule for Newtown; the merest glance at the indicators on those instruments would have shown that the situation did not make sense.

In the meantime the 17-year-old porter, who had accepted the up express from Newtown had proceeded to the west ground frame to set the road. This was his usual duty, and on arrival at the frame he found the points set for the down platform line. Trying to reverse them for the up road he found them locked. This surprised him a little, and he was still more surprised, on coming out of the box to see the down train standing in the station. Nevertheless he was about to shout to the signalman to give him the bolt-lock release so that he could set the points for the up train when he saw the stationmaster signalling the down train away. This youth, at the west ground frame, was the only person who had taken any part, so far, in the handling of the up express, and he had not told anyone that he had accepted it and authorised the issue of a tablet to it at Newtown. It is true the consequences of his action were there for anyone to see on the tablet instrument indicator; but in fact no one had looked at it. This youth, whose unauthorised action in accepting the train was the result of lax supervision rather than any fault of his own, could draw only one conclusion when he saw the stationmaster signalling away the down train. It was that he, or the signalman, had been able to cancel the acceptance of the up express, and was sending the down train on. The youth, without any further consideration, pulled off his slot on the down advanced starting signal, thus allowing it to be lowered for the down train to proceed.

In actual fact no one had been in the tablet room at all since the porter had accepted the up express from Newtown, and the arrival of the down train had been completely unrecorded, so far as tablet instruments were concerned. Thus there had been no one in the vicinity when there came the 'train entering section' signal for the up express from Newtown. This event, which would surely have alerted everyone to the real situation, took place at 11.59 a.m. (according to Newtown); but the ring was not heard by anyone and it went unacknowledged. It was an appalling fact therefore that no one at Abermule knew that the express had actually entered the Newtown-Abermule section. Then, at about 12.3 p.m. just as the down train was starting the 15-year-old clerk went into the tablet room to give 'train entering section' to Newtown, and 'train out of section' to Montgomery. And it was only when this boy looked at the instruments that anyone realised the terrible mistake that had been made.

The stationmaster telephoned Newtown, to find out the whereabouts of the express, because no one had received the 'train entering section' signal four minutes earlier, and as the down train was only just starting away an attempt was made to attract the enginemen of No. 82 by working the up distant signal violently up and down. But the men on this engine, who had accepted the 'wrong' tablet without troubling to look to see what they had been given did not see this attempt to attract their attention; and the general impression was that they were not looking out at all. The driver and fireman of this engine, in their carelessness in not looking at the tablet, and in steaming away from Abermule without keeping a good lookout paid for it with their lives. Although an accident was now almost inevitable, and the crash that eventuated was bad enough in all conscience, it might have been much worse had not the enginemen of the express been as diligent and alert as the men on the down stopping train were otherwise. The outcome was a hideous head-on collision; but through their own alertness the enginemen of the express survived, and were subsequently able to give a clear account of the last minutes before the crash.

Abermule is four miles from Newtown, and the express had accelerated in good style and was running at about 50 m.p.h. when it reached the usual point for shutting off steam, prior to slowing down for the tablet exchanging at Abermule. Passing under a bridge on a short length of 50 chain curve the driver saw some smoke ahead, and a moment later sighted the oncoming train only 300 yards away. He made a full brake application, and whistled and then got down on to the footplate step on his side. His fireman did the same on the other side of the engine. They both hung on until the very last minute, and then jumped clear, and saved their lives. It was considered that at the time of the collision both trains were travelling at about 30 m.p.h. The express was running on a falling gradient of 1 in 123, and the damage to rolling stock was more extensive in this train than in the other. The casualty list included 17 killed and 36 injured. Both engines were destroyed. The boilers were torn off the frames, and lay quite separately, and the first four coaches of the express were telescoped and shattered.

Enough has been written of the chain of events leading up to this shocking affair to highlight the lack of supervision at Abermule, that allowed two well-intentioned youths to

Quintinshill, 1915 The fire almost under control: one of the rearmost coaches of the troop train, a Great Central 12-wheeler, little damaged in the collision, but gutted by fire

Quintinshill The mass military funeral of the dead soldiers, in Carlisle

Abermule, 1921 The splintered wreckage of the up express

Sevenoaks, 1927

The Pullman car *Carmen*, jammed across the piers of Shoreham Lane bridge

Sevenoaks, 1927

The 2–6–4 tank engine *River Cray* after the derailment

Sevenoaks

The work of salvage. The wrecked engine can be
seen ahead against the cutting side. An almost
demolished coach in the foreground, after lifting

Charfield, 1928   An aerial view of the smouldering ruins, after the fire under the bridge. The express engine is just discernible amid the smoke on the left

Charfield

The mangled wreckage of burnt-out carriages piled against the bridge. The chimney and smokebox of the G.W.R. goods engine can be seen through the arch

Ashchurch, 1929

Rescue work by night after the collision in dense fog, between the Bristol-Nottingham night express and a goods train

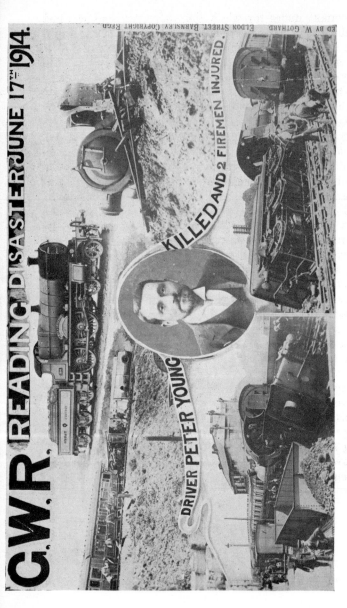

Reading, 1914 An interesting contemporary 'montage' of the accident, which the author saw shortly after it occurred

undertake duties for which they were not qualified, and without any guidance or checking; while the enginemen of the down stopping train neglected to carry out the most elementary safety precautions needed on single lines. Had any one of the various blunders made on this tragic occasion been discovered in time the accident would have been avoided. But one mistake followed another right up to the very last minute.

The enquiry was conducted by Col. Sir John Pringle and, quite apart from the seriousness of the Abermule collision in itself, the practice of single line working on the Cambrian Railways came under more than usual scrutiny. Only three years earlier a very bad, but little known accident had occurred at Parkhall, near Oswestry, when two goods trains had met in head-on collision. In that case enquiry revealed the startling fact that two tablets had been issued *for the same section*! How it was done was never fully established, and the fact that no passenger train was involved and that the only death was one of the firemen made the accident pass almost unnoticed by the general public. But the Board of Trade, which was then responsible for regulations and safety procedures on railways, took a very serious view of it. In the case of Abermule, however, the working of the tablet instruments was entirely correct. It was the human element that failed so disastrously.

Sir John Pringle made the recommendation that to increase the safety of working on single lines there should be electric interlocking between the tablet instrument and starting signal. This would make it impossible to clear the starting signal unless a tablet, or other token, had been withdrawn from the correct instrument for the section that was being entered.

10

The Sevenoaks derailment

After the crop of serious accidents due to excessive speed on curves that had marked the years 1906-7, there had been a welcome immunity from this particular kind of accident, and public apprehension over any individual feat of high speed running, whether safe or otherwise had receded to the point where it was virtually negligible. In the years immediately following the grouping of the railways in Great Britain it was France, and not our own country that suffered a series of accidents on curves. With the enterprise of the Great Western to point the way there was a general urge to speed up, and the publicity departments of the newly established 'Big Four' companies lost no time in telling the world of any specially meritorious piece of running. At the same time there were certain developments, arising from the grouping, which would have given rise to genuine apprehension if their implications had been appreciated.

On the former London, Brighton and South Coast Railway the use of large tank engines on express trains had been general since the introduction of Earle-Marsh's celebrated 'I3' class 4-4-2 tank engines in 1908. The practice had extended to the designing of the very fine 4-6-2 tanks *Abergavenny* and *Bessborough* and Marsh's successor, L. B. Billinton, had gone one better with the huge 'L' class 4-6-4s introduced in 1914. These engines at first gave a good deal of trouble from unsteady riding. There was indeed a derailment at Hassocks serious enough for the Brighton Company to set up an independent technical enquiry by Messrs. C. J. Bowen-Cooke and W. W. Grierson. Some of the trouble was traced eventually to water in the tanks surging about when the engines were running at speed. This defect was cured on the first two engines of the class by introducing baffle plates, and when the time came for more engines of the class to be built, from 1922 onwards they were very satisfactory from the riding point of view. All the Brighton express tank engines had to run hard on occasions, and from the enginemen's point of view the tank engines were considerably better than the Marsh 4-4-2 tender engines, which were just as lively in their riding as their more celebrated counterparts on the Great Northern Railway.

In the programme of locomotive standardisation that had been worked out on the South Eastern and Chatham Railway from 1914 onwards a design of 2-6-4 tank had been included as the probable answer to the haulage of the Kent Coast expresses of the future. Efficient superheater tank engines had for some years been used on the longest runs made on the Brighton line, and the crack trains on that route made longer non-stop runs than anything envisaged on either the Folkestone or the Margate lines of the S.E. & C.R. Tank engines were particularly suitable for train working in the busy London terminal areas. They occupied less platform space on arrival, and did not need turning before starting away on a return working. This latter was something of an academic point. In practice drivers always seemed to prefer running chimney first, and if they could get to a turntable would always turn their engines. In view of Brighton experience with tank engines and the building of more engines of the Maunsell 'K' class 2-6-4 design after grouping the use of some of the latter engines on the Folkestone expresses seemed a perfectly logical development. They were not used on the 80-minute Charing Cross-Folkestone non-stops, but on trains making an intermediate stop at Ashford. Despite their excellent valve gear and economical usage of water it was found that their tank capacity was not really adequate for the longer non-stop runs with the 300-ton trains then conveyed.

On August 24th, 1927, engine No. 800 *River Cray* was on

131

the 5 p.m. from Cannon Street to Folkestone booked to run non-stop over the 56 miles to Ashford in 65 minutes. The load was a normal one of eight coaches—seven ordinary vehicles and the Pullman car *Carmen*. The latter was one of those built specially for service on the S.E. & C.R. which unlike the great majority of British Pullmans were painted in a livery of crimson lake, to match the old S.E. & C.R. carriage style. The trailing load was one of 250 tons tare, well within the capacity of the engine. The train made normal speed in the early stages of the run, in fact a little time had been lost on the long climb to Knockholt, partly on account of a slight signal check at Orpington. The driver, W. H. Buss, was a very experienced man having been a driver for 30 years, but the fireman, although with 10 years' experience had not been mate to Driver Buss before, neither had he ever been on a 'River' class 2-6-4 tank engine. The driver had, therefore, to give him an occasional word of advice, and the first instance of this was just after they had passed the summit point at Knockholt, and had commenced the fast descent through Polhill, towards Sevenoaks.

Buss was aware of the tendency of these engines to roll, and half-way through Polhill tunnel he told his fireman to reverse the dampers and put a little coal on, so that it should not be necessary to do any firing when running down the lower part of the bank, at a speed of 55 to 60 m.p.h., and run the risk of being thrown about while so engaged. What actually happened on the engine is best described in the driver's evidence in the subsequent enquiry:

'The engine ran steadily without any unusual movement through Polhill tunnel to Dunton Green Station where he estimated that the speed attained was from 55 to 57 m.p.h. About half-way between Dunton Green and Sevenoaks, when steam was still applied, the engine running as usual, he heard a knocking noise in front of the engine and immediately closed the regulator. After the usual clattering noise due to shutting off steam had ceased, the knocking noise began again, and he then applied the brake with full effect. He thought he made this application just where the catch points are situated on the down line. He had not felt any extraordinary movement or lift of the engine wheels before he heard the knocking noise mentioned. He thought this noise was made by the Bissel front wheels being off the rails to the left, and held strongly the opinion that it could not have been the leading coupled wheels of the engine. He did not feel that the continuous brake was getting a hold upon the wheels until the engine was near the Shoreham Lane overbridge.'

A serious rolling motion had been initiated when the engine passed over a pair of trailing points at the south end of Dunton Green Station. The alternate dipping and lurching action, at a speed of about 60 m.p.h., together with the effect of travelling round a gentle left hand curve led quickly to the derailment of the pony truck of the engine; but from the marks on the chairs it is evident that this leading pair of wheels continued to travel close to, and parallel with the rails, for a distance of some 500 yards. Then unfortunately the engine came to a pair of trailing catch points; the derailed wheels burst these points open, and the engine and the whole of the train was derailed. The line runs in a shallow cutting at the particular spot, and with strongly-built modern rolling stock the effects of the derailment might not have been very serious, but for the misfortune that in that cutting there was a road overbridge carrying the Shoreham Lane, and that overbridge had separate arches for the down and up lines, with a central pier in the six-foot way.

That overbridge and the existence of the central pier turned what might have been no more than an alarming incident into a disaster. The bridge was about 100 yards beyond the catch points, and although the engine was then completely off the road it was still travelling at considerable speed when its left hand leading end came into violent contact with the abutment. It nevertheless passed through, and took the first two coaches with it. The couplings broke between the second and third coach, and again between the third and fourth. The latter became jammed askew under the bridge, and seriously crushed. The first vehicle in the

133

train was the Pullman car *Carmen,* and although this was thrown against the northern face of the bridge, and ended in a position athwart both down and up lines, its massive construction withstood the tremendous forces of impact remarkably well, and the casualties inside were not so severe as might have been expected. Nevertheless the vehicle was extensively damaged and in clearing the line afterwards it was broken up on the spot. The casualty list was 13 killed; 21 seriously injured and detained in hospital, while a further 40 persons were less seriously injured, or found suffering from shock effects.

This was an accident in which the engineering interest, both as regards the track and the locomotive, was profound, and the outcome was far-reaching on both accounts. The two chief officers concerned were the Chief Mechanical Engineer, R. E. L. Maunsell, who was responsible for the design of the locomotive, and the Chief Engineer, G. Ellson. Both were formerly South Eastern and Chatham men, Ellson having been Maintenance Engineer. At the time of the grouping he had been appointed deputy to A. W. Szlumper, and had succeeded him as Chief Engineer not many months before the accident. It is important to emphasise that although the engine actually concerned was relatively new, and had covered little more than 40,000 miles in traffic the design dated back to 1917, and was one prepared expressly for service on the South Eastern and Chatham Railway. After the accident both engines and track immediately came under suspicion. In the course of the Ministry of Transport Enquiry, conducted with consummate skill by Col. Sir John Pringle, it was revealed that there had been several reports of bad riding by the 2-6-4 tank engines, and in consequence certain modifications were made to the springing of the bogie and of the leading pony truck.

Prior to the disaster near Sevenoaks there had been three cases of derailment of the 'River' class tank engines, all on the Swanley-Maidstone-Ashford line which, although a secondary route, was used frequently for conditional boat train workings. The significant fact about all the reports of trouble with the 'River' class engines was that all related to lines of the former S.E. & C.R., and that in using these engines on the Brighton line no complaints of bad riding had been received. At the time of the Sevenoaks derailment Maunsell was on holiday, and in his absence the General Manager, Sir Herbert Walker, gave instructions for all the 'River' class engines to be withdrawn from traffic pending inquiries into their performance. But at a very early stage in Sir John Pringle's investigations the main suspicions began to shift from the engine to the track, and he obtained the assistance of Mr. H. N. Gresley—as he then was—Chief Mechanical Engineer of the London and North Eastern Railway, in carrying out some completely independent tests on the riding of certain Southern Railway locomotives, including the 'River' class.

A section of the former Great Northern main line between St. Neots and Huntingdon was chosen for these tests. There was a particular point in choosing this stretch because it included the curving length beside the River Ouse, just south of Offord station. There are three points of reverse on this section connected in each case by transitional curvature. The formation of the road was then gravel throughout, and the bottom ballast on the inside of the curves consisted mainly of broken slag to depths varying between 13 and 17 in. below the sleepers. The drainage was well provided for, and the ballast was clean, and of first-class quality. This description, which is taken from Sir John's report merely confirms the general impression at the time that the track of the Great Northern main line was of very high quality. And over this section trial runs were made with three Southern locomotives, namely:

(a) 2-cylinder 2-6-4 tank No. 803 *River Itchen*

(b) 3-cylinder 2-6-4 tank No. 890 *River Frome*

(c) 'King Arthur' class 4-6-0 No. 782 *Sir Brian*

The load in each case consisted of two coaches, one being the L.N.E.R. dynamometer car. Gresley himself rode on the footplate on all tests. With the tank engines six runs were made in each direction. On the up line the engines ran chimney first, and on the down line bunker first. The 'King Arthur' made two runs only, both on the up line travelling, of course, engine first. The tank engine trials were made some with tanks half empty and some with tanks full. The results were remarkable. Engine No. 803, whether running forwards or backwards gave an immaculate performance, while No. 890, although somewhat livelier on its springs than No. 803 when running forwards, gave a very steady ride backwards even though speed was worked up to no less than 83¼ m.p.h. The detailed report of Mr. Gresley on the running of these two engines is in such contrast with the general opinion formed of them on the Southern Railway that it is quoted in full.

These trials constituted a triumph for Maunsell so far as the design of the locomotives was concerned, though at the same time, from his long and intimate experience with the S.E. & C.R. he would have known that track conditions on the latter line were not to be compared with those on the Great Northern. Sir John Pringle commented on the track near Sevenoaks as follows:

'The original ballast used on this road, both top and bottom, which possesses weight, is in itself clean; but as may be imagined, presents a poor support for sleepers carrying heavy traffic. Binding of some sort, in the shape of ash or soil was utilised to render this bottom ballast more stable. Kentish ragstone is now used for the top ballast, but over the section of road concerned, binding material has also been used with stone. The present bottom ballast under the sleepers, for a width of about 18 inches on each side of the rail, is composed, I understand, of half ragstone and half beach ballast, the remainder being beach ballast mixed with binding. The quality of the ballast, and in particular of the bottom ballast, is inferior in rigidity and holding capacity to that which nowadays is to be found on first class roads. The bank itself (constructed of chalk) is of good width, and appears substantial in character. But the level of the bottom of the left-hand ends of the sleepers on the down track is generally flush with the level of the cess. The level of the cess

London and North Eastern Railway, October 16th, 1927

No. of Trial	Engine	Direction of Running	Road Up	Condition of Tanks and Bunkers	Speeds m.p.h.	Observations
1	803	Forwards	Down	Nearly empty	67¼-73¼	Engine ran without roll or lateral motion on straight and on curves except for a slight roll at about 55¾ Mile Post and again a lesser roll at 54¾ Mile Post
2	803	Backwards	Up	Nearly empty	67-73½	Engine ran quite smoothly and without any rolling or lurching
3	890	Forwards	Down	Nearly empty	73½-77	Engine rather more lively on its springs than 803 and not quite so steady. A slight roll was noticeable at 55¾ Mile Post and at 54¾ Mile Post: otherwise she ran smoothly and did not roll
4	803	Backwards	Up	Nearly empty	77½-83¼	A very satisfactory trial: engine ran, if anything, steadier than 803 bunker first, and there was no rolling or lurching although 83¼ m.p.h. was attained
5	803	Forwards	Down	Full	72½-78	Engine ran steadier than when empty on No. 1 trip. In fact, considering speed, it could be regarded as being on this trip a very steady, comfortable riding engine
6	890	Backwards	Up	Full	68-77½	Running of engine very steady and smooth throughout trip
7	890	Forwards	Down	Full	74-77½	Not quite so steady as engine 803, trip 5, but better than when running with tanks and bunkers empty on trip 3
8	890	Backwards	Up	Full	69¾-79	Engine ran very steadily
9	803	Forwards	Down	¾ Full	56¾-59¾	These trials at reduced speed were carried out at the suggestion of the Chief Engineer of the Southern Railway with a view to learning whether at lower speeds, any periodical oscillation might be set up. The engines ran quite steadily and without any noticeable oscillation
10	803	Backwards	Up	¾ Full	62¼-66¼	
11	890	Forwards	Down	Nearly empty	61½-68¾	
12	890	Backwards		Nearly empty	57½-64¾	

on the inside of the curve is too high. The explanation is that the ballast has sunk or been driven by heavy loading into the formation. The result is that there can be no drainage from the top or bottom ballast except through the bank.'

Sir Herbert Walker was naturally keeping in very close touch with all aspects of the enquiry and, upon learning of the excellent performance of the Southern locomotives on the L.N.E.R. line in contrast to their behaviour on the Eastern Section of the Southern, he asked for a similar series of trials to be carried out, not on the S.E. & C.R. line but on one of the fastest running sections of the Southern system, namely between Waterloo and Basingstoke. The section between Woking and Walton-on-Thames was chosen, as one habitually the scene of high speed running, and also including some slight curvature in the neighbourhood of Weybridge. In addition to Mr. Gresley, and Mr. J. L. M. Moore, Assistant Inspecting Officer of the Ministry of Transport, that very distinguished 'elder statesman' of the railway engineering world, Sir John Aspinall, was also present throughout the trials. Before the trials took place special maintenance gangs gave close attention to both the down and up fast lines. As on the L.N.E.R. there were no speed restrictions on the test lengths. The formation in the cutting (between mile posts 18 and $18\frac{1}{2}$) is marl; it is the same also in the vicinity of mile post 19. Elsewhere, mainly on embankment, the formation is sand. Bottom ballast was stated to be laid to depths of from 16 ins. to 18 ins. below sleepers. In some places Meldon stone is used; at others there is from 6 ins. to 9 ins. of Thames ballast on which is laid from 3 ins. to 6 ins. of Meldon stone.

The performance of the tank engines tells a very different tale from that on the L.N.E.R., as will be seen from Gresley's report. In his report to Sir John Pringle, Gresley commented thus:

'There is a very marked difference in the conditions of the sections of the tracks of the London and North Eastern and Southern Railways over which the trial runs were made.

Both the Tank and Tender engines ran with remarkable

138

No. of Trial	Engine	Direction of Running	Road	Condition of Tanks and Bunkers	Speeds m.p.h.	Observations
1	803	Forwards	Up	Nearly empty	44½-63	Only moderate speed was attempted on this run; engine rolled slightly at several points and was not so steady as on L.N.E.R.
2	803	Backwards	Down	Nearly empty	34½-69½	Only moderate speed was attempted. Engine rode steadier than in No. 1 trip. Down road appeared to be in better condition than up road
3	890	Forwards	Up	Nearly empty	51½-77¾	Engine rolled at several points on this trip, but quickly recovered itself, five oscillations being the greatest number occurring together in close succession. These oscillations or rolls were the worst experienced in any of the trials. Some were on the straight road, others on entering curves, and again where super-elevation of outer rails changed. I did not regard the rolling as actually dangerous but if it had increased instead of abated, should have promptly applied the brake
4	890	Backwards	Down	Nearly empty	31-69¾	Engine rode much better than on the up road, the speed was lower than in preceding run, and the road in better condition. There was a slight roll at 19¼ Mile Post
5	803	Forwards	Up	Full	50-77½	The engine rolled to about the same extent as engine 890 on trip No. 3 and at the same places
6	803	Backwards	Down	Full	31-73½	Engine ran fairly steadily and better than when empty
7	890	Forwards	Up	Full	52½-68	Speed reduced on this trip owing to instruction received from Chief Engineer, but rolling still considerable at bad points
8	890	Backwards	Down	Full	33½-70¾	Engine running was fairly satisfactory and seemed rather better than on Trip 4 when empty. There were some vertical oscillations but no rolling to speak of. (Sir John Pringle rode on the footplate)

steadiness at high speeds on the London and North Eastern track. The curves are all transition curves, and the general condition of the road was superior to that of the Southern. I am satisfied that on the London and North Eastern section over which the trials were made both Tank and Tender engines could run regularly with safety at any speed which they could attain.

'On the trial section of the Southern Railway the rolling of both Tank and Tender engines was excessive at high speeds; the rolling of the engines at some places when running on the straight line was quite as great as the worst roll experienced on curves.

'It seemed clear to me that this rolling was caused by irregular depression of the road at various points, apparently owing to the sleepers not being properly packed, and to defective drainage.

'The rolling of both Tank and Tender engines at speeds of 70 m.p.h. is greater than I consider to be safe for regular working on roads in a condition similar to that of the Southern Railway over which the trials were made.

'If the location of the irregular depressions in the road previously referred to should coincide with the rolling periods of engines, a dangerous and unstable condition would arise. As it is not so likely that such irregularities would occur as close to each other as to coincide with the shorter rolling periods of Tender engines, there is less probability of this dangerous condition arising with Tender engines than with Tank engines.

'Both the Tank engines are well designed efficient engines, and on a road well laid and well maintained are suitable for working express passenger trains.'

I have not mentioned, until now, Gresley's comments upon the working of the 'King Arthur' class 4-6-0, as they are not strictly relevant to the accident at Sevenoaks. But Sir Herbert Walker was naturally anxious to have the riding of this class of engine examined. On the L.N.E.R. at speeds of 75 to 81½ m.p.h. the engine ran steadily without any roll or lurch; but the vibration on the footplate was so severe that it was impossible to obtain any record with the Accelerometer, used for measuring the lateral and vertical acceleration in a roll or lurch. On the Southern up to a maximum speed of 86 m.p.h., Gresley reported:

'The vibration was, if anything, worse than on the London and North Eastern. At the places where rolling occurred with the Tank engines, there was considerable rolling and lurching with the Tender engine, and the riding can be described as being very rough and uncomfortable.'

The experience on the S.E. & C.R. line, and the high speed tests between Woking and Walton showed clearly that all was not well with the Southern permanent way. Ellson was a man of somewhat highly-strung, nervous disposition, and the disaster coming so soon after he had succeeded to the office of Chief Engineer led to him suffering a nervous breakdown. It seemed as though he was constantly overawed by the tremendous personality of Sir Herbert Walker, and his relations with Maunsell were frequently strained. As soon as Sir John Pringle's report was available Sir Herbert summoned Maunsell and Ellson to hear their views. It is said that both men blamed the other. There was, of course, a joint responsibility for the accident. On the locomotive side there is no point in having an engine that rides perfectly on a good track, if there is not a good track to run on. Sir John Elliott has told how Sir Herbert Walker cut short the wrangle between these two chief engineers:

'Well, gentlemen, a number of people have lost their lives on our railway, so there must be something wrong somewhere. Maunsell, we will withdraw the whole of this class (21 'River' tanks) of locomotives from traffic for the time being, and it may be wise to convert them into tender engines. Let me have the cost. Ellson, please prepare for me for the next Board your estimate of the cost of re-ballasting the whole of the boat train route between London and Dover.'

And so the handsome 'River' class tank engines disappeared, to become part of the 'V' class 2-6-0 series. It is sometimes thought that the construction of new 2-6-0s with

6 ft. diameter coupled wheels was the *result* of the Sevenoaks accident. Actually, however, before the accident occurred a decision had been taken to build the new batch of 6 ft. mixed traffic engines as 2-6-0 tender engines, rather than 2-6-4 tanks, and the conversion of the 'Rivers' to tender engines was a natural outcome. But far more important than the disappearance of the 'River' class was the vast improvement made in Southern permanent way as a result of the revelations contained in Sir John Pringle's report, thus:

'My examination, however, of the down track in the vicinity of the scene of this accident, and the actual survey made of the gauge and level of the rails, leads me to conclude that there was an insufficiency of hard and clean ballast foundation, a lack of proper drainage, and irregularities in the level and gauge of the rails, sufficient to set up serious rolling and lateral motion on tank engines travelling at high speeds. I cannot help believing that the heavy rainfall in the morning of the day of the accident may have caused the track to go down rapidly under traffic, and have occasioned some of the irregularities subsequently observed and measured.'

Among other comments, he also made these:

(*a*) The necessity for permanently strengthening the road bed on some sections of their main lines of railway, in order to meet present-day traffic conditions, does not appear to have been fully realised. Loading has been increased, and heavier and more powerful locomotives have been designed and built, to haul these heavier loads at the same or higher speeds. Betterment in the type of road bed, and class of maintenance, becomes correspondingly of importance.

(*b*) Sufficient attention does not appear to have been paid at all events on certain sections of their railways, by the Permanent Way Staff to instructions issued by the Chief Engineer with regard to the superelevation required upon curves, and to the necessity for maintaining it. The erection of permanent pillars alongside important curves showing the cant required, and the further supply to gangers of combined gauge and level reading tools, would appear to be advisable.

(c) More frequent riding on the footplate of engines travelling at high speeds by Permanent Way Officers and Inspectors, particularly in wet weather, would keep them better informed of the condition of the road bed, and the need for action.

These were strong words to a major railway company, in the year 1928, when the report was issued; but they had the desired effect, and Southern permanent way, using a splendid rock ballast from Meldon quarry, subsequently attained a very high standard.

11

Running through Signals: three cases for A.T.C.

The collision and fire near Aisgill on the Midland Railway, in 1913, more than any other single event aroused railway and public conscience to the need for something more than semaphore signalling for the protection of heavy main line traffic. As mentioned in Chapter Seven, however, opinion among railway officers was not then in favour of a system of automatic train control such as that in process of development on the Great Western Railway, and with the outbreak of war in 1914 the general question of some adjunct to the wayside signals fell into abeyance. After the war the administrative problems prior to, and immediately after grouping naturally claimed an inordinate amount of the attention of senior railway officers, but then, under the new organisation a committee was set up under the chairmanship of Col. Sir John Pringle to advise and recommend a policy concerning automatic train control in general. In the meantime the well-known Great Western system had been brought to a high degree of reliability, and its use was being extended to cover the entire main line network of that company.

In the meantime while committees met and senior managements argued accidents that could have been prevented by some means of automatic train control continued to occur. An ever-present difficulty in railway operation was the incidence of weather conditions that made observation of signals difficult. Drivers anxious to maintain their schedules were sometimes inclined to run harder than was expedient in fog; while with large modern locomotives having short chimneys and the soft blast arising from good valve gears, the exhaust steam was tending to cling to the boiler, and drift down into the driver's view. Difficulty of this kind was experienced with the 'King Arthurs' class 4-6-0s of the Southern, and it was generally considered to be the cause of the derailment of the 'Royal Scot' one Sunday morning in 1931, at Leighton Buzzard, when that train was being crossed from fast to slow line on account of line occupation for engineering work at some place ahead. If indeed exhaust steam was beating down and obscuring the driver's lookout an additional warning in the cab would have alerted him to the fact that he was being crossed over, and needed to reduce speed considerably.

Rather more than two years prior to this relatively minor accident however, in October 1928, there had occurred the first major disaster in Great Britain since Quintinshill. I am aware that Abermule and Sevenoaks had occurred in the meantime, but of Charfield Sir John Pringle wrote that 12 years had passed since an accident with so many deplorable features had taken place. There was a tragic parallel also to the incidents of Hawes Junction and Aisgill, in that Charfield was followed quite shortly by a very similar collision not far away, at Ashchurch—both again on the Midland line. Charfield was an affair of the early hours of an autumn morning. It had been a clear, still night and mist was rising in the fields and drifting towards the railway. The West of England main line of the Midland is always busy, and between Gloucester and Yate it was also used by certain Great Western trains. On this particular morning there were four trains all fairly close together: a Midland goods from Birmingham to Bristol: a Great Western fitted goods from Wolverhampton to Bristol: a Midland parcel train from Leicester to Bristol, and finally the Midland night mail from Leeds to Bristol.

Control was keeping a close watch on the working, and the Birmingham goods was shunted at Charfield, and the Wolverhampton goods at Berkeley Road to clear the line for the parcel train, which was a fast one and which would otherwise have been delayed by the slower trains ahead. The

parcel train duly passed through, and then the signalman at
Charfield rang Control to ask about the forwarding of the
two goods trains. As a result the Birmingham goods was
sent forward from Charfield, but before leaving this train
drew into Charfield station and spent five minutes taking
water, Signalman Button, of Charfield, had not reckoned
with this. He had hoped to get rid of both trains, and had
accepted the G.W.R. train from Wolverhampton from
Berkeley Road, and it was on its way. If he had sent both
trains on the mail would undoubtedly have been delayed,
and so reluctantly he realised he would have to shunt the
Great Western goods back into his lay-by as soon as it
arrived.

To appreciate what happened subsequently some reference is needed to the Midland system of block working, in
conjunction with track circuiting, which had been standardised on the line since the days of Hawes Junction. The line
was equipped with Langdon's rotary interlocking block
which ensured the correct sequence of operations on the
instruments. Furthermore, the starting signal at the box in
rear could be lowered only when release was obtained from
a treadle actuated by the previous train passing a definite
clearing point at the box in advance. Thus the starting signal
at Berkeley Road South Junction could not be lowered until
the previous train had passed the release treadle at the Charfield clearing point signal. Certain signals also had electrical
repeaters in the box, and there was a track circuit in rear of
the outer home signal.

The Great Western goods arrived at Charfield at 5.13 a.m.
and as it drew past his box the signalman shouted to both
driver and guard to set back into the refuge siding. The
train had passed his release point treadle, and so 'Train out
of section' was sent back to Berkeley Road South Junction.
Already the mail was close at hand, and exactly one minute
—according to the train register book—after the Great
Western goods had arrived, and before it had commenced
to set back the express was accepted from Berkeley Road.
The signalman was correct in doing this, because there was

146

the necessary quarter mile interval between the clearance point and the down outer home signal. In accepting, however, signalman Button realised that the Great Western goods would not have shunted clear in time to give the mail a clear run, and that a check, if not a dead stop was almost certain.

In passing one must comment upon the cumbersome procedures then needed in order to sidetrack a goods, or other slow train. The 'horror of facing points' had persisted from the nineteenth century, and to get clear in a case like that existing at Charfield meant drawing ahead and then setting back over a trailing crossover into the lay-by. It was a lengthy process, and the Great Western was no quicker than usual in carrying it out. It so happened too that an up empty wagon train was also approaching Charfield. The signalman was anxiously watching the progress of the shunt back movement, at the same time taking an occasional glance at his down line circuit indicator. This latter would tell him that the mail was at hand, and as a keen railwayman he was naturally impatient for the moment when he could reverse his siding points and pull off his down line signals for the mail. Suddenly, as he was expecting the track indicator changed from 'clear' to 'occupied'. The mail was now approaching; but then to his horror he saw it quickly go back to clear—so quickly indeed that it was evident that the mail was running fast, and was in fact running clean through his signals.

The circumstances could scarcely have been worse. On the down line the Great Western goods was setting back into the sidings and on the up line the empty wagon train was slowly trundling through. Into this death trap charged the mail at about 60 m.p.h. It was hauled by a Midland class '3' 4-4-0 No. 714, and consisted of eight wooden-bodied, gas-lit coaches. The engine hit the wagons of the Great Western goods first, and then being deflected crashed into the up goods train ploughing itself to a stand, on its side, amid the splintered wreckage of two goods trains. But worse than this was the fate of the coaches of the mail train. At the very point of collision a low overbridge spanned the tracks, and the wooden coaches piled up in a heap under this bridge, and promptly took fire. It was fortunate that there were not many passengers in this night train, or the death roll would have been much heavier. As it was the terrible fire raged for 12 hours, and 15 persons perished.

In the subsequent enquiry attention naturally became focused on the aspect displayed by the distant signal. One thing is certain; it could not have been cleared by the Charfield signalman, for the line ahead was not cleared and the lever was physically locked. On the other hand there was the frank and straightforward evidence of the driver and fireman of the mail. This was no repetition of Aisgill, where a driver took a perfunctory look at the distant, misread it and went on regardless, in perfectly clear weather. Driver Aldington and Fireman Want on engine No. 714 were very much on the alert, in the dark hour before dawn on this misty morning. After Berkeley Road, Want was looking ahead, and the driver crossed from the right hand to the left hand side of the engine to look over his fireman's shoulder and make certain of the signal. Both men were absolutely certain it was showing green. If this was actually the case, and both driver and fireman were excellent witnesses, how it came to be so was a mystery, because the levers of all the down line signals had not been moved.

Automatic train control could probably have prevented the accident, and in the 15 years that had elapsed since he conducted the enquiry into the Aisgill disaster Sir John Pringle had completely changed his views about the Great Western system. At the time of Charfield he strongly recommended its adoption. So far as the accident itself was concerned the Inspector emphasised how all the elements of time and chance had been hostile. If only the driver of the L.M.S. goods had told Signalman Button he needed water, that train would never have been let out of the lay-by; the Great Western goods would have run through, instead of having to be sidetracked and the mail would have followed. If the mail had arrived 10 seconds later than it did it would have got through. It would have been a hair-breadth escape;

148

but nevertheless, an escape. The existence of that overbridge made the effects of the collision on the coaches of the mail train far worse than they would have been otherwise. It was a monument of ill-luck.

By this time in this story of severe accidents my own association with railways was bringing a keener and more vital interest than that of a railway enthusiast reading the news in the paper. Reports were eagerly scanned by us young trainee engineers, and the same questions always used to be discussed: was it anything to do with the signalling? Whose apparatus was installed at the locality—and so on. Furthermore, in my own case, through interest in locomotive running I was getting to know, by sight at any rate, many of the express drivers who worked into St. Pancras and King's Cross. Both stations were very busy between 1 and 2 p.m. The L.N.E.R. drivers had their names engraved on the engine headlamps, while the Midland men had their names on tablets fitted into a slot on the sides of the engine cab. In this way I came to recognise by sight many of the celebrated footplate men of the day, who worked from Kentish Town, Leicester and Derby on the one line, and King's Cross, Grantham and Doncaster on the other.

Then in January 1929 came the news of another bad accident on the West of England main line of the Midland, again in the early hours of the morning. Once again a goods was in course of carrying out the laborious process of setting back, in this instance from the up to the down line at Ashchurch. It was foggy at the time and a Bristol-Leeds express came up, hauled by a Midland compound No. 1060. The load consisted of 10 bogie vehicles and four six-wheelers. This train over-ran signals and crashed at full speed into the goods. The driver was killed, but it was thought that he had not realised he was running through a patch of fog and that the distant signal would be hard to see. There was tremendous damage to rolling stock, but fortunately no fire, and with a sparsely filled train only three other persons besides the driver were killed. The driver was a Derby man, Crabtree by name, who regularly worked into St. Pancras and who I knew well. Automatic train control would undoubtedly have averted this accident.

One of the most extraordinary cases of running through signals, with disastrous results took place on the Edinburgh to Glasgow main line of the L.N.E.R. at Castlecary on December 10th, 1937. It was a bad winter's evening and many railwaymen who were concerned said that the conditions for operating traffic were as bad as they had ever seen; snow was falling heavily at the time and with darkness coming on around 4 p.m. one had the added difficulty, from the point of view of signal observation, of not knowing whether one was running through heavy snow that was blanketing the view, or if it were the darkness of the night and that no signals were in the vicinity. It seems from what various witnesses said after the accident had occurred that snow showers were intermittent, but very heavy while they lasted; and during those showers the visibility was often less than 50 yards.

The familiar trouble of snow blocking points was the starting point in the chain of events that led to the accident. At Gartshore a delay awaiting the clearance of points led to a goods train being stopped on the main line at Dullatur, and this in turn reacted back, so that the 2 p.m. express from Dundee to Glasgow experienced adverse signals at Castlecary. The line was not clear beyond. The signalman at Castlecary, Sneddon by name, said afterwards that the worst snow had been between 2.30 and 3.20 p.m., and was beating against the windows of his cabin; but that during that time he had always been able to see all the signals under his control that were normally visible. One gained the impression, from his evidence, that he did not consider the visibility was bad and that no additional precautions were needed. Nevertheless when the Dundee train approached at about 4.30 p.m. the line forward from Castlecary was still not clear, and all the Castlecary signals were against it.

Because of the bad conditions of visibility the driver of this train missed the distant and the home signal and when the signalman saw that the train was still steaming he threw

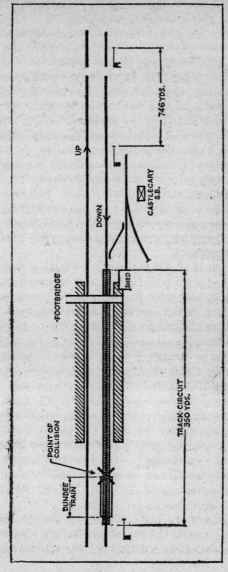

Fig. 9. Plan of tracks and down line signals at Castlecary.

open the window of his box, exhibited a red lamp and blew a whistle to attract the attention of the driver. As the train was travelling at a considerable speed, even though its driver was alerted to the aspects that were being shown by the signals it took a little time to pull up, and Signalman Sneddon then made the most extraordinary blunder. Because the train had been travelling fairly fast and it had passed out of his immediate sight, he assumed that his warning of a red lamp and whistle had failed to attract the driver, and that the train was running away. He said afterwards that he expected there would be a collision with the goods, which he knew to be still standing at Dullatur East. Actually the driver of the Dundee train was very much on the alert and to the signalman's red lamp and the whistle he acted with such promptitude that he stopped with the tail of his train only 294 yards beyond the signalbox. It is true that he slightly overran the starting signal, which was also at danger, but only by a matter of 18 yards.

The signalman did not watch the track circuit indicator that he had in his box. He had received no whistle or other acknowledgment from the driver as he passed, to confirm that he had seen the red lamp; he watched the tail light of the train to about the middle of the station platform after which it disappeared from sight owing to the existence of a goods shed in between. Without taking any further action to confirm what had actually happened he sent the 4-5-5 bell signal to Dullatur (train running away on right line), and then sent for the stationmaster to tell him what he imagined had happened. Never was a disaster premeditated by such careless assumption as this. The stationmaster did not appear to take any greater precautions than the signalman had done, to ascertain what had happened to the Dundee train and immediately afterwards Sneddon became concerned with the approach of the 4 p.m. express from Edinburgh to Glasgow.

He telephoned Greenhill Junction the box immediately east of Castlecary to confer with the signalman there about the advisability of accepting the Edinburgh train. The latter signalman questioned him on several points: had he sent the emergency signal to Dullatur? Had he got the requisite clearance beyond the home signal? Had he seen the tail lamp? Were all his signals on? To all these questions Sneddon replied 'yes', and as both men were anxious not to delay the Edinburgh train unduly they agreed that there was nothing in the regulations to prohibit the acceptance of that train. In view of the weather conditions however the Greenhill man suggested putting down detonators, in addition to keeping all the signals at danger. This again was a terribly unwise procedure. Consider the circumstances: the signalman at Castlecary imagines—quite wrongly—that the Dundee train has run past all his signals and is about to collide, if it had not actually done so, with a goods train which was standing in the section ahead; and yet just for the sake of advancing a succeeding express from Greenhill to Castlecary he decided to accept another train that would, in any case, even if it had stopped, have approached very closely to what could have been a serious collision.

All the time snow was falling, visibility was a great deal worse than this signalman seemed to appreciate, and he had already had a case of one train running past signals due to this bad visibility. Nevertheless the result of the conversation between the signalmen at Greenhill and Castlecary was that the Edinburgh train was accepted. It came on at full speed, and like its predecessor from Dundee missed the first two Castlecary signals through bad visibility. Sneddon once again showed a red lamp and his detonator duly exploded. But instead of stopping harmlessly, as the Dundee train had done, even though slightly over-running the starting signal, the Edinburgh express ran headlong into the standing Dundee train and the result was the worst accident on British railways since Quintinshill.

Circumstances at the moment of collision can be better imagined than described. The Edinburgh train was a heavy one, consisting entirely of modern L.N.E.R. stock with massive underframes and teak bodies connected throughout with the equally massive buck-eye couplers. The speed was

estimated at about 70 m.p.h. and the train was hauled by a
Gresley 'A3' class Pacific No. 2744 *Grand Parade*. The
driver had time to do no more than shut the regulator, apply
the brake and the sanders before his engine struck the standing train. The Edinburgh express ploughed for nearly 100
yards into this latter train, smashing the rear coaches almost
beyond recognition; but the force of the impact was so terrific that the first three coaches of the Edinburgh train completely overshot the engine and tender, the third finishing
immediately above the engine boiler. Fortunately there was
no fire, but the work of rescue was made very difficult by the
snow and darkness.

In all 35 persons were killed and 179 injured. The driver
and fireman of the Edinburgh express, Messrs. Anderson
and Kinnear had miraculous escapes, seeing that their
engine was practically buried under wreckage. But there was
no 'jack-knifing', and the tender remained completely in line.
There is no doubt that the construction of the tender itself
and its high sides had the effect of causing the succeeding
coaches to ride over the top, and over the top of the engine
itself rather than to crush the tender, and with it, the men on
the footplate. The fireman was injured though not very
seriously, but the driver escaped practically without harm.
This was another case in which I knew some of the people
concerned. Just over seven years later I had a footplate pass
to ride the down 'Aberdonian' express from Edinburgh to
Dundee, and on that morning our driver was Davie Anderson who was very much involved at Castlecary in December
1937. As if this were not enough, about six years later I met
him on the footplate once again, when I rode through from
King's Cross to Edinburgh on the 'non-stop'. It was then
known as 'The Capitals Limited', and Davie Anderson was
our driver from Tollerton to Edinburgh.

At Castlecary a great deal of evidence and the attempts to
establish the responsibility for the disaster centred upon the
aspect displayed by the distant signal. Anderson was known
to be a very reliable and vigilant engineman and only on the
previous day he had stopped in the course of working an

express train because he was not sure of the aspects being displayed by a signal in conditions of indifferent visibility. After the accident he maintained that he thought that the distant signal was showing clear, though the Inspecting Officer felt that both he and the driver of the Dundee train, who also ran past signals, were driving at a speed greater than the bad weather conditions justified. But there was another point which threw an element of doubt on the case. The Castlecary signalman maintained that his track indicator went to 'clear' after the train had passed his box. In fact that train stopped with its rear standing on the track circuit. In such conditions it is highly unlikely that the track circuit would have cleared itself so as to cause the indicator to clear, and the Inspecting Officer felt that far from justifying Sneddon's action, in assuming that the Dundee train had run right past and out of his control, this evidence tended to reinforce the view that Sneddon had acted in a somewhat irresponsible manner.

But all the circumstances of this accident combined to emphasise the need for some kind of automatic warning, linked very closely with the distant signal. Had a system of automatic train control such as that used on the Great Western Railway been in operation at Castlecary, it would almost certainly have alerted the driver of the Edinburgh express, and prevented him having any doubts as to what aspect the distant signal was displaying. Again the northern Companies came in for a form of mild criticism for not having adopted, just as it was, the Great Western system of automatic train control. Unfortunately there was at that time a good deal of parochialism among the railway companies and a reluctance to adopt what other administrations had found to be very satisfactory. While the Great Western was installing automatic train control over the whole of its main line network and equipping every one of its locomotives, the northern lines were still discussing and experimenting. The Castlecary accident greatly accelerated the process of development, and before the outbreak of World War II the L.M.S.R. and the L.N.E.R. had agreed to combine in developing the Hudd system of inductive automatic train control, and it is not without significance that the Glasgow to Edinburgh main line of the L.N.E.R. was selected for an extended trial.

Another aspect of railway equipment which received a good deal of publicity at the time of the Castlecary accident was the method of constructing the coaches used on express passenger trains. On the continent of Europe so many casualties had occurred from accidents in which wooden coaches were involved that at the time of Castlecary there was a strong newspaper campaign in progress in this country towards the general adoption of all-steel coaches, such as were then general in America and coming increasingly into use in this country. On the L.N.E.R. Sir Nigel Gresley was strongly against this movement. He felt that if all-steel coaches were used and were thrown violently about in collision the casualties inside them would be far more severe than in the form of coach that he had standardised on the L.N.E.R., namely, a massive steel underframe and a heavily built teak body. The way in which coaches of this kind stood up to the terrific impact of the Castlecary accident provided some evidence to the strength of his argument, though the cost of construction of coaches of this kind was high. There is no doubt, however, that lives were saved in the Castlecary accident by the existence, from end to end of the Edinburgh express, of the buck-eye couplings which helped to keep the train in line and avoided all but the very worst tendency to telescope.

12

Accidents on the Great Western

In the period between 1915 and the outbreak of World War II there was scarcely an official report upon a railway collision that did not contain some reference to the Great Western system of automatic train control, and there is no doubt that the inspecting officers of the Ministry of Transport would like to have seen it adopted generally on the railways of this country. But there was a definite resistance to doing so on the part of the other companies, partly through the Great Western use of a contact ramp for initiating the indications in the cab. It was felt that a contact system was not to be relied upon in all weathers, though there was no evidence in support of this objection in the records of performance on the G.W.R. But it was important to see that the principle of the system was being generally accepted, and a brief reference to this is necessary for an appreciation of what it failed to prevent in the accidents recalled in this chapter.

The system is based wholly upon the indication displayed by the distant signal, and the ramp was mounted in the track approximately 440 yards ahead of that signal. The physical act of passing over the ramp imparted an upward movement to the collector shoe on the locomotive, and this upward movement did two things: it opened the A.T.C. brake valve; and it would cause a vacuum operated siren to sound in the cab. If the distant signal was in the caution position the ramp was dead, and passage over it did nothing more than move the shoe upwards. But if the distant signal was clear, current was applied to the ramp. This was collected as the engine passed over, and the current applied to the locomotive equipment forestalled the opening of the brake valve and the sounding of the siren, and rang the 'all-clear' bell instead. The important item was the 'fail-safe' feature inherent in the system. If current failed to be picked up the warning was given instead. There was no possibility of getting a false clear.

The audible warning in the cab, and the associated brake control was provided only at the distant signals, though the importance of doing this was plain enough when one merely turns back to the preceding chapter of this book and considers the events leading up to Charfield, Ashchurch, and Castlecary. But the fact that it was confined to the distant signal explains why it could not have prevented the first accident now to be described. This was not in any way a 'disaster' in the sense that most incidents described in this book can be regarded. But I recall it, because after the lapse of more than 50 years it remains the *only* railway accident that I have ever seen personally. It occurred at Reading in the morning of Saturday, June 17th, 1914. On that morning a race special from the West of England, bound for Ascot, stopped at the up main platform to reman. By a coincidence, the engine was 4-4-0 No. 3379 *Reading*, of the 'Bulldog' class, and the train was being held at the platform while the up main line—the centre road—was cleared for the morning Worcester-Paddington 'flyer'.

Someone on the platform, anxious to get the special away, and without looking at the platform starting signal gave an ambiguous hand signal. This was mistaken by the fresh crew for the rightaway, and the train moved off, passing the danger signal, and it was entering upon the main line just as the express came up at full speed. The engine *Reading* had only just fouled the main line, and the Worcester engine, 4-4-0 No. 3819 *County of Leicester* struck it no more than a glancing blow. But at the speed the express was travelling it was enough. The 'County' was derailed, overturned, and came to rest almost at right angles to the track, and the driver was killed. My home was then at Hurst, and as I returned from school at midday, from the South Eastern and Chatham station, I had a panoramic view of the wrecked trains, on the Great Western embankment. It was one of those scenes never to be forgotten!

From this recollection of boyhood I pass on to something infinitely more serious, the collision near Shrivenham on January 15th, 1936, when the up Penzance 'sleeper' ran into some stationary wagons, on a dark cold night, several hours before dawn. At 5 a.m. a loaded coal train of 53 wagons, and hauled by a standard 2-8-0 engine, left Highworth Junction, Swindon, and made steady progress eastwards. Although the Penzance express was due shortly afterwards the coal train would normally reach Shrivenham in plenty of time to be switched on to the up goods line there and continue to Knighton Crossing, a further $2\frac{1}{2}$ miles east of Shrivenham. There was no question of a shunt back to clear the main line, as in the tragic cases of Charfield and Ashchurch; the train could enter the relief line direct by a facing connection. Actually the train was signalled on the main line through Shrivenham, and was turned on to the goods line at Ashbury Crossing box, 1,192 yards east of Shrivenham signal box.

The signalman at Shrivenham, W. Head, watched the mineral train approaching, and at the same time a down train of milk empties was passing. He observed the tail lamp of this latter train, and thought he had also observed the tail lamp of the Aberdare coal train. He gave train out of section for this train to Ashbury Crossing at 5.15 a.m. and accepted the Penzance express at 5.18 a.m. The signalman at Ashbury Crossing was called to the telephone just as the coal train was turning on to the goods line, and he had to look after it to see the tail lamp. He saw what he took to be a white light reversed by the guard, but he did not immediately give 'train out of section'. Instead he looked down the line towards Shrivenham, and as there was a good view right to the station, and this line was empty, he assumed all was well, and gave 'train out of section' at 5.18 a.m. at which time also Shrivenham accepted the express.

At 5.22 a.m. Shrivenham received 'train entering section'

from Marston Crossing, but a minute later the signalman heard a loud bang, and the up distant signal lever was badly shaken. At first he thought cattle were on the line; but realising in any case that something unusual had happened he threw all his down line signals to danger, and thereby stopped an empty stock train which was approaching at full speed. The casual way in which this signalman and his colleague at Ashbury Crossing had observed the passage of the Aberdare coal train proved fatal. That train *had no tail lamp* when it passed, for the simple reason that there had been a breakaway between the 48th and 49th wagons, and five wagons and the brake van had come to rest in the open country some 1,000 yards west of Shrivenham box. As such they were completely unprotected by the signalling system. A track circuit extended 500 yards in rear of the home signal, but the wagons lay beyond this, and were undetected. They were about 500 yards inside the distant signal, but that offered no protection. Thus when Shrivenham sent 'train out of section' to Marston Crossing, the lock on the starting signal at the latter box was released and there was nothing to prevent the express being accepted and signalled forward.

The last line of defence was the guard of the coal train, left marooned with five wagons in open country. This man was clearly not giving proper attention to his duties, and was not keeping the good look-out he should have done, seeing that he had not worked a train over that route for four months. He admitted he did not see Marston Crossing Box; but soon after he noticed they were slowing down, and when they stopped he assumed they were at Shrivenham home signal. All the evidence suggests that he had a full nine minutes after stopping to investigate and take protective action; and it is clear that the real situation only dawned on him when it was too late. He then had time to do no more than run back about 70 yards, waving a red lamp, when the express came up at about 55 m.p.h. It was a nine-coach train, hauled by engine No. 6007 *King William III*. Much of the force of the collision was taken by the frame of the goods brake van; it was driven into the three rearmost wagons,

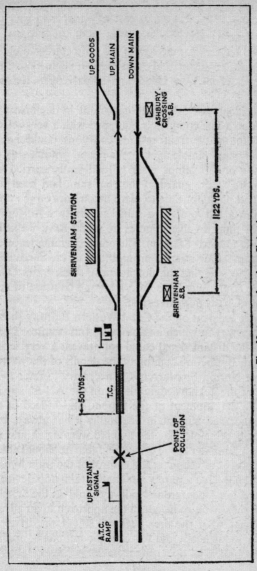

Fig. 10. Layout of tracks at Shrivenham.

which were piled into a heap. The engine ploughed its way into this obstruction, and turned over on its right side, and the two leading coaches shattered themselves upon the engine and tender. But the rest of the train consisted mainly of steel framed coaches, and casualties were light. The driver and one passenger were killed, and 10 passengers seriously injured.

The accident was extremely important in demonstrating that even on a line completely equipped with a very reliable form of automatic train control collisions could not be avoided if such simple, yet fundamental routines as the observance of tail lamps were not diligently carried out. Furthermore, if the guard of the coal train had been fully alert he had plenty of time to place detonators on the track, and exhibit a red lamp at a sufficient distance to stop the express in time. In five minutes he could have walked at least ½ mile towards Marston. The one redeeming feature of this unhappy affair was the promptitude of the Shrivenham signalman in stopping the down empty stock train. Otherwise there could only have been a second collision of great severity and many more lives lost.

The next accident on the Great Western Railway showed yet another way in which an automatic train control system based on the distant signal could not prevent a very serious derailment. But before coming to the details of the wartime disaster at Norton Fitzwarren it is necessary to refer to the working of the acknowledging lever on the A.T.C. apparatus. In the development of the system, and indeed of any system concerned with main line traffic it has always been an accepted principle that the audible warning should primarily be a reminder to the driver, and that he should always have the power of retaining full control of the train himself. One could not have a purely automatic train-stop device, as on the London Underground railways, and so the acknowledging lever was introduced. In the approach to an adverse distant signal, when the siren begins to sound, the driver has the power to silence it and forestall the automatic application of the brakes by operating the acknowledging lever. He has thus been audibly alerted, and having acknowledged this it is then up to him to act upon the signal indication he has received. Only if he fails to acknowledge is the control of the train taken out of his hands and the brakes applied.

The acknowledging lever is also used to silence the siren and forestall a brake application in those instances where the distant signal is 'all clear', but where for some reason current is not picked up from the ramp by the collector shoe, and a warning instead of an 'all clear' is received in the cab. When riding on the footplate of Great Western locomotives I have many times seen the acknowledging lever used in this way. It was this practice, safe and perfectly legitimate in ordinary circumstances that was one of the factors that led to disaster on the night of November 4th, 1940. At that time the blitz on London was at its height, traffic by all regular passenger trains was extremely heavy, with naval, military and air force personnel travelling to and from units, on leave and such like; and on the night in question the 9.50 p.m. express from Paddington to Penzance was conveying a very heavy and full complement of passengers.

This was one of the time-honoured services of the G.W.R. For very many years there had been a 9.50 p.m. from Paddington, and the service ran unchanged throughout the war, and until the complete alteration of the service to the West of England in diesel days. On this particular night the train was running late, as it frequently did during the war years; but it had not been unduly delayed by air raids, nor had it been diverted from its usual route via Bristol. There were times, of course, when the incidence of severe air raids, and damage on the line, caused extensive diversion; but the delay on this particular night in November 1940 was due only to ordinary traffic circumstances. Nevertheless the conditions were far from normal, and the driver who, as usual, was working through from Paddington to Newton Abbot on a double-home turn was an Old Oak man. Although he himself was in good health his home circumstances had been very much disrupted when his house was damaged in one of the London air raids.

On reaching Taunton 68 minutes late the train was routed into the down relief platform which leads out westwards on to the down relief line. The down main line passes through the centre island platform. The train was in its normal course so far as using the down relief line platform was concerned, and its normal route afterwards was to take the crossover road on to the down main line immediately to the west of Taunton station. But as the train was so late, and the 12.50 a.m. newspaper express from Paddington was running on time, the signalman at Taunton Station West Box decided to signal the 9.50 down the relief line and to allow the newspaper train to have a clear run through. He judged that very little further delay could occur to the 9.50 by this procedure, for by the way the newspaper train was running it would be practically clear of Norton Fitzwarren by the time the 9.50 had proceeded thus far. The latter train consisted of 13 vehicles, and was drawn by a 'King' class locomotive No. 6028 *King George VI;* on this engine, as normal on the Great Western Railway, the driver's place was on the right-hand side.

In tracing out the sequence of events that led to the disaster, the story is complicated by the fact that the driver, who survived the accident, had obviously been so affected, both by his experience at home, and by the shock of the accident itself that his evidence was confused in certain respects, and unreliable in others. The enquiry was conducted by Col. Sir Alan Mount, who showed great sympathy towards this unfortunate man, but who was forced to regard some of the points mentioned as unacceptable.

It is now necessary to refer to the layout of the signals immediately west of Taunton station, and these are shown in diagramatic form in the accompanying plan. Four signal boxes were concerned: Taunton Station West Box; Taunton West Junction Box; Silk Mill Crossing; and Norton Fitzwarren. The home signals for Taunton Station West were immediately beyond the end of the platform, and to facilitate sighting from locomotives with right-hand drive, the signals for the down relief line were bracketed out so as to

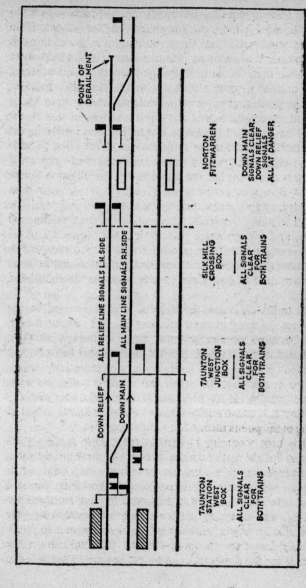

Fig. 11. Layout of tracks from Taunton to Norton Fitzwarren.

stand clear of the station awning, and to be readily visible. The home signal for the down main line was slightly ahead of the down relief line signals and stood to the right of the main line. When viewed from the footplate of a locomotive standing in the down relief line platform the group of signals was quite clear, and readily discernible as to their meaning.

The particular point of evidence which Sir Alan Mount found unacceptable was the driver's statement that shortly after he brought his train to rest in Taunton station he saw the home signal for the diversion line, from relief to main, go to green. This would have been the normal route of the train in question; but the signalman in the Taunton Station West Box was perfectly clear as to what he had done, namely, to give precedence to the newspaper train and send the 9.50 along the relief. This man was a good reliable witness, and for the same reason Sir Alan Mount found unacceptable the driver's statement that he had received the warning siren when he was leaving Taunton, which he would have done if he had been crossing from the 'down relief' to 'down main' line. Actually all signals were pulled off for both trains. Of course the fact that the distant signal was off did not guarantee that an 'all-clear' would be sounded in the cab. I have personally noted many occasions on Great Western engines where the 'all clear' signal has not been picked up because of a faulty contact, or some other reason. But if at this stage the driver had received a siren he would have been perfectly in order in acknowledging and cancelling it, because all the signals were clear and he could see they were so.

He frankly admitted afterwards that when leaving Taunton he did not realise that he was on the relief line and not on the main, and, by an unlucky chance the disposition of the signals between Taunton and Norton Fitzwarren was such that travelling under this mistaken impression there was little to appraise him of his error until it was too late. Referring once again to the diagram, apart from a gantry of signals across the tracks at Taunton West Junction, where the signals for both relief and main line were above the right-

166

hand side of the respective lines, all the relief line signals, right up to the point of derailment, were on the left-hand side, and all signals for the main line, until Norton Fitzwarren itself, were on the right-hand side. Between Taunton and Norton Fitzwarren, in the ordinary way of working this train, the driver would have seen all his signals after leaving Taunton on the right-hand side of the line; and on this unfortunate night, which was very dark and stormy, when he believed that he was travelling on the main line, he was sighting all the usual signals for a normal run from the right-hand side of his engine; and in the particular circumstance he does not appear to have realised that he was sighting them across one track, instead of on his immediate right as normal.

The signals for his own line were all on the left-hand side. These he was unaware of, and the case was complicated by the fact that he received clear A.T.C. signals at Taunton West Junction Box and at Silk Mill Crossing. It was only when he was approaching Norton Fitzwarren that he received an adverse distant signal, accompanied by the warning siren on the A.T.C. apparatus; but his subsequent evidence was so confused that he said he did not recall clearing the A.T.C., or in fact, receiving a warning. There was no doubt he must have received the warning and cleared it; otherwise the brakes would have been applied in plenty of time, and the train stopped. It was evident that on approaching Norton Fitzwarren, and seeing a clear signal on the *right-hand side* of the line, that he became somewhat confused. But what finally brought him to the realisation of his error was that in the immediate approach to Norton Fitzwarren he was overtaken by the newspaper train running at high speed. Then he realised where he was, and the danger that was imminent.

The train had accelerated smartly from Taunton despite its heavy load, and in the two miles from rest had attained a speed of about 45 m.p.h. When the driver finally realised the danger he had only about 300 to 350 yards before reaching the crossover road leading on to the main line. The points here were, of course, normal, to permit the passing of the newspaper train; the relief line ended at the catch points at the entrance to the crossover, and these latter points were set to protect the main line. The driver's action appears to have been rather slow, even in the face of this emergency, and speed had not been reduced very much when the train ran through the catch points and the engine fell over on soft ground beyond the end of the rails. The driver was practically unhurt, but the engine had fallen over on its left side and the fireman was killed.

Although the engine was no more than slightly damaged there was very serious destruction to the leading coaches of the train and the first six were all severely damaged, some being telescoped. The casualty list amounted to 27 killed and 56 seriously injured; but the circumstances might have been infinitely worse had the 9.50 p.m. train been fractionally later. The latter train was running at about 60 m.p.h. when it overtook the 9.50, and one can only imagine how much worse the death roll would have been had the newspaper train fouled the wreckage, which was flung in all directions after the crash. As it was the guard of the newspaper train felt something hit his van. He applied the brake and the train stopped beyond Victory Siding. After consultation with the driver this train proceeded to Wellington, when a thorough examination was made. It was only then that the men of the newspaper train heard of the derailment, and realised what a lucky escape they had had.

A.T.C. did not enter very prominently into the factors leading up to this accident. It was primarily due to the driver misinterpreting the signals at the west end of Taunton station, and continuing in the mistaken belief that he was on the main line instead of the relief. In his report to the Ministry of Transport, Sir Alan Mount had many comments to make upon the sighting of the signals. While the actual sighting from the footplate of a 'King' class engine was generally quite satisfactory, he felt that the positioning of some signals to the left of the line and some to the right—generally because of structural clearances at the particular locations—could lead to a certain amount of confusion though he did not consider that the signals which were mis-read by the driver admitted of any misunderstanding. It was in the subsequent disposition of signals along the line that he felt some criticism might be made.

Had the positioning been completely standardised, on one side or the other, there would have been better chance of the driver realising his mistake long before he got to Norton Fitzwarren. He would then have been fully on the alert, ready for the Norton Fitzwarren signals, at which he would have expected to be stopped to let the newspaper go ahead. The only other point that might have given the driver a false impression, though at the very last minute, was the ordinary routine action of the signalman at Norton Fitzwarren. He had accepted both trains, but of course kept all his relief line signals at danger. When the 9.50 approached and his track circuit indicator on the rear of the home signal showed 'track occupied' he lowered the home signal to allow the train, as he thought, to proceed up to the starter. He was surprised to see the train run through the station at practically the nor-mal speed of a train that had started from Taunton, and having done so, the accident happened almost immediately afterwards. The driver may have seen the lowering of the home signal as he approached, but the point was not raised in evidence.

When Nationalisation of the railways took place in 1948, it was realised that the traditional place for the driver on Great Western locomotives, the right-hand side, would have to give way to the practice universal everywhere else in Great Britain. There was great opposition to it among men of the former Great Western Railway. This was no more than natural, because they had grown up with it, and apart from the unfortunate accident at Norton Fitzwarren the Great Western had a very fine record of safe operation. But in modern conditions with colour light signalling, the driver's place on a steam locomotive was unquestionably on the left-hand side, and men of the former Great Western Railway

169

had to accustom themselves, much against their will, to working British standard locomotives with left-hand drive. But at the time the Norton Fitzwarren accident occurred, in 1940, colour light signalling had scarcely begun to appear on the Great Western Railway except at one or two large stations, and in his comments on signal sighting Sir Alan Mount was very careful not to express any view as to whether the left-hand, or the right-hand side was preferable on lines then almost wholly equipped with semaphore signals. What he criticised was the positioning of the signals, some on one side of the track and some on the other; and in this he undoubtedly made a very strong point for standardisation throughout any particular railway.

Less than a year later, on July 2nd, 1941, there was another very unfortunate accident on the Great Western Railway, once again in the early hours of the morning, and once again involving a West of England express. The locality this time was Dolphin Junction, one mile east of Slough station, where there were crossover roads from main to relief lines, and vice versa; in other words there were two double crossovers. This was a curious case of muddled working on the part of the signalman concerned, and although one of the locomotives involved—a Stanier '8F' 2-8-0—was not fitted with the Great Western system of A.T.C., it is doubtful if the accident would have been averted if the down freight train had been hauled by a standard G.W.R. locomotive. The first step in the chain of circumstances leading to the accident was reminiscent of Quintinshill, as it resulted from the late running of an express passenger train, the 6.20 p.m. from Plymouth to Paddington. A Government stores train had been sent on ahead of this train from Reading, but when the signalman at Dolphin Junction learned how relatively close behind the special the express was running, he seems to have been struck with an unfortunate fit of indecision, in his anxiety not to delay the express unduly.

It was too late to divert the stores train on to the relief line; but he realised that the express would quickly close in on the former, and suffer delay from adverse signals. Recalling that nothing had passed on the up relief line for over an hour, and following some enquiries as to the occupancy of that line, he decided to divert the express. The situation was complicated by the fact that he had already accepted on the down relief line, the 1.30 a.m. freight—Old Oak Common to Severn Tunnel Junction—itself running some 40 minutes late. By the time Signalman Welch, at Dolphin Junction, had received acceptance from Langley for the express, on the up slow line, he had received 'Train entering Section' for the down freight. Langley is about 1¼ miles from Dolphin Junction, and with the freight running at about 30 m.p.h. and travelling under clear signals it would have reached Dolphin Junction in about 2 minutes from the 'Train entering Section' signal.

At this point there was complete disagreement in the subsequent evidence. Signalman Welch asserted that he kept all his down relief line signals at danger, whereas the driver of the freight engine, with left-hand drive was quite positive that the Dolphin distant signal was clear. He referred particularly to the good look-out from the left-hand side at this location, which gave a clear view of the Dolphin distant signals for both main and relief lines. After assuring himself that the distant was 'off' he crossed the footplate to supervise his fireman's remedy for a leaky coal spray pipe; but he was quite sure he did not mistake the 'main' distant signal for the relief distant. When he sighted the home signal at danger, at a distance of 300 to 400 yards, he assumed that the signals had been reversed because of some emergency ahead. But he had an unbraked train of 62 wagons, and although he acted promptly enough it had not reduced the speed very much when he came to the actual junction.

In the meantime Signalman Welch, in his anxiety to cause a minimum of delay to the up express, had taken a totally unwarranted risk. In his evidence he said he watched the lights of the approaching freight train to make sure it was stopping, before he reversed the points. This is a matter which should have had the utmost care, because the two parallel crossovers were free of each other, so far as the mechanical interlocking was concerned. This practice was always regarded as debatable. At a single junction there would be no doubt: the down line points would also have had to be reversed, to provide trap-point protection in case of over-run. But with a parallel crossover, as in this case, an over-run, while protected from an opposing move on the up direction crossover line might foul the down main line, and cause even worse trouble. The Inspecting Officer, Major G. R. S. Wilson, was convinced that when Welch reversed the points for the up crossover road, and pulled off the appropriate signals, he could not have seen the freight train at all, and that he took a chance that it would pull up in time.

The express, consisting of eight coaches, and hauled by a 4-6-0 locomotive No. 4091 *Dudley Castle*, had been standing at the Dolphin up main home signals about two minutes when the signal to cross over on to the up relief line was cleared. The driver put on steam, and made the usual smart getaway that one would expect from a 'Castle' with a relatively light load, and collided head-on with the freight precisely on the diamond crossing. The combined speed of the two trains was estimated at 30 to 35 m.p.h.; but the momentum of the freight was much greater than that of the express, and *Dudley Castle* was driven back about four yards. The two leading coaches of the express took the force of the collision, and were telescoped for about two-thirds of their length. Five passengers were killed, and six persons were seriously injured, including the driver of the freight train.

At the time of the subsequent enquiry a point was made that the engine of the freight train was not fitted with A.T.C. apparatus. But if, in fact, the signalman at Dolphin Junction had originally pulled off his down relief line signals for the freight, and changed his mind after the driver had sighted the down relief line distant signal, an A.T.C. system based on the distant signal would not have helped. This is not to disparage the value of the Great Western, nor of the British Railways automatic warning system, which are invaluable

172

aids to the safe working of trains. But the examples quoted in this chapter are enough to show some of the loop-holes that still exist, and which will continue to demand alertness and diligence on the part of all concerned with the movement of trains.

13

Blunders with 'Lock and Block'

The midday London newspapers of April 2nd, 1937, carried banner headlines. There had been a collision on the Southern Railway in the height of the morning rush hour in a most dramatic location: just where the Brighton lines leading to Victoria cross the approaches to Stewart's Lane locomotive depot, and the South Western main line. But to anyone familiar with the technical equipment of the line in question the fact that a severe rear-end collision had occurred at all was more disconcerting than the elevated position where it occurred. For this line had for 30 years been equipped with Sykes 'Lock and Block' apparatus; and the interlocking for the signal levers with the block working, and the electric interlocking with treadles actuated by the passage of the train would appear to have made this section of the line as near foolproof as practicable, while retaining semaphore signals.

At the time rapid progress was being made with the modernisation of signalling on all the London suburban lines of the Southern Railway, substituting multi-aspect colour light signals and continuous track circuiting for semaphores and manual block. Naturally there are priorities in such a programme, and those priorities were settled largely by reference to the existing signalling equipment rather than by the density of traffic carried on the lines concerned. The approach to Victoria, over the tracks of the former London, Brighton and South Coast Railway was one of the heaviest used sections of the entire Southern Railway system—particularly that from Battersea Park into the terminus where

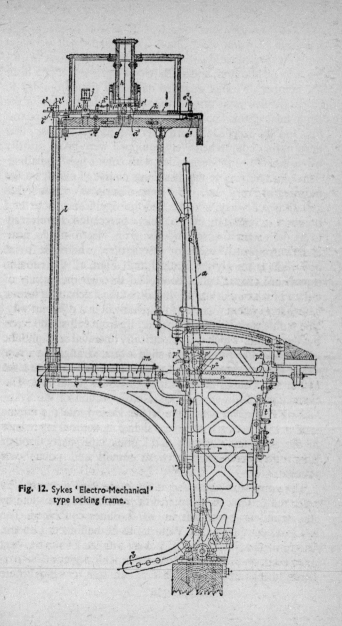

Fig. 12. Sykes 'Electro-Mechanical' type locking frame.

the South London line merges with the quadruple-tracked line from Croydon, via Balham. Traffic had much increased since the electrification of the main lines to Brighton, Worthing and Eastbourne, and at Battersea Park signal box itself the number of trains signalled daily had risen from 712 to 838 in the five years prior to the accident. But because of the equipment of this line with Sykes 'Lock and Block' apparatus, and its excellent record over the past 30 years, other lines not so comprehensively equipped were given priority when it came to modernisation with colour light signalling.

Before referring to the disastrous course of events on the morning of April 2nd, 1937, some description of the Sykes system is necessary, in order that the significance of several blunders in operating may be fully appreciated. In referring to modern signalling schemes the term 'electro-mechanical' is now frequently used for installations where the point operation is mostly mechanical and where all the running signals are colour lights, controlled through the agency of circuit breakers worked off the tails of the mechanical levers. The Sykes system was electro-mechanical in a different way. The points were worked mechanically from full-sized levers, but the signals, which were electrically operated semaphores, were worked from miniature slide levers, arranged in a row above the mechnical levers for the points at about the level of the block-shelf, in an ordinary manual signal box. The accompanying drawing shows a cross-section of the Sykes locking frame, on which the letters kk indicate the miniature locking between the signal slides; m, the locking trough for the point lever locking, and l, one of the shafts through which the interlocking between signals and points was effected.

The apparatus concerned at Battersea Park was installed when the L.B.S.C.R. completed the re-modelling of Victoria station and its approaches, in 1907-8. Battersea Park was the last box, coming out of Victoria, to be equipped with the electro-mechanical type of locking frame. The next one, travelling away from Victoria, Pouparts Junction, had a purely mechanical frame, though still fully equipped with

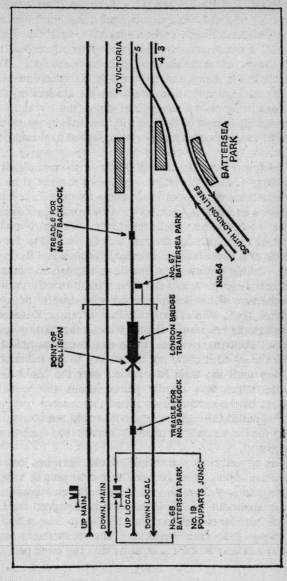

Fig. 13. Layout of tracks and signals at Battersea Park.

the 'Lock and Block' apparatus. The electro-mechanical boxes all originally had a miniature form of 'Lock and Block' working in conjunction with the signal slides. This was still in use at Battersea Park, but Victoria itself had, not many years before the accident, been equipped with a form of relay block, manufactured by the W. R. Sykes Interlocking Signal Company, that eliminated the mechanical connections between instruments and slides. But owing to the intended equipment of the line with colour light signals this form of modernisation had not been applied to the outlying boxes.

The function of 'Lock and Block' is to ensure that in signalling trains all the various operations required from the signalman are carried out in the correct sequence, and that a positive interlock is made between the working at adjacent boxes. To make the various interlocks more clearly understood the accompanying diagram may be referred to, for the specific case of the boxes at Pouparts Junction and Battersea Park. Taking the up main line in particular, the man at Pouparts Junction would not offer a train forward until he saw the arm of his semaphore indicator drop to the clear position. If the man at Battersea Park accepted, this would automatically release the electric lock on the starting signal lever at Pouparts Junction. Once this lever was pulled to lower the signal it could not be restored to the full normal position until the train had passed over the backlocking treadle, which was usually placed about 150 yards in advance of the signal. This ensured that when a train had been signalled through the apparatus could not be released ready for the acceptance of another train until the first one had passed.

It is nevertheless a principle of all signalling that the signalman should never be prevented from putting a signal to danger *at any time*. This could be vital in emergency, and so the apparatus was designed so that the lever could be moved back far enough to restore the arm to danger, but not far enough to free the interlocking. The question then arose, with 'Lock and Block': supposing that for some perfectly

178

legitimate reason a signalman having offered a train forward, and had it accepted, found that he wanted to hold it, or because of traffic circumstances carry out a different movement. Once the starting signal lever had been pulled it would be backlocked in the 'clear' position, and there would be no means ordinarily available to the signalman to release. It was to meet such a case as this that the releasing 'key' was designed by Mr. Sykes. While accepted as a necessity, to avoid inordinate delays to traffic, it was realised at the outset that the introduction of the releasing key constituted a source of danger. In fact there were collisions on the Metropolitan Railway at King's Cross, and at Glasgow Central (low level) in 1903 which were both due to improper use of the releasing key.

In the early installations the W. R. Sykes Interlocking Signal Company sought to prevent that misuse by fitting a shutter over the keyhole in the instrument. On the introduction of this arrangement H. Rayner Wilson, at one time Signal Engineer of the Lancashire and Yorkshire Railway and the author of several standard works on signalling wrote, enthusiastically: 'the shutter can only be removed in order to allow the key to be used by the joint action of the signalman on either side sending a releasing current simultaneously, and they in turn can only send the current after resetting their instruments to normal, providing, of course, that the block-sections are unoccupied. The key being used must be taken out of the instrument at once to re-establish communication. Thus it will be seen that three men are required to act in concert in order to cancel one train, so making the risk of collision impossible.'

By the time the 'Lock and Block' installation was put in at Victoria a new form of cancelling had been devised, referred to as the co-operative or button system. In the ordinary way cancellation still required the co-operative action of three men; but the box at Battersea Park was in a peculiar position, in that it was the last of the electro-mechanical plants. Cancelling was therefore co-operative with Battersea Pier, but not so with Pouparts Junction. A further factor had to be considered in the interests of the expeditious working of traffic, and that was the possible failure of the cancelling apparatus. One would have the awkward situation of a signalman having become locked up, maybe from some quite legitimate circumstance, but yet being unable to free himself, by the regular co-operative procedure laid down, because the cancelling arrangements had a fault in them. The Southern Railway operating authorities felt that with such an intense traffic to handle a failure of this kind could not wait the attention of a linesman; and relying therefore upon the sense of responsibility of the men in charge of busy main line signal boxes they issued, in June 1932, the following instruction:

'In the event of the special cancelling apparatus failing, the signalman must break the seal of the instrument case and move the slides in order to restore the instrument and lever to the normal position, immediately calling the Linesman to put the instrument in order and re-seal the case. The failure must be reported in due course.'

The year of issue of that instruction was that in which main line electrification to Brighton was inaugurated; and it was no doubt the possibility of delay to the intensified service that led to it. It was, nevertheless, a rather extraordinary thing to do. As 'The Railway Gazette' remarked, editorially: 'Although it is easy to be wise after the event, we cannot help feeling that it ought never to have been issued. If it is unthinkable that a signalman should be permitted to open a point detector relay case and short circuit the detection because he believes—or even positively knows—that everything is right for a proceed signal to be shown, it seems to us equally dangerous to allow him, merely because he is persuaded that something has failed, to interfere in any way with the very mechanism that should be his safeguard.'

On the morning of the accident Battersea Park box was in charge of a relief man, Childs by name. He was an experienced man, who had served 14 years in that capacity, and had been passed as competent to work 60 different boxes. But shortly before 8 a.m. he was confronted with an awkward situation. A train off the South London line, the 7.37 a.m. London Bridge to Victoria was approaching the station and Childs was intending to give this train precedence over the 7.30 a.m. London Bridge to Victoria, via Tulse Hill, which he had accepted from Pouparts Junction. But when he went to clear signal No. 64 (see diagram) for the South London train he could not draw the slide out far enough because he had neglected to reverse points 5, leading from the South London line on to the up local line from Pouparts Junction. It would appear however that the locking and slides were worn to such an extent that although the slide was 'locked' he was able to pull it out far enough to 'jump' the Sykes intermediate lock apparatus to the locked position, as if the signal had been properly cleared, but not far enough to clear the signal.

It was at this stage that he evidently became flustered. The London Bridge train had arrived from Pouparts Junction, and was standing at signal 67, and he still had the South London train at signal 64. He therefore tried to obtain the necessary release by co-operation with the man at Battersea Pier box. The latter received the appropriate bell signal and pressed the correct button; but there was no response from Childs. The latter in turn failed to get a release, and there is a strong probability that in his hurry to co-operate with the Battersea Pier man he pressed the wrong button. In any event his attempt to get the signal 64 released was abortive, and as time was passing he decided the cancelling apparatus was out of order, and determined to use the authority given by the instruction of June 1932. He therefore cut the seals; removed the end panel of the mechanism case, and freed No. 64 lever by hand. He was thus able to bring the South London train into the station. It left at 8.1½ a.m. and then he reversed the points No. 5 prior to clearing signal 67 for the London Bridge train to proceed.

But it was not so much the clearance of the signal for the South London train, as other events that led so soon to the serious accident. The man Childs, had, by his own mistake, failed to get cancellation of signal 64 by the proper means, and had hastily resorted to cutting the seals. What else he did, no doubt quite by accident, while he had the front panel off will never be known. His evidence, though very lengthy, was largely unacceptable to Col. Mount. The official report states: 'In some way or another, either while directly inserting his arm in the case, or indirectly by his hand coming against the resetting button as he forced the front panel in place again, Childs must have cleared the "train on" indicator for the up local line. The switch-hook also cannot have been over the plunger, because the block indicator fell at Pouparts Junction. Childs could not account for its being off, nor would he admit recollection of having cleared the "train on" indicator or of sending any release to Pouparts Junction, but he did admit that "both these things must have happened". He thought he might have pressed the block plunger inadvertently with his chest, and declared he sent no bell signal to Hillman at Pouparts Junction. He did recollect seeing the switch-hook on the plunger when he pulled No. 67 for the London Bridge train, but could not remember when he turned it. He asserted quite positively "I still think I never made a mistake in any shape or form . . . I say the block bells were never sent".'

Whatever he did resulted in the gross irregularity of clearing the control on the Sykes up local line block plunger, previously used to accept the waiting London Bridge train, and the false lowering of the electric semaphore indicator at Pouparts Junction. The rest is simply told. Immediately the signalman at Pouparts Junction saw his up local line indicator clear he offered the 7.31 a.m. Coulsdon North to Victoria train. It was accepted at once. Its driver, who had a remarkable escape, said the Pouparts Junction distant signal was 'on', but all the other signals at that box were clear, and he continued at about 40 m.p.h. Battersea Park distant signal was 'on', but as he came round the curve towards the viaducts over the other railways he sighted signal 67 'off'. This must have been the precise moment that Childs had cleared that signal for the London Bridge train to start.

Conditions of visibility were however bad, and this driver

was naturally so little expecting to find another train standing on his own line that at first he thought the London Bridge train was an 'empty stock' standing on the down line. But soon he realised what it *really* was, and made an emergency brake application. But with only 50 yards to go a collision could not be avoided, and the crash took place at a speed estimated at 30 to 35 m.p.h. Both trains consisted of two 3-coach motor sets with two trailers between. The rear motor-coach of the standing train was telescoped and the casualty list was 10 killed, and some 80 injured.

'The Railway Gazette' aptly summed up the circumstances of this complicated affair thus: 'The Battersea Park signalman was undoubtedly the human factor that erred, but it was the irregular signal locking, and the authority he was given to interfere with the mechanism, that started him on his career of blunders.

'As we had expected, the abolition of manual signalling on this and other heavily worked sections of route where it yet remains is under consideration, and as it is only a matter of time before this is done, possible improvements to the existing apparatus present no great interest. It has admittedly given good service under trying conditions for a long time, but the great increase in traffic of recent years, resulting in a corresponding increase in the number of movements to be made by the signalman, has reached the limit of capacity of hand worked apparatus, and automatic working is becoming indispensable. Lock-and-Block, at least from section to section, will still be used elsewhere, however, and the question of cancelling therefore remains of importance. To place it on a satisfactory footing the principle, adopted some time ago by certain lines in India and elsewhere, should be applied, and all cancellation of block acceptance made impossible once a train has passed the section signal in the rear. In this way the danger of two men getting at cross-purposes on the telephone and cancelling under a misapprehension is removed.'

As might well be expected, the instruction about cutting the seals and releasing locked levers by hand was immediately withdrawn. Furthermore, the seals were replaced by padlocks. No one except a skilled linesman was thenceforth able to open the instruments. Nevertheless, the releasing key for the Sykes 'Lock and Block' apparatus was involved again in a very serious accident on the Southern Railway 10 years later on October 24th, 1947. On that morning there was dense fog on the Croydon area, but the working had not been unduly delayed. At that time although there was continuous multi-aspect colour light signalling from Coulsdon to Brighton the section between Coulsdon and the approaches to Victoria was only in process of conversion, the work having been delayed by the war. The two boxes concerned in this case were South Croydon Junction and Purley Oaks, $1\frac{1}{4}$ miles apart, and lying on a gradient of 1 in 264 descending towards Croydon. This again was a case of tragic misuse of the Sykes releasing key.

The 7.33 a.m. electric train from Haywards Heath to London Bridge, running on the up main line was brought to a stand at Purley Oaks starting signal, and it was kept waiting there about seven or eight minutes. Actually the signalman had completely forgotten the train, which had not been accepted by South Croydon Junction. This man who was in charge at Purley Oaks was a porter-signalman. He had been passed as competent to work this busy main line box in the previous May, and from that time until five weeks before the accident he had taken duty partly as porter and partly as signalman. In the last five weeks he had taken full-time duty as signalman in place of one who was ill. The signalman in the next box to the south, Purley North, had not received the 'out of section' signal for the Haywards Heath train; and after an interval of time he rang up Purley Oaks and asked 'how he was looking on the up main'. A few seconds later following some unintelligible exclamation on the telephone he received 'train out of section', and so he offered the 8.4 a.m. Tattenham Corner to London Bridge electric train. It was accepted at once, and the train left Purley station at 8.34 a.m.

That telephone call from Purley North to Purley Oaks

jerked the porter-signalman in the latter box to the realisation that he had not cleared the Haywards Heath train on his instruments. He turned round from the telephone, jumped to the conclusion that his Sykes plunger was locked, and made the fatal mistake of using the releasing key. He certainly did not carry out regulation 7 of the Lock and Block rules which reads:

'Signalmen are specially cautioned not to use the release key or other means of release unless they have clearly ascertained that no train is in the section and that such release is absolutely necessary and can with safety be given. Whenever a signalman is offered a train and finds that his Sykes plunger is locked he must first assure himself, beyond all measure of doubt, by consultation with the signalman at the box in the rear (even if that means delay to traffic) whether his inability to use the plunger in the normal manner is due:

   (i) to a train having been accepted or being already in the section; or

  (ii) to a shunt movement having been made from a siding to the main line within the area under his control; or

 (iii) to some failure of the apparatus.

At the same time he must have a clear understanding with the signalman at the box in the rear as to the description and whereabouts of the last train, signalled to him before he uses the release key or other means of release to free the plunger.'

Having cleared the plunger, most irregularly, without consultation with either of his colleagues, north or south, he was, of course, able to accept the Tattenham Corner train. At that very moment however South Croydon Junction at last sent the acceptance signal for the Haywards Heath train, which was still standing in Purley Oaks station, completely obscured from the signal box by the density of the fog. The porter-signalman did not seem to grasp the significance of the bell code ring from South Croydon Junction. Having made the gross error of clearing his instrument by a totally unjustified use of the key the call from South Croydon Junction did not remind him of the Haywards Heath train that was still standing in the station. Instead, the out-of-section ring came just at that very moment when he was preparing to clear all his up main signals for the Tattenham Corner train. The starting signal was released by receipt of the out-of-section ring, and the Purley Oaks man was able to clear that signal the moment he touched the lever. He also pulled off the up main home and the up main distant, to give the Tattenham Corner train a clear run through.

The circumstances so far as train running was concerned were now a precise parallel of the Hawes Junction disaster on the Midland, on Christmas Eve 1910. The driver of the Haywards Heath train, which had been standing in Purley Oaks station for seven or eight minutes, saw that starting signal clear—just as the drivers of the two Carlisle light engines had done; he took it that it was his belated signal to proceed, and started away. In the meantime the Tattenham Corner train approached Purley Oaks, running under clear signals, just as the Midland Scotch express had done, and went through at about 40 m.p.h. There were now two trains in one section, and it only needed an adverse 'distant' at South Croydon Junction to slow the first train down to walking pace. The gap between them was closed, and the second train crashed into the first at about 45 m.p.h. In the morning rush hour both trains were crowded, with the first carrying about 1,000 passengers, and the second 800. In the circumstances, although the casualties were heavy, it is really surprising that they were not more so. A total of 32 passengers was killed, and 183 injured.

The enquiry on behalf of the Ministry of Transport was conducted by Col. Sir Alan Mount assisted by Brigadier C. A. Langley, and very naturally the report included a great deal of comment upon the Sykes releasing key, and the stringent instructions as to the use of it. Sir Alan observed that he knew, 'of no other instruction which gives warning that improper use of apparatus may incur dismissal'. The fact remained however that the installation had been in service for 50 years, and some of the equipment was becoming worn. Signalmen were aware of certain wrong-side failures of the Sykes treadle, and there may have been a tendency for men of short experience to jump to the conclusion that the apparatus itself was wrong. Pertinently, Sir Alan Mount commented:

'The accident would not have occurred had colour light signalling and track circuiting been in use, and it was proposed to commence to equip the line between Battersea Park and Coulsdon in 1940, but the war postponed the work.

'Approval has been given recently for it to proceed, and plans are well in hand. The present signalling has been in use for over 50 years and it is probably true to say that no other mechanical system could have coped so efficiently with such heavy main-line and suburban electric services. It is essential, however, that more modern equipment should be provided to deal with increased traffic, afford even greater safeguards against human error, and ease the manpower position.'

14

Hairbreadth Escapes

In the foregoing chapters the story has been told of accidents in most of which many factors combined to produce the ultimate disaster. Instances have been recalled in which fundamental mistakes were made, and yet there were chances that catastrophe could, up to the last minute, have been averted had not some consummating blunder occurred. The title of this chapter—'Hairbreadth Escapes'—indicates another side to the picture, and covers three incidents that came to my own notice in years before World War II.

In 1898 on the Midland Railway there was an alarming and unprecedented accident at Wellingborough. A porter's barrow fell off the platform on to the down main line just as a London-Manchester express was approaching at full speed. Despite the efforts of two men, who endangered their lives in so doing, the barrow could not be retrieved in time. The bogie of the engine was immediately derailed, and at a crossing just beyond the end of the platform the whole engine was derailed, and a destructive accident occurred in which five passengers and both enginemen were killed.

One Saturday afternoon in the summer of 1935 I was riding the engine of the up 'Queen of Scots' Pullman, non-stop from Leeds to King's Cross. It was a busy day and we were running hard to get time in hand to offset the effects of a special stop that had to be made at Peterborough. We had a Great Northern 'Atlantic' and the usual load of seven Pullmans, and after a slight reduction of speed over Muskham water troughs we were approaching Newark accelerating rapidly on the level and doing about 65 m.p.h. The fireman

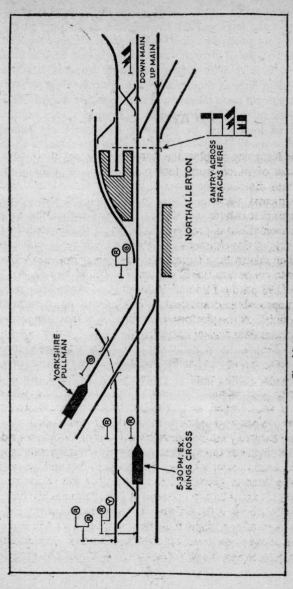

Fig. 14. Layout of tracks at Northallerton.

was putting a bit on, while the driver and I, respectively at the right and left hand cab glasses, were looking ahead.

We were probably not 300 yards from the platform end, when a couple of porters with a four-wheeled barrow piled mountains high with luggage solemnly trundled it across both main lines at the far end of the station while we were bearing down upon them at a rate of 95 ft. per second! They got over safely, and as a minor incident in a very exciting piece of locomotive performance it immediately passed from my mind, at the time. But the plain fact remains; those porters had about 25 seconds to get clear. A slip, or a trolley wheel caught in the rail on the level crossing, and we should have had a second Wellingborough!

In the autumn of that same year there was a hair-raising incident at Northallerton. The old Leeds Northern line, running from Harrogate to Stockton, passes beneath the East Coast main line just north of Northallerton station, and there are burrowing junctions that connect with the Leeds Northern line without any surface crossings. At that time three-indication colour light signalling was installed south of Northallerton, but immediately north of the station the old semaphores still remained. The sketch plan shows the track layout and signalling as then existing.

The 'Yorkshire Pullman', then leaving King's Cross at 4.45 p.m. ran via Leeds and Harrogate, and continued to Newcastle, calling only at Darlington north of Harrogate. On this occasion it was running a little behind time, so much so that it was likely to join the main line at Northallerton only just ahead of the 5.30 p.m. dining car express from King's Cross to Newcastle. This latter train used the main line throughout, and made a considerable faster time than the Pullman, which made the detour via Leeds. Nevertheless the 'Yorkshire Pullman' had on this occasion been given priority at Northallerton. The road was cleared for it, and it had commenced to traverse the connecting spur from the Leeds-Northern line, at Cordio Junction, to the main line at Northallerton south.

The train was hauled by one of the original Gresley

190

Pacifics of Class 'A1'. When first built, and for some time afterwards, these engines were equipped for right-hand drive, as had been customary on the Great Northern Railway. On that evening, too, the 5.30 p.m. from King's Cross was also hauled by a 'Pacific' with right-hand drive. This latter was a very famous engine individually and was being worked by a driver whose name was then a household word among railway enthusiasts. But in view of what happened I think it is wise, even after more than 30 years, not to reveal the names of either engine or man.

It was autumn, and by the time the two trains had got into those latitudes darkness had fallen, and on a clear night, as I can testify from experience on the footplate, those colour light signals south of Northallerton were not the easiest of signals to read. There were locations, at junctions and crossings from main to relief lines, where more than one signal was mounted on the same post, and the indication to the driver was given by a combination of lights. When sighted at long range—and on the York-Northallerton line the sighting was often very long, especially on a clear night—the green and red lights tended to mingle. The optical combination of red and green produces a white light, and sure enough these junction signals seen at night, at extreme range, did present a hazy disc of white light. As one drew nearer the configuration of the lights was resolved, and one could see the disposition of the green and red lights distinctly. This 'sorting out' took place well before one reached the signal itself; but the first sight was often very indistinct. The sighting of signals was made more difficult for an engine with right-hand drive, because the line of sight cut off by a long boiler like that of the Gresley 'Pacific' was considerable.

The aspects displayed by the various signals presented to the two approaching expresses are shown in the accompanying diagram. The Pullman was running up the gradient from Cordio when the driver heard an unusual noise, that made him look over his shoulder. He was horrified to see the 5.30 p.m. from Kings Cross coming down the main line at full speed, steaming hard. With the utmost promptitude he made an emergency application of the brakes, and reversed the engine. Mercifully he stopped just clear as the London train roared by. Northallerton sent the emergency signal 'Train running away on right line', and the flyer was duly stopped farther down the line. What had happened was this: the driver had seen ahead of him, from his stance on the right-hand side of the cab, the double-green indication of the semaphore signal at the far end of the Northallerton platform which was the correct signal for the Pullman and also the green of the colour light bracket signal at the entrance to the station. He had missed all the intervening colour lights, which of course were very convenient for observation from the *left-hand* side of the engine. The fireman was stoking and did not see them. But for the vigilance and very prompt action of the Pullman driver there would have been a terrible accident. Hit by a train having the momentum of the 5.30 p.m. from King's Cross the terrific impact would almost certainly have knocked the Pullman down the high embankment.

The incident happened just before the introduction of the high-speed 'Silver Jubilee' service between King's Cross and Newcastle, and an officer of the L.N.E.R. expressed the view to me at the time, that if the accident had occurred the shock to public opinion would probably have been such as to compel the postponement of the 'Silver Jubilee' debut. In any case it led to a change in the arrangements for the ever-famous Press run of the new train on September 27th, 1935.

From these examples of hairbreadth escapes while running I pass on to an episode of a different kind. During the weekend of 20th and 21st June, 1936, in the Newtown district of Montgomeryshire events moved more like the scenario of an American screen melodrama than happenings on a British railway. The whole of England was swept by storms of great violence, but in these Welsh hills both rain and thunder were of an almost tropical intensity. Conditions were bad enough on the Saturday when the river Severn overflowed and Newtown itself was flooded to an unparalleled extent, but so far the railway had suffered no harm.

Shrivenham, 1936 The wrecked 'King' class engine No. 6007, and overturned carriage

Shrivenham The shattered remains of the leading coaches

Southern Electric Collisions

Wreckage on the viaduct at Battersea after the collision on April 2, 1937

The collision in fog, near South Croydon Junction, October 1947

Harrow, 1952 View from down electric line platform showing the wrecked engines of the down express

Harrow The fearful destruction of engines and stock: the locomotives of the carriages between the platforms

Harrow Clearing the line. Night work among the ruins

Harrow

View looking north from the damaged footbridge

Lewisham, 1957

Destruction of modern stock, under the heavy overbridge that collapsed

Through this district the main line of the one-time Cambrian Railways, then part of the Great Western, follows the Severn valley, and it then carried a large proportion of the holiday traffic to the Cambrian Coast resorts. Newtown has already figured in this book, as one end of the single-line section where the tragic head-on collision took place in January 1921.

Late on the Sunday afternoon things were beginning to look ugly at Scafell, a hamlet some two miles west of Newtown where the line was double-tracked. The tiny station here was one of the few in charge of a stationmistress and the lady in question was the wife of a retired permanent way man, ex-Ganger Haynes. At 6 p.m. the thunderstorms culminated in a terrific cloudburst in the hills south of the Severn valley. This caused the rivers to rise so rapidly that Haynes feared for the safety of the railway. It was not the Severn that seemed the most potential source of danger, but the Dulais river which comes down from the very hills where the cloudburst had taken place. So at the height of the storm, Haynes and his daughter went out to keep watch at the bridge. One can pause here to admire the sense of responsibility and devotion of a retired man to turn out in such appalling conditions.

Just at the point where the Dulais enters the Severn it is crossed by the railway, running on a 20 ft. embankment, the foot of which is washed on the north side by the waters of the Severn. At that time the bridge over the Dulais river was a solid masonry structure with an arch of 25 ft. span. When Haynes and his daughter arrived on the scene the neighbouring fields were already flooded, and the little river which was normally nothing more than a turbulent mountain stream was a really terrifying sight. An incredible volume of water was sweeping down, carrying all before it; bushes along the bank were being torn up as if they were tender seedlings, and the force of this onrush was scouring out the banks and bringing great pressure on the abutments of the railway bridge.

Dulais farmhouse, just on the Newtown side of the river,

was completely marooned, and the ground floor rooms were already flooded to a depth of five or six feet; and in the hope of being able to help the unfortunate people there Haynes and his daughter crossed the railway bridge. They were hardly over when a still more unexpected thing happened. On the Scafell side of the Dulais river was a group of huge venerable elms; under the tremendous wind these were waving like so many reeds, when suddenly one of them was completely uprooted by the rush of water. By some extraordinary freak of wind and water it was borne downstream in a perfectly upright position, and a few seconds later had crashed into the railway bridge. It struck the parapet, which was at once destroyed; the tree rebounded and was then dragged under the arch by the force of the current. Its passage ripped away the brickwork at the crown of the arch, and immediately the whole bridge collapsed. A curious point noted by Haynes was that the downstream side of the arch fell first.

The situation had now become one of extreme danger. The telegraph wires were undamaged and hung like the rails across the breach in the line. There was nothing, as yet, to those responsible for signalling the trains to indicate that anything was wrong. The block system between Newtown and Moat Lane Junction was still intact. On Sundays the latter station was switched out and the next signal box open was at Caersws, about six miles west of Newtown. Haynes immediately thought of the up mail, which by that time would have left Aberystwyth and be well on its way; but he and his daughter were in the worst possible position to do anything. There was a telephone at the station house at Scafell, but between them and that telephone was that tremendous breach in the line 60 ft. long, across which the tracks were suspended in mid-air. Even these intrepid people could not face the hazard of trying to crawl back across that fragile 'suspension bridge' above the raging waters of the Dulais river.

The quickest way of giving the alarm was for one of them to walk the two miles along the line to Newtown, and send warning from there. The storm was then, if possible, worse than ever, and yet, amid darkness almost of night, in torrents of rain and incessant thunder, Miss Haynes set out to walk two miles down the line to give the alarm. It was by no means certain that she could get through. The way might easily be barred by floods or another washaway; so Haynes attempted to get back to his home by way of the road, which ran parallel to the railway and about a quarter of a mile away.

By going a short distance from the course of the river he was able to wade across the flooded fields, and eventually he got to the road. This also was under water, but he managed to cross the river. He was hardly over when this bridge too was swept away. All the time the mail train was getting nearer. There were no signals at Scafell and the bridge was approached on a curve from a deep cutting; speed was usually 50 to 55 m.p.h. at this point, and travelling thus on a dark evening of minimum visibility the driver would never have been able to see the breach in time. But when at last Haynes reached his home and telephoned through to Caersws he learned that his daughter had been in time, and the train was stopped.

By what margin tragedy was averted I cannot precisely say. One loses all sense of time in a situation like that faced by Haynes and his daughter. Later that year, when the new permanent bridge was put into service I had the pleasure of meeting them both, and I realised that the exact time Haynes reached home, and the exact time his daughter reached Newtown were to them very minor details in the night's events! The main thing was that their cool-headed action in the face of extreme danger saved the situation. One would have thought also that when Haynes got home, and had telephoned to Caersws signal box, his work for the night was over. Not a bit of it! Sunday evening is proverbially a bad time to find people in a hurry, but Haynes managed to get into telephone communication with the Bridge Foreman at Caersws, and from his railway experience was able to tell him the exact nature of the washaway. This was of no little help later in the evening when plans were made for bridging the gap. And then, as if he had not rendered enough service, Haynes went out onto the main road to warn motorists of the broken bridge, and continued to do so until 2 o'clock the next morning!

The scene now moved to Divisional Headquarters at Oswestry, 30 miles away to the north. Later that evening the Bridge Foreman at Caersws was able to get into touch with the Divisional Engineer by telephone, and largely due to Haynes' report he was able to describe very clearly what had happened. A breach in the main line called for very rapid action, especially as the full summer service was due to come into operation in a fortnight's time. So that very night a little conference of three, hastily summoned, prepared a scheme for a new bridge and before midnight the necessary material had been ordered by wire. To have constructed a new permanent bridge to deal with traffic at normal speed would have meant delaying the re-opening of the line for many weeks, and so a temporary structure was decided upon. This would carry a single line of rails and necessitate all trains crossing at dead slow speed; but after all the great thing was to get the line open again.

On the morning after the storm the country was an unforgettable sight. The course of the Dulais river was one continuous trail of destruction. What remained of the railway bridge was lying out in the Severn; a filling station on the main road had been completely smashed up, and petrol pumps, a tea shelter and other debris lay all over the surrounding fields. In order that the railway service could be restored, arrangements were made for a fleet of buses to operate between Newtown and Caersws, and on the Tuesday after the washaway, in spite of delay in getting the requisite material at such short notice, reconstruction work on the bridge began.

15

Two B.R. Catastrophes

On January 1st, 1948, the railways of Great Britain were nationalised, and from that time there began a gradual process of standardisation of operating practices and engineering design intended to eliminate the considerable divergencies that had existed between the privately-owned companies of the Grouping era. It was bound to be a slow process. One important aspect of standardisation was the need to extend the use of automatic train control to all main lines in the country. As earlier chapters of this book have shown, the initial hesitation of the Government Inspecting Officers towards the Great Western system changed to whole-hearted approval from the 1920's onwards, and in many a report on collisions elsewhere there were statements that an audible warning system, with brake control, based on the aspect displayed by the distant signal, would have almost certainly averted an accident. Even so, there were certain circumstances, as related in Chapter 12, in which the Great Western system having a similar basis was powerless to prevent disaster.

In the years immediately following the end of World War II there were many eminent men who felt that control based only on the distant signal was not enough, and that some form of continuous indication was the ultimate answer. At the same time, while the Great Western system provided a reliable brake application in the event of a driver ignoring an adverse audible warning, it was noted that in the U.S.A., where a very great amount of experimental and development work had been done between the two world wars, all modern tendencies were to eliminate the brake control feature and to rely on continuously controlled cab signals. On one freight line indeed, such confidence was placed upon the cab signals—without brake control—that the wayside signals were dispensed with. On the nationalised British Railways however decision was reached at a fairly early stage to standardise upon a system of audible cab signals based upon the aspect of the lineside distant signals, and to incorporate the automatic braking feature in the event of a warning being disregarded, from any cause. In other words the principle of the Great Western system was accepted in its entirety.

In view of its wide application, and the advanced stage to which its various components had been developed there were many who felt that its details should also have been accepted, and its installation on all main lines made a matter of high priority. Prior to nationalisation however the northern lines had not been able to accept the contact ramp method of connection between engine and the trackside equipment, and on the Southend line of the L.M.S.R. the Strowger-Hudd system of inductive pick-up had been developed to provide indications and controls that were the same in principle as those included in the Great Western system. But experience with the Southend installation had suggested many points where improvements were desirable; and once the principle of cab signalling and brake control had been accepted by British Railways a team of engineers was set aside to carry out the development and produce apparatus that should be capable of universal application.

It is well known that after nationalisation partisan feelings for the practice of one or another of the privately-owned companies ran high, and great was the disappointment and annoyance among men of the former Great Western Railway, and its supporters, that instead of adopting the well-tried contact ramp system time and money should be spent in developing something that was not then proved, to any appreciable extent; and that considerable delay must inevitably result before the new standard system could be applied to an extent that would provide security over a wide area of railway operation. Nationalisation took place in January 1948; but by the summer of 1952 developments had reached the stage of fitting a 'mock-up' of the new apparatus to the ex-L.N.E.R. class 'A4' Pacific engine No. 60007 *Sir Nigel Gresley*, and an experimental installation of the new form of track inductors was being made over a short stretch of the East Coast main line. Having regard to the engineering tasks involved in implementing the decision of the Railway Executive, as it was then, the work had not been slow. But in October 1952 a catastrophe suddenly highlighted the entire project.

On the morning of October 8th, in weather that was seasonable but which could not be called foggy, an early suburban train, from Watford to Euston, was making its usual stop at Harrow and Wealdstone; and at the up main line platform many passengers were joining the train. It was fully protected in rear, with the distant, outer home, and inner home signals all correctly at danger. Then, inexplicably and at full speed there bore down upon that standing train the up Perth sleeping car express running $1\frac{1}{2}$ hours late, and headed by the Stanier 'Pacific' engine No. 46242 *City of Glasgow*. There was scarcely time to comprehend the full horror of what had happened before the 7.55 a.m. express from Euston to Liverpool and Manchester, double-headed with a 'Jubilee' class 4-6-0 *Windward Islands* piloting the brand new 'Pacific' No. 46202 *Princess Anne*, came tearing in from the south end at about 60 m.p.h. and ploughed into the wreckage of the first collision.

The result was indescribably terrible. In many ways the two collisions were a ghastly echo of Quintinshill, except that in the first one the fast-moving express struck the rear of a standing train instead of a massive locomotive, and the casualties were mainly in the 'local'. But the down express, double-headed as at Quintinshill struck a far more formidable obstacle than the scattered wreckage of the troop train, and under the footbridge at Harrow there piled up the most terrible wreck ever seen on a British railway. It is fortunate that the down express was sparsely filled with passengers that morning; otherwise the death roll, bad as it was, would greatly have exceeded the actual total of 112. Among the dead were the driver and fireman of the *City of Glasgow*, and with their deaths vanished any possibility of establishing the reason why their train ran past all the Harrow signals with no appreciable slackening of speed. Col. Wilson, who conducted the enquiry on behalf of the Ministry of Transport, was placed in exactly the same position as his predecessors, who had to deal with Salisbury, Grantham, and Shrewsbury.

Many people, engineering and otherwise stormed indignantly into print. Why had the Railway Executive not adopted the G.W.R. system of A.T.C., which would almost certainly have prevented the accident! There was talk of 'criminal neglect'. One railway journal went so far as to write: 'The answer, many believe, could be found in a stubborn refusal to adopt something which another company had conceived. We would like to think that such petty reasoning could be dismissed as ridiculous. That there are technical difficulties, particularly with electrified track, is acknowledged, but there is no evidence of any real effort having been made to overcome them.' One can understand these strong words, written by an editor who was an eye-witness of the disaster, and who toiled for many hours in helping to extricate some of the injured. At that time the developments in hand were not generally known; but news of the experimental installation on the East Coast main line spread like wildfire, and J. H. Currey, the engineer in charge of the work, has told how he arrived at King's Cross after lunch on the very day of the Harrow accident to ride the locomotive on its second trial run, and 'was flabbergasted to find most of London's press photographers on the platform'.

When Col. Wilson's report was published, at the end of June 1953, 'The Engineer' had a leading article that opened with these words: 'Major disasters on the British railways by their very rarity never fail to arouse feelings of particular horror, and for some little time afterwards the burden of many letters in the national and in the technical press is to seek means whereby "it could never happen again". Sometimes, as in the case of the Armagh runaway collision in 1889, the public conscience had been so deeply stirred as to secure adoption of increased safety measures by Act of Parliament; but those who have studied the reports of the Government inspecting officers over the past 40 to 45 years cannot fail to have noticed the frequency with which some form of automatic train control has been recommended. In retrospect, those officers appear to have been little more than voices crying in the wilderness. But now the catastrophe at Harrow last autumn appears to have done for A.T.C. what Armagh did for automatic continuous brakes, and for the absolute block system; and the British Transport Commission is now prepared to consider financial authority for a scheme that will eventually cost some £17 million.'

Nevertheless, the announcement, while reassuring to the extent that it indicated that urgent action was at last to be taken, was not so reassuring on a long term basis, and on September 11th, 1953, 'The Engineer' returned to the subject, under the heading of a leading article entitled 'More thoughts on A.T.C.' This article so aptly summarises current thought that it is worth quoting in full:

'It was perhaps no more than natural after the catastrophe at Harrow last autumn that attention came to be concentrated largely on the warning aspects of automatic train control and cab signalling. The burden of many letters in the press has been to see the establishment of means to warn a driver and fireman who were heading towards such a holocaust; and the Inspecting Officer of the Ministry of Transport indirectly sets his seal upon this particular trend of thought by his view that, in connection with a system of multi-aspect colour light signals, there is no need to differentiate between the double-yellow and the single-yellow of the lineside signals in the audible signals provided in the cab. In his view the same "warning" indication can be given for both. Now it seems to us that a very important point in railway operating practice is here involved. The long and difficult history of signalling evolution seems likely to repeat itself with the general adoption of A.T.C. in this country, and in view of the large sums of money concerned the point cannot, in our view, be over-emphasised. In the early days of railways, signalling was installed primarily as a means of warning a driver, and indicating to him in precise terms where he must stop. Similarly today the "warning" value of A.T.C. seems uppermost in the minds of those charged with the development of the new standard system. But in the case of signalling, once the means of warning had been developed to something near perfection, railway operating men found in the multi-aspect day colour light signal a means of expediting the flow of traffic in busy areas. Modern electrically-controlled signalling has come to be regarded as a predominant part of the equipment, without which the more intensive services could not be run. Signalling technique has progressed a very long way beyond giving a simple "yea" or "nay" to the driver. With four-indication colour light signals he is now told the state of the line ahead.

'With A.T.C. as now proposed on a national basis it seems that the clock is to be put back. In early experimental days on the Great Western, and elsewhere, the hope was expressed in some quarters that audible cab signalling coupled with control of the train brakes would make distant signals unnecessary. Nowadays, however, there is general agreement that A.T.C. and audible cab signalling should be a supplement to the wayside signals—never a substitute for them. But it is now proposed that the same audible cab signal should be given for both the double-yellow and single-yellow of a multiple aspect system as for the distant signal in mechanical territory. If one regards A.T.C. only as a last line of defence where a driver is ignoring signals, all well and good. The wayside signals are displaying a warning aspect, either preliminary or final, and the driver is given an audible indication to supplement those wayside indications. But the use of colour light signals, particularly in misty weather, has proved of such inestimable value in keeping trains on the move, that it seems a pity that differentiation between the yellow and the double-yellow is, apparently, not to be made in the new standard arrangement of A.T.C. On some lines, as mentioned in Col. Wilson's report on the Harrow accident, the installation of multi-aspect colour light signals was considered an acceptable alternative to A.T.C. The close spacing of the signals, particularly in the electrified suburban area of the Southern Railway, keeps drivers constantly on the alert, and it was considered that the chances of signals being misinterpreted, or missed altogether, were thereby lessened considerably. In the North Eastern Region we have known of express passenger and fast freight trains running at 55 to 60 m.p.h. continuously on the 'double-yellow', and their drivers knowing from the aspects of the signals sighted whether or not they are gaining or losing on the train in front and knowing also that from such speeds there is adequate braking distance should a 'single-yellow' be sighted. Those are examples of the advantage taken of modern signalling to keep trains on the move.

'In view of the deep significance attached by drivers to the difference between the "single-yellow" and the "double-yellow" on routes where they are continuously installed, and the operating advantages derived from it, we feel it can only be a matter of time before some differentiation is called for in the audible cab signals of the new standard A.T.C. system. In this respect it is perhaps significant that the British railway with by far the longest and most extensive experience of A.T.C., had in mind, prior to nationalisation, some new works, including four-aspect colour light signals, and to operate in conjunction with these the standard system of A.T.C., and cab signalling was adapted to give a different audible signal for "yellow" and "double-yellow". We described this system in our issue of November 14th, 1947, but it is not clear at the moment how the inductive system proposed as the standard for British Railways could be extended to provide the same additional facility, if at any time such extension should prove to be desirable. We feel that the possibility of adding to the proposed standard system should be given serious consideration at this early stage. There is one last point we would make, and although it lies in rather a different direction it certainly forms part of the general interest, not to say anxiety, on all matters concerning A.T.C. at the present time. The Railway Executive has, in certain aspects of its work, been very frank in publishing results of tests on Regional and standard equipment, especially in the case of steam locomotives. In view of the widespread public and technical concern over A.T.C. at the present time, it would be of great interest if the Executive could publish full results of the tests on existing equipment, so that engineers could appreciate fully the reasons why neither the L.M.S. inductive system nor the well-tried Great Western contact systems were acceptable for installation on a national basis, and lengthy experiments had to be made on something that is new and untried.'

Since then, of course, the British Railways Automatic Warning System, as it is now called (A.W.S.) has been brought to a high degree of reliability, and installed on some of the most important trunk lines in the country. But the reference in the article in 'The Engineer' to the Southern Railway's use of closely-spaced multi-aspect colour light signals has a particular poignancy in leading up to a reference to the last disaster to be mentioned specifically—the terrible rear-end collision near Lewisham, on the main line of the former South Eastern and Chatham Railway, on December 4th, 1957. It is remarkable that in this case, as at Harrow five years earlier, the cause of the accident was extremely simple, in contrast to the complications and multiple responsibility involved in some of the events described earlier in this book: the driver ran through signals.

The circumstances were certainly difficult. The evening was foggy, and because of late running and delayed movements of stock in the London area the driver and fireman on the 4.56 p.m. express from Cannon Street to Ramsgate had not had time to take water during the turn-round time. The engine was being 'nursed' until the first passenger stop, at Sevenoaks. The engine was a 'Battle of Britain' class Pacific

No. 34066 *Spitfire*, and from London Bridge on the down fast line this express was following the 5.18 p.m. suburban electric train—Charing Cross to Hayes (Kent). Between New Cross and Lewisham the four-aspect colour light signals dated from 1929; but the principles on which they were installed have remained unchanged. The plain fact emerged: the Ramsgate express closed in upon the local train; passed first, a 'double-yellow', then a 'single-yellow' without appreciable reduction of speed, and it was only when they were actually passing a 'red' that the driver began to apply the brakes. Then it was too late, and the engine ploughed into the back of the electric train just at the point where the Nunhead 'flyover' crosses the main line. There was then not only a very serious collision, but the steam train fouled the columns supporting the bridge, demolished them, and the 'flyover' collapsed into the wreckage.

I need not enlarge upon the terrible results of the collision, which so far as the casualty list was concerned was the third worst in British railway history. The death roll, 90, was exceeded only by Quintinshill and Harrow. Nor need I refer to the tragic proceedings that ensued when the unfortunate driver of the express was tried for manslaughter. The significant point is that in extenuating circumstances he failed to heed the warnings of a series of colour light signals, and no factor could be discerned in the lengthy enquiry that ensued that could relieve him of sole responsibility for the accident. Points were made about the difficulty of observing signals sometimes from the Bulleid 'Pacifics' in foggy weather, and to the fact that the signals on this particular section were installed at a time when most of the locomotives working over the line had right-hand drive. But as the prosecuting counsel pointed out, if there was a known trouble with visibility on that class of locomotive, that should have been an additional reason for special care and caution on a night like that of the accident.

And so, once again we come back ultimately to the human element. Sometimes its failure is inexplicable as in this last case; sometimes, as at Grantham, Shrewsbury and Harrow we shall never know what the causes were; and at times there was sheer carelessness, as at Quintinshill. Some of the saddest cases are those where a conscientious man makes an honest mistake, like Signalman Sutton, at Hawes Junction, on Christmas Eve, 1910. But the introduction of track circuiting, various forms of automatic train control, and continuous colour light signals has made the railway incomparably safer in operation, and in another very important respect there has been outstanding progress. Reports of earlier accidents in this book, and dramatic pictures of the pitiable scenes that came afterwards, show clearly that although many of these accidents occurred at no more than moderate speed casualties were often severe through the virtual disintegration of the small wooden coaches of which passenger trains were then composed.

Quite apart from the risks of fire the coach bodies were crushed and splintered, with dire results to the occupants, and one can only imagine the conditions that ensued in a smash like that in Wigan station with the night tourist express in 1873, when a whole group of these vehicles ran amok from an initial speed of at least 50 m.p.h. One of the engravings reproduced in the plate facing page 23 shows vividly what happened to one of these carriages that landed upside down on the station platform; it had concertina-ed. The first strong indications of a great improvement in carriage construction came at the time of the Preston derailment in 1896 when despite a most alarming smash, at considerable speed, only one person was killed. And to appreciate to the full the extent to which carriage construction has progressed today one can refer in particular to the derailment of an up night express near Hest Bank on May 20th, 1965, at a speed estimated at around 70 m.p.h.

The initial cause, here, was a broken rail; but it was the result of the accident rather than the cause that is of the greatest interest in relation to my own theme. The broken rail was in the section of line including Hest Bank water troughs. The fault occurred at night, so that the driver came upon the danger quite unawares. The diesel engine and the first three coaches of the train passed the break safely; but in so doing the gap in the rail top lengthened and probably the alignment or level must have been affected, because the fourth coach was derailed to the left, and it dragged the succeeding ones after it. The couplings between the third and fourth coaches broke, and after passing the end of the water troughs the leading derailed coach swung further to the left. When it came to Hest Bank station the left hand wheels ran up the platform ramp and overturned the coach to the right between the platforms. Three other coaches suffered likewise, but the last five coaches, although derailed, remained upright, and in line. Of course by that time the brakes were fully applied, and both the derailed and the un-derailed parts of the train were quickly brought to rest.

Recalling mid-Victorian accidents like Staplehurst, Wigan, and Penistone, it does not need much stretch of the imagination to picture what would have happened if the train concerned at Hest Bank in 1965 had been composed of the rolling stock of 90 to 100 years earlier, and not fitted with continuous automatic brakes. A derailment at 70 m.p.h. followed by violent overturning of the coaches on to one side! Yet in this recent case, in which the enquiry was conducted by Col. McNaughton, there were no deaths and only *eleven* persons sustained minor injuries, such was the strength of the coaches in which they were travelling. This feature was to be demonstrated still more remarkably in certain subsequent accidents.

The results of the accident, so far as the train and passengers were concerned, were very interesting in the light of the past history reviewed in his book; but the cause of it—a broken rail—would appear to be symptomatic of a new age in British railway working. It is not that broken rails are something new in themselves, but since the introduction of diesel traction, a trouble, not experienced with steam locomotives, had developed in the form of incipient wheel spin. With steam no driver was under any delusion as to what was happening when his engine started to slip; but slipping can take place almost imperceptibly with diesel locomotives,

207

and in his report on the Hest Bank derailment Col. McNaughton stated that during the years 1963-64 426 wheelburnt rails had been removed from British Railways track. He emphasised that wheel burns were liable to arise whenever heavy trains had to restart where the rail conditions are poor; and Hest Bank, where the overspill from water troughs and the salt spray from Morecambe Bay combined to make the rails slippery, is a case in point. Of the 426 wheelburnt rails removed from British Railways tracks 28 were definitely broken and a further 170 were cracked. On the diesel-electric main line locomotives running on British Railways there is an illuminated indicator in the cab to warn the driver that wheel slipping is taking place; and in addition to this some locomotives have safety circuits incorporated in their controls to reduce the engine power automatically if slipping occurs. But the fact that slipping can be more or less imperceptible on these locomotives makes it a point that needs very careful watching, and no doubt trouble from this source will tend to lessen as greater experience in running diesel-electric locomotives in this country is obtained.

The fact that a new trouble should be developing to exercise the minds of all who are concerned in the running of trains at this comparatively advanced stage in railway development is, however, no more than symbolical of the need for constant vigilance and ready adaptability in the minds of all concerned. The Inspecting Officers of 100 years ago were concerned with such things as time-interval block, trains without adequate brake power, faulty permanent way, and sometimes faulty machinery on trains which caused broken axles and broken tyres. Today, now that the art of signalling is advanced to such an extent, and that brake and rolling stock construction have reached a very high degree of reliability, the use of diesel and electric traction is tending to bring in new problems with a gravity that was emphasised in the disastrous results of a broken rail at Hither Green, as described in Chapter 17.

16

The Didcot High-speed Derailment

In years to come, when the assessment of the gravity of an accident is likely to be made upon little more than the bare statistics of damage and casualties, the derailment of the 9.45 a.m. express from Paddington to Bristol on the morning of September 27th, 1967, could well be regarded as no more than a minor affair. So it was in respect of the casualty list; but as a hairbreadth escape from an absolute catastrophe it must surely rank ace-high. The fact that I was a passenger in the train certainly places the experience among those which I have no desire to repeat. The train in question is one of the hourly series now provided between London and Bristol, on which the intermediate stops other than at the major stations are varied from train to train. On this particular service Didcot was omitted, and a non-stop run made from Reading to Swindon.

To secure increased productivity the rosters of enginemen had not many months previously been changed; this particular train was remanned at Reading, and taken forward by a Westbury man, E. Biggin, who had worked the 07.32 diesel multiple-unit train from Westbury to Reading. This was not a case of single-manning; there was a second-man on the engine. On leaving Reading we were immediately crossed over from the main to the relief line, because of engineering work, farther west. I had a compartment to myself, in the eighth coach, a corridor first, and had been at work throughout from Paddington, with certain papers spread on the adjoining seats. I was not logging the run in any detail, and apart from noting the crossover from 'main' to 'relief' at Reading west end I recommenced work and took no further notice until we had passed Cholsey and appeared to be running at an unusually high speed for the relief line. It subsequently transpired that this Westbury driver had not previously worked over the relief line, and was unaware that the speed limit was 60 m.p.h. throughout. The driver himself said afterwards that he drove the train at 68 to 70 m.p.h. under clear signals, being under the impression that the maximum speed permitted on the relief line was 70 m.p.h.

When we approached Didcot station without the slightest slackening of speed I began to get concerned. Recalling that in the fairly recent changeover of the signalling from mechanical to colour light there had been some track alterations I wondered if a high-speed junction had been laid in, to enable full-speed transition from relief to main to be made. A friend wrote afterwards to sympathise, with what he called 'the instant agony of apprehension you must have undergone'. Crossover there certainly had to be, because the relief lines end at Foxhall Junction. But while I was quickly turning this over in my mind the coach in which I was travelling was suddenly but very smoothly swept to the left, and then in a split-second all was chaos. Amid loud crashes and sickening lurches the coach was thrown from one side to the other. I had time to realise that here was I, who had written a book about accidents, now in the thick of one myself, and I got my feet wedged against the opposite seat to brace myself against the violent movement, and to lessen the chance of getting my legs trapped if any collapsing of the coach took place endways.

All this takes much longer to write down than it did actually to happen; but after the first furious seconds at the moment of derailment the coach somehow became stabilised, tilting right over to the right, and sliding on its side; and from my corner right down almost on the ballast, I was able to see something of what was happening outside. We were still travelling quite fast. Something ahead of us was obviously derailed, because a perfect fountain of granite chippings was being flung out, like spray from a pick-up scoop on water troughs. Although so much ballast was flying about the windows in my compartment were unbroken, and after about 400 yards running on our side we came to rest, and I realised I was safe and completely uninjured. The corridor side of the coach was upwards, and after collecting my scattered papers, and other effects I was able to make a ladder out of the seat cushions, and climb up. Willing hands hauled me into the corridor, and in a moment I was clear of the wrecked coach, and down on the track.

The scene was an astonishing one, and the manner of our going from the moment of derailment readily explained. The engine, a 'Warship' class diesel-hydraulic, No. D853, and the first five coaches were on the rails, standing on the down main line as if nothing had happened. The buffet car, sixth on the train, was still upright but it had been dragged crabwise between the fifth coach, which had reached the down main line safely, and the up main line the rails of which had guided the rear bogie. It was this derailed bogie which was throwing up the torrent of granite chippings. Both the seventh and eighth coaches had their bogies torn clean off in the derailment; both had gone over on to the right-hand sides, and been dragged along thus until the train stopped. We in the eighth coach were fortunate in that the coach body slid on the right-hand rail of the up main line, and this kept it tilted slightly upwards. This undoubtedly saved much breaking of windows. The ninth coach, the last in the train, had broken clean away, apparently at the moment of derailment, and was lying some distance back, on its left-hand side —also minus all its wheels.

It was an extraordinary experience for me, having for many years studied the circumstances of railway accidents, to find myself down on the line amid the scattered wreckage of my own train. I am no expert ambulance worker, and the serious casualties were fortunately few, and having helped one or two passengers who were bleeding from minor injuries and cuts from broken glass, I immediately began a study of the wreckage, and of the damaged track. Inciden-

211

tally, I think it was this immediate pre-occupation with the technical aspects of the crash that staved off any effects of shock, and enabled me to travel on to Chippenham as soon as transport was available, and do a full afternoon's work. The casualty list was 1 killed and 23 injured—remarkably few, having regard to the speed at which the derailment took place. In the previous chapter of this book I referred to the way in which modern coaching stock can withstand the effects of derailment. Here again was another case, comparable with Hest Bank. The bodies of the three coaches that had their wheels torn off although badly strained were not collapsed in any way, and the casualties were due to the violence of the motion immediately following derailment and the breaking of windows. All three coaches however were 'a write-off', and after removal to the side of the line they were scrapped where they stood.

Precisely the same question was asked afterwards as was asked after Preston, Salisbury, Grantham, and Shrewsbury: why was the driver running at such a speed, where a limit of 25 m.p.h. is imposed? One must first consider the signalling. The layout at Foxhall Junction is controlled from Reading power signal box through a remotely controlled relay room at Didcot. Since December 1966 the signal controlling the turn-out from down relief to down main line has been a three-aspect colour light, equipped with a junction indicator. There are three alternative routes from this signal: the principal route, through the two subsequent crossover roads leading to the down main line, and the other two cover the low-speed movements into the sidings of the Central Electricity Generating Board. These latter two have approach controls, and indications on the junction indicator; but the principal route had no approach control and no junction indicator aspect. If the road was clear, as on the morning of the accident, this signal was showing green. It was up to the driver's route knowledge to observe the very severe speed restriction that negotiation of the route, through the two successive crossovers, entailed.

In his Report to the Minister of Transport Major P. Olver,

who conducted the enquiry, refers to Driver Biggin's evidence thus:

'In anticipation of being returned to the Down Main Line at Moreton Cutting he had shut off power, but he was not returned there and he knew that the next point he could then be returned to the Down Main Line was beyond Didcot Station.

'Biggin maintained that on approaching Didcot, he shut off power and reduced speed to between 55 and 60 m.p.h. through the station, and that he made a full brake application soon after leaving the platform. He admitted that he misjudged the distance to the crossovers at Foxhall Junction and said that the locomotive traversed the first crossover at 50 m.p.h. After reaching the Down Main line, just before the train came to a stand, he looked back and saw the extent of the disaster that had occurred at the rear end of the train.'

Against this I can only quote my own statement to Major Olver. I was not able to attend the Inquiry in person, as I was abroad at the time; but this is what I wrote, and this was subsequently included in Major Olver's Report:

'On leaving Reading I noticed that we were put over on to the Relief line, and at first we were running at fairly reduced speed. I took up my work again, and it was not until we were approaching Didcot that I realised we were travelling unusually fast for the Relief line. Our speed would have been quite normal for main line, on which the alignment is, of course, perfect for high speed travel. I did not take a precise reading, but passing through Didcot station I judged the speed to be between 70 and 75 m.p.h.

'At this stage I grew very apprehensive because there was no slackening off. I did not then know the exact nature of the layout at Foxhall Junction, and in the few seconds that remained I was expecting some brake application. I am quite positive, however, that there was none, and then the coach in which I was riding—the last but one in the train—was suddenly swept to the left and all was chaos immediately afterwards.

213

'Two points stand out very clearly in my recollections of the affair:

1. There was no brake application by the time my coach took the first set of facing points.
2. There was no appreciable reduction in speed between Didcot station, where we were travelling at 70 to 75 m.p.h. and the point of derailment.

'The fact that I was so near to the end of the train would suggest that the engine and the leading vehicles had all negotiated the first crossing and part of the second crossing before any application of the brakes was made.

'After that, of course, it was impossible to know whether the brakes were being applied or not in our coach because we had lost all our wheels; in any case, an emergency application would have been made when the last coach broke clean away and turned over on its left-hand side.

'I would not be dogmatic, and assert that the driver did not apply the brake earlier; it is only that I was expecting a brake application every second after we had passed Didcot station and am confident that none came.'

A witness of this accident 'from outside' was Platform Inspector T. C. Gibbard, who was on Platform No. 5 at Didcot as the train approached. He told Major Olver that, 'He stood back from the platform edge when the train passed through the station at a speed considerably greater than normal for a train travelling on the Down Relief line. He estimated that it was travelling at about 70 m.p.h. and was certain that the brakes were not being applied as the train passed him; nor did it appear to slow down at all as it approached Foxhall Junction.

'Gibbard said he expected to see the locomotive turn over as it traversed the first crossover of the junction, but the train successfully negotiated the crossover until the last vehicle became derailed and turned very slowly on to its left-hand side.'

Major Olver comments:

'Despite Driver Biggin's and Second Man Wilson's evidence to the contrary, there is little doubt that the express passed through Didcot station at about 70 m.p.h., and that the brakes, if applied at all, were not applied until immediately before the locomotive started to traverse the first crossover. Had the former reduced the speed of the train to between 55 and 60 m.p.h. through the station and then made a full brake application soon after leaving the platform, as he stated in his evidence, the speed of the train would have fallen to 25 m.p.h. before the locomotive reached the first crossover.'

One repeats the inevitable question: Why did the driver proceed as he did? All the evidence went to show that he really did not know the road. He had learnt it, from Reading to Swindon in January 1967, travelling over it on the 3rd, 4th, 5th and 7th of that month, and signing for it on the 13th, preparatory to working this particular duty. His link at Westbury was so arranged that the drivers concerned worked the turn for one week in every 12, and from his first trip on April 7th, covering the turn for a driver on a rest day, he had worked the train on 14 occasions prior to the day of the accident. On all these runs he had been routed on the main line throughout, including the two days immediately prior to the accident; September 25th and 26th. Although he resigned his route card on July 25th, Major Olver's Inquiry showed that his knowledge of the relief line was sketchy. He had travelled over it only twice, in the cab of a diesel multiple-unit between Reading and Oxford, but had *never* travelled from Didcot to Foxhall Junction on the relief line. However, on one of the days that he travelled to Didcot he walked along the down relief line towards the junction to observe its layout. As Major Olver observes: "his knowledge of the route was insufficient for him to drive a train safely over."

After Didcot the Inspecting Officer was thus able to extract the explanation for this high speed derailment that was precluded by the deaths of the drivers concerned in the previous historic cases at Salisbury, Grantham, and Shrewsbury; but one can imagine that it would almost have needed a microscope to measure the difference between safety and total disaster at Didcot. Comment has often been made about Great Western luck in the avoidance of serious accidents, and that even in the wartime disaster at Norton Fitzwarren the chance of something infinitely worse was missed by seconds, when the newspaper train just got clear before the Penzance sleeper ran through the catch points. Never, one imagines, was Great Western, or Western Region luck more on the side of safety than on the morning of September 27th, 1967; for at such a speed it was little short of a miracle that the locomotive got through two crossovers in succession without overturning. The track layout at Foxhall Junction *had* been changed. Originally one crossed in one long sweep from the down relief to the down main, intersecting the up main immediately on a diamond crossing. In the new layout there are two crossovers, one from down relief to up main, and a second from up main to down main. The engine and the first five coaches got through safely; but by what slender margin the wheel flanges remained below the top of the rails, or by what few degrees of tilt the overturning angle was not reached, can only be a matter for conjecture. Fortunately the track was in superb condition and at the actual turnout from the down relief line it was little disturbed.

Major Olver's 'Remarks and Recommendations' fall under two broad headings, both of extreme importance in modern railway operating conditions: first, the signalling arrangements at the junction, and secondly the arrangements made for route learning by drivers. Taking the signalling first, the critical signal at the junction, R. 180, was provided strictly in accordance with the standard principles established by the British Railways Board. In this case, because the difference in maximum speeds permitted on all routes was less than 10 m.p.h. there was no approach control on the principal route. Approach control *was* provided for the routes leading into the C.E.G.B. sidings, because of special conditions obtaining just beyond the actual junction. The other factor was that in accordance with established principles the junction indications were given only for the subsidiary routes, that is, into the C.E.G.B. sidings. Major Olver felt that the application of these principles in the particular layout at Foxhall Junction could have been misleading, particularly in the case of a driver whose road knowledge was poor. He continues: '. . . a driver running along the Down Relief line and crossing to the Down Main line could receive a plain Green aspect at Signal R. 180, located about ¼ mile before the crossovers, having also received Green aspects at the previous two or more signals. Travelling beyond the signal, a driver would see facing turnouts on the track, both to left and to right, but he would also see the track carrying straight on ahead of him. In my opinion, a driver having received Green aspects through Didcot, including one at Signal R. 180, could momentarily overlook the fact that the principal route lay via the crossovers to the Down Main line, and mistake the Up Goods loop for the continuation of the Down Relief line. In this case he would see no reason to reduce speed unless he actually noticed the facing crossover in front of him set to take his train up to the Up Main line and thence to the Down Main line, by which time it would be too late to make any effective reduction in speed.'

He then adds a note of the important alteration in practice that has subsequently been made: 'The question of the signalling of diverging junctions where the principal route is not the straight route has subsequently been the subject of discussion between the Inspecting Officers of Railways and the Officers of the British Railways Board, and it has been agreed that in such cases a junction indicator should be provided for the principal route, but that the provision of an approach control is unnecessary unless the difference in speed over the diverging routes is greater than 10 m.p.h. I am satisfied that this arrangement is suitable on the Down Relief line at Foxhall Junction, where Signal R. 180 is some 365 yards from the first crossover and the sighting distance of the signal is at least ¼ mile, thus giving the driver ample braking distance to reduce his speed from the line speed of 60 m.p.h. to the 25 m.p.h. limit over the junction. However, occasions may arise where the signal may, of necessity, have to be sited nearer the junction, or the sighting distance is limited, and the provision of an approach control may then be advisable in addition to the junction indicator.'

On the subject of route learning, it was emphasised during the enquiry that a driver on being asked to learn a particular route was given as much time as he required to learn it and was not obliged to sign to acknowledge that he knew the route, including the signalling, permanent speed restrictions and limits, and other relevant matters, until he felt fully confident to drive over it. With the remodelling of the railways, however, including the large scale introduction of multiple aspect signalling, many more drivers today are required to learn new routes than in the past, when most route knowledge was acquired over a considerable number of years, when younger men were working on the footplate as firemen or 'passed cleaners', with drivers of long experience. The reorganisation of many links has resulted in the need for more drivers to learn new routes.'

In connection with the extensive track remodelling that has been carried out recently at such centres as Paddington, Reading and Cardiff, the Western Region had arranged route learning classes. These were initially to familiarise all drivers with the new track layouts and signalling in the respective station areas and immediate surroundings, but they have been continued in order to assist other drivers who are learning the routes in these areas. These classes, held during normal working hours and normally of one or two days' duration, are run by Traction Inspectors who illustrate all the various routes by means of wall charts and coloured slides showing individual signals. Drivers subsequently walk the routes in concentrated areas, such as Paddington, and ride in the cab to learn routes in more open areas. The Western Region is also equipping a single diesel power car for route learning by groups of drivers under the instruction of a Traction Inspector, who will point out the various signals, speed limits, gradients and other matters that are essential for the drivers' route learning.

Thus Didcot, a hair-raising experience for me personally, and for many others, was in the long run, a 'crowning mercy' not only that the locomotive did not overturn and thus precipitate a complete wreck of the train, but that two important facets of modern operation were highlighted. As such Didcot, though a small one from the casualty point of view, takes a definite place in this chronicle of Historic Railway Disasters.

17

Hither Green, December 1967—A Broken Rail

One of the most disconcerting things about a study of rail-way accidents is the way in which history can repeat itself in the second and third generations. The details will probably vary, but the overall pattern can be most alarmingly similar. An earlier chapter of this book deals with the derailment near Sevenoaks on August 24th, 1927, when one of the Maunsell 2-6-4 tank engines of the 'River' class left the road on the left-hand curve between Dunton Green and Seven-oaks station. The liability of those engines to roll was known in a general kind of way; but on good track they were quite steady, at speeds very much higher than that prevailing at the time of the derailment. The prime cause of the accident however was the state of the track, which the Inspecting Officer, Sir John Pringle, considered unsuitable both in ballasting and in standards of maintenance for the fast traffic and heavy locomotives it then had to bear.

The Southern Region of British Railways as successor to the Southern Railway is subject to extremely severe track usage, both in frequency and speed of trains, and from the almost universal employment of multiple unit trains for main line and local services. In these the relatively high un-sprung weight on the wheels of both electric and diesel-electric sets, that results from using axle-hung traction motors, has a far more punishing effect on the track than steam locomotives, and in his Report to the Minister of Transport on the Safety Record of the Railways in 1966 Colonel McMullen, commenting on rail-end fractures said:

'It will be noted that this category of fracture in particular is appreciably greater on lines where electric multiple-unit trains operate than on other lines, due possibly to the heavy battering which the rail ends receive from this type of traction.' This is a generally accepted view, and it certainly provides a major part of the conditions permanent way men on the Southern have to contend with, as part of their daily occupation.

Traffic on the Southern is also deeply characterised by its commuter business into and out of London in the peak hours. The trains are very heavily loaded, with a high proportion of passengers standing, yet run to quite sharp timings. Comfort of travel, as one understands it in long distance train services does not exist, and a certain amount of rough riding of the stock, in addition to the overcrowding has been accepted, if not appreciated, as the normal order of things. Some trains, and some routes were naturally worse than others in both these respects; but apart from the odd newspaper article about rough riding, the majority of passengers viewed the Southern services with an air of mild tolerance, and as a quick, rather rigorous way of getting to and from their daily work. I have mentioned the attitude of passengers prior to the tragic evening of Sunday, November 5th, 1967, because they were to play a considerable part in the events that followed.

On that evening the 7.43 p.m. express from Hastings to Charing Cross was, as usual, made up to a 12-car train, with two 6-car diesel-electric sets. These trains were specially designed for the Hastings line, over which full electrification was not considered to be justified by the traffic. Because of tight clearances in certain tunnels south of Tunbridge Wells these train sets had to be built to a reduced overall width, and there were certain other features of their design, arising from this loading gauge restriction, that were revealed subsequently. Manning arrangements on the Southern are complex, and on this turn the driver who worked the train from Hastings was relieved at Sevenoaks. The first man, E. G. Baines, had a good run up, though arriving at Sevenoaks about 4 minutes late on account of checks. Earlier in the day he had driven another train into the London Area and noticed nothing unusual about the track. He was relieved by Driver Purves, who had worked through from Hastings to Charing Cross on the 5.43 p.m. train from the former station on the same day. It had been a normal trip. On arrival he returned to Sevenoaks.

Taking over the 7.43 p.m. ex-Hastings from Driver Baines, at Sevenoaks, all went normally at first. These trains are limited to a maximum speed of 75 m.p.h., and from that speed Purves reduced to 60 m.p.h. as prescribed, for the curve through Chislehurst. After that he put on power again and rapidly accelerated to about 70 m.p.h. by the time he had entered Elmstead Woods tunnel and commenced the fairly steep descent that extends past Grove Park and Hither Green sidings to the commencement of the London Area proper. On this gradient, 1 in 120, at first and slightly easing after Grove Park, Purves shut off power and allowed the train to coast at a steady speed of about 70 m.p.h. The next few minutes are best described in his own words, as given in the Report of the Ministry of Transport Enquiry:

'Driver Purves said that when driving trains on the Up Fast line it was normal custom to apply the Westinghouse brake between Grove Park and Hither Green, "near the beginning of the concrete sleepers", and just before reaching the Continental Goods Depot, in order to reduce the speed of the train to 60 m.p.h. to comply with the restriction in the Inner London area from Hither Green onwards. On this occasion, in preparation for making this brake application, he placed the brake handle into the lap position and soon afterwards he felt a drag on the train. He thought that he might inadvertently have thrown the handle slightly into the Westinghouse position and made a small brake application so, to use his own words, he "waited for the thing to sort itself out" before making another application. In retrospect, however, he thought that he had not put the handle into the Westinghouse position and that the drag was caused by the derailed coach.'

222

'Soon afterwards, however, the drag became severe and there was much snatching until there was a severe snatch with a "terrific bang". The brake cylinder pressure gauge "shot up" to 50lb./sq. in. and the brakes came hard on, and the coach stopped a short way ahead. Purves realised that the train must have become divided but he did not realise until he looked out after stopping that the division had occurred behind his motor coach.'

Behind him a terrible wreck had occurred, and his motor coach was actually the only vehicle in the entire train that had remained on the rails. What had happened was this: the leading pair of wheels of the third coach in the train struck a small wedge-shaped piece of steel that had broken away from the end of a running rail, and those wheels, and they alone were derailed. From a subsequent examination of damage marks on the track it was established that the train ran like this for about a quarter of a mile. The derailed wheels ran parallel to and close to the rails, striking some of the concrete sleepers of the continuous welded rail existing at this location, and jumping over others until they struck the crossover of a diamond crossing 463 yd. from the point of the initial derailment. Contact with the crossover lead caused complete derailment of the third coach. It overturned on to its right-hand side and caused both the second and fourth coaches to overturn. General derailment of the rest of the train followed immediately, with severe damage to coaches two to five inclusive. There was some jack-knifing with coaches six to nine, with less severe damage, and the last three coaches remained roughly in line, though all were derailed. The casualty list was a grievously long one, 49 killed and 78 injured.

The public reaction was immediate, and although much of it was irrelevant, it was understandable enough. The general inference was that the accident had been caused by bad riding of the stock and excessive speed. Colonel McMullen, then Chief Inspecting Officer of Railways, took the enquiry himself, and both he and the Minister of Transport received a very large number of letters criticising the track, and the rolling stock used on the Hastings line trains, and suggesting that the trains ran at excessive speed. A considerable number of letters was also published in the daily press, all on the same theme. But whatever other factors may have been contributory, in varying degrees, it was quickly established that the prime cause of the accident was a broken rail, and a very great part of Colonel McMullen's enquiry was rightly devoted to establishing the cause of this fracture.

Considerable progress had been made on the Southern Region with the installation of continuous welded rail on the main lines; but on the Southern in particular, it was the practice to insert short closure rails, for convenience, where the prefabricated lengths of c.w.r. stopped short of point connections. On the up fast line, to the south of Hither Green, there is a crossover from the up slow line, and between the trailing points and the section of c.w.r. there were two closure lengths, the first 34 ft. and the second 30 ft. long. These had fishplated joints. These closures were laid in standard flat-bottomed track on concrete sleepers except for one isolated exception. At the joint between the 34 ft. and the 30 ft. closure rails the concrete sleeper at the leaving end of the 34 ft. length had cracked, and it had been replaced by an ordinary 10 in. by 5 in. wooden sleeper. The c.w.r. on the up fast line and the closure rails were laid in February 1967. At the time of relaying the ballast had been cleaned, and new limestone ballast added; but a cross-section taken after the accident shows that there was only 2 to 6 in. of clean ballast under the joint sleepers, and even this did not extend across the full width of the track, as shown in the accompanying drawing.

During the very detailed and expert examination of the track that took place after the accident it was not considered that the ballast alone had contributed to the conditions that eventually led to the fracture of the rail-end. The main contributory cause of the trouble was considered to be the replacement of the faulty concrete sleeper beneath the running-off end of the 34 ft. closure rail by a wooden one of a shallower section. However well the packing may have been

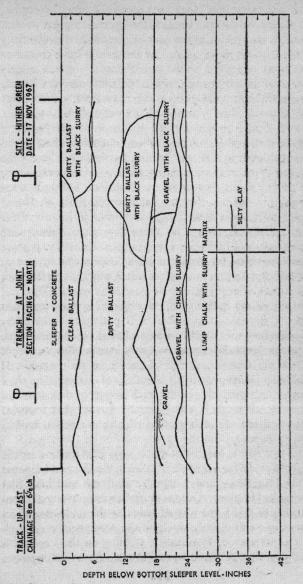

Fig. 15. Track cross-section beneath sleeper level, Hither Green derailment, November 1967.

done at the time of replacement, some differential deformation of the ballast beds beneath the concrete sleeper on one side of the rail joint and the wooden sleeper on the other had almost certainly taken place and this would have given rise to a 'pumping' action on the rail joint as a whole. The general run of the evidence did not indicate this was very severe, though in the prevailing conditions of traffic it was the principal cause of the fracturing of the rail-end. Witness after witness, from the Chief Civil Engineer of the Southern Region, downwards, referred to the 'punishing' effect of the multi-unit electric stock on the rails, particularly where there was any break in the continuity, as at points and crossings, and at rail joints. Nevertheless conditions had been considered suitable for the maximum speed limit of certain classes of train to be increased to 90 m.p.h. in July 1967. This undoubtedly had a far more damaging effect on the track than the Chief Civil Engineer and his staff expected; the deterioration was much more rapid than was envisaged, but unfortunately an insufficient watch was kept on the state of the track after the 90 m.p.h. speed limit was allowed.

So far as the design of the multiple-unit stock was concerned, with axle-hung motors it is perhaps a little extraordinary that this practice has prevailed on the Southern, despite the gradual increase, not only in maximum speed but also in the general average of passenger train speeds. It would seem that successive generations of civil engineers had accepted this punishing of the track as part of their terms of reference, although it was generally known that overseas railways made use of bogies on which the traction motors were suspended from the sprung portion of the bogie. It is also significant to recall that as long ago as in the last decade before World War I Sir John Aspinall, the General Manager of the Lancashire and Yorkshire Railway, and his Chief Mechanical Engineer, George Hughes, were actively engaged in trying to find some way of reducing the damaging effect of multiple-unit electric stock on the permanent way, from their experience of fast electric running on the Liverpool-Southport line. Aspinall was of course himself an engineer, and was probably more interested, and certainly better fitted professionally, to co-ordinate the work of the different engineering departments, when the equipment of one was having an unduly adverse effect on the equipment of another.

In his enquiry into the causes of the Hither Green accident Colonel McMullen paid close attention to the many reports of rough and dangerous riding of the stock. There are, as previously mentioned, some design considerations that affect the riding, and the following reference to this is made in the official report:

'On account of restricted clearances in tunnels on the Hastings line, the coaches on these diesel electric sets, which were built specially for use on this line, are restricted to an overall width of 8 ft. $0\frac{3}{4}$ in. In common with other stock that runs on some sections of the Southern Region where clearance difficulties obtain, the side movement at cantrail level has to be restricted to 3 in. and in order to enforce this restriction, the bogies are of a special design; they include, among other things, coned rubber stops to limit the side-to-side movement of the bolster relative to the bogie frame and which come into action when the side movement exceeds $\frac{3}{4}$ in. either way. Any track irregularity which causes the bogie to move sideways more than $\frac{3}{4}$ in. relative to the body will therefore cause sharp contact with the coned rubber stops which exert a progressively stopping action to the movement. Should the sideways movement exceed 1 in. in the case of motor bogies and $1\frac{1}{2}$ in. in the case of trailer bogies, the bolster comes into sudden contact with flat hard rubber stops and imparts a certain degree of shock to the vehicle. In particular a low rail joint will cause the bogie to turn abruptly into the joint and out again, and this will impart a sharp sideways movement to the coach body which will increase in proportion to the lowness of the joint and the speed of the train.'

Of the practical effect of these design features several passengers gave evidence, and the remarks of two of them may be quoted here:

'Mr. G. Dean, a company director, who had travelled on

227

the Hastings line periodically over a period of 10 years, joined the train at Battle. He was travelling in the fourth coach, the trailer first, of the leading set. There was only one other passenger in his compartment but he thought that the second class coaches were well filled. Mr. Dean said that up till near Hither Green it seemed a normal run but he added "on that line coaches always swayed a lot and I have always had an uneasy feeling that they were going too fast". When the train got near Hither Green his coach started to sway more than usual and there was a noise that sounded to him as if the train was running over splintered glass. The coach then started to rock very much more until suddenly there was a crash, the lights went out and the coach turned over on its right-hand, the corridor side. Mr. Dean was fortunate in being unhurt. Mr. Dean repeated that it was usual for these trains to "sway and rocket all over the place". In his opinion the train in which he was travelling was going too fast, but not faster than these trains usually travelled.'

Mr. J. C. Reitchel, Vice-Chairman of the Uckfield Rural District Council, had been a regular traveller on the Hastings line for over 30 years and had, in recent years, travelled from Wadhurst to London usually several times each week; he regularly occupied a seat in the sixth coach (motor brake second) of the train. He was not travelling on the train that became derailed but said that in his opinion and in the opinion of many other passengers with whom he travelled, the trains ran too fast. He added that there were, before the accident, some particularly bad stretches of track, near Grove Park and the site of the derailment on the Up fast line and approaching Sevenoaks on the Down Fast line, where trains swayed badly. In his opinion the swaying and speed had increased during the weeks just before the derailment.

Clearly there was an all-round disposition to blame the rolling stock as much as the permanent way, and Colonel McMullen did exactly the same as Sir John Pringle had done after the Sevenoaks derailment of August 1927, namely to carry out riding tests on a different section of railway altogether. After Sevenoaks it was of course the behaviour of the locomotive that was suspect; after Hither Green it was the entire train. In both cases however tests were carried out on the East Coast main line as well as certain sections of the Southern system. In 1927 Mr. H. N. Gresley—as he was then —acted as assessor, and he rode personally on all the locomotives under observation. In view of my earlier reference to Lancashire and Yorkshire Railway anxieties about the riding of the stock it was most interesting that Sir John Aspinall, then approaching 80 years of age, was invited to attend the trials. In 1967 Colonel McMullen asked the Director of Design, British Railways Board, to carry out the tests. These were made as follows:

2nd December, 1967	Southern Region Tonbridge-Ashford-Tonbridge-Cannon Street-Tonbridge.
6th January, 1968	Eastern Region King's Cross-Hatfield-Grantham-Hatfield-King's Cross.
7th January, 1968	Southern Region Grove Park-Tonbridge-London Bridge-Chislehurst- and also Ashford-Dover and return (three runs).

The methods of tests were not the same throughout, but varied as follows:

(i) In the test on 2nd December a portable universal vibrograph was used in two positions on a motor coach and one position on a trailer coach to record lateral and vertical accelerations at selected train speeds and locations.

(ii) In the test on the 6th and 7th January accelerometers were fitted in lateral and vertical planes in much the same positions as before and an axlebox on the trailer coach was instrumented. The signals were recorded on a multi-channel recorder.

(iii) Whereas in the December test recordings were made at only one test position at a time and for short periods of time (20 seconds) at each location, the comparative tests between

Eastern and Southern Region, in January, were arranged differently. The unit was run at different constant speeds over sections of approximately four miles of track. Several recordings were made, each of 40 seconds duration. In this way, several values of mean ride index were obtained at the same speed but on different sections of track. Average values were calculated from the band width and scatter of points.

Some explanation of the term 'ride index' is necessary, of which the values represent constant sensation values which depend upon frequency and acceleration. In this latter it is the acceleration of an oscillation, and not the acceleration of the train along the track that is referred to. The general significance of the ride index values quoted subsequently is as follows:

Ride Index	Comment
2.0	Good
2.5	Almost Good
3.0	Satisfactory
3.5	Just Satisfactory
4.0	Tolerable
4.5	Not Tolerable
5.0	Dangerous

The results obtained from the test on 2nd December were as follows:

Average ride index values for motor coach and trailer coach

	45 m.p.h.	75 m.p.h.
Lateral	2.2	3.2
Vertical	2.4	3.2

The results obtained from the tests on 6th and 7th January were as follows:

Average ride index values for motor coach and trailer coach

	Eastern Region		Southern Region	
Speed, Mile/h	45	75	45	75
Lateral:				
Main line, welded	2.0	2.8	2.8	3.5
Main line, jointed	—	—	2.8	3.4
Vertical:				
Main line, welded	2.3	2.8	2.3	3.5
Main line, jointed	—	—	2.7	3.1
Lateral:				
Suburban, jointed	2.3	—	2.2	2.7
Vertical:				
Suburban, jointed	2.6	—	2.7	3.1

The differences in the lateral ride index between the two Regions shows the index on the Eastern Region was better than on the Southern Region by 0.8/0.7 over the speed range on the main lines. There is little difference between welded and jointed track on the Southern Region. The vertical ride index is similar on both Regions on welded track at the lower speed range, but it is 0.7 greater on Southern Region at 75 m.p.h., and the index on welded track is higher than on jointed track. Both lateral and vertical ride indices are similar on both Regions on suburban lines.

Colonel McMullen comments as follows:

'The above results indicate that the set rode well on the Eastern Region, but that on the Southern Region the riding was not so good. The index of 3.5 on the Southern Region is completely acceptable from a safety point of view, and having regard to the age of the stock, it is acceptable from the passenger comfort point of view, though the riding could not be described as really comfortable. Even bearing in mind the different nature and configuration of the Eastern Region and Southern Region main lines over which the tests were conducted, the results indicate that the condition of the track on the Southern Region is significantly inferior to that of the Eastern Region main line. The difference was particularly noticeable on c.w.r. and when running over points and crossings.'

231

This was the conclusion reached also in the 1927 trials, when the unfortunate 'River' class 2-6-4 tank engines gave an impeccable ride on the East Coast main line, taking the succession of reverse curves near Offord at speeds of around 80 m.p.h. to Gresley's entire satisfaction. So far as the Hastings line diesel-electric multiple-unit trains are concerned, Colonel McMullen summarises the position thus:

'Regarding the riding qualities of the Hastings line rolling stock, the test run on the East Coast main line of the Eastern Region by a random unit, not specially prepared, that had run 50,000 miles since its last overhaul, indicated that the ride was, from the accepted classification better than "satisfactory"; for stock designed and built over ten years ago I consider that this is creditable. I was in the train and found that the ride was comfortable and reading was easy. The riding of this stock on the Southern Region was not so good, from the comfort point of view, and the reason for this is the reaction of the bogies, which are specially designed for these trains and other electric multiple-unit trains to meet the clearance difficulties on the Region, to unfavourable track conditions. From the safety point of view, however, the riding qualities are well within the acceptable limits. All units of the Hastings line trains are fitted with the same type of bogie which is known as the Mark IV. The axle loads of the traction bogies of the motor coaches are much the same as those of motored axles of electric multiple-unit stock, though the axle loads on the other bogie that supports the weight of the generator, which is fully sprung, are higher.'

After Sevenoaks both locomotives and track came in for equal share of blame, and Sir Herbert Walker issued the most far-reaching directives to both departments. In 1968 the train-sets were exonerated so far as riding was concerned and all the blame was put on the track. But the design characteristics of the multiple-unit stock used on the Southern are another issue altogether, and the criticism of them in the official report raises a problem the solution of which may take many years to attain.

18

Hixon Level Crossing, January 1968

The frequent incidence of level crossings on the railways of
Britain has been a perennial source of danger, though with
the various forms in use until recent years—gated and fully
interlocked, gated and hand-worked with warning signals,
and the 'occupation' or farm crossing—accidents involving
appreciable loss of life have been relatively few. Cases have
occurred when vehicles have accidently crashed the gates,
and burst on to the line of railway in the path of an oncoming train, and others have occurred at occupation crossings.
In the great majority of cases the principal victims were the
road users, except where the obstruction suddenly imping-
ing upon the line was such as to derail the train. None of
these incidents reached major accident, let alone disaster
proportions. There had been nothing to compare with the
terrible accident that occurred at Hixon crossing, Staffordshire, on Saturday, January 6th, 1968. The circumstances
were so unprecedented, the crash itself so violent and the
reaction from both the public and the press revealing so
much confusion of thought that on January 16th, 1968, an
Order was made under Section 7 of the Railways Act, 1871,
for a formal inquiry to be made, the findings of which were
required to be presented to Parliament by the Minister of
Transport.

The new factor, that led to so much public concern, was
that this appalling accident took place at a crossing recently
equipped with automatic half-barriers. The whole question
of the introduction of this type of level crossing protection
was raised, and the Report submitted in due course to Par-

liament most succinctly reviewed the circumstances. It re-called the decision of the Ministry of Transport and British Railways to send a joint working party, under the leadership of Colonel McMullen, to make a close study of continental level crossing protection methods, in particular visiting France, Holland and Belgium. That was in 1956, at which time the late Colonel G. R. S. Wilson was Chief Inspecting Officer of Railways. The terms of reference of that working party are clearly defined in a letter from Colonel Wilson to Colonel McMullen on September 25th, 1956:

'Before you leave for the Continent I feel that it may be helpful to the party and their work for me to recapitulate very briefly the considerations which have led to the arrangement of this visit to study problems in connection with the design and working of lifting barriers at public road level crossings.

'First of all I should say that there is no doubt in anyone's mind of the very high standard of safety to road and rail traffic which has been maintained over the years at our public level crossings with their alternatively closing swinging gates worked by gatekeepers or signalmen on the spot. The wisdom of Parliament in insisting on this form of protection by legislation in the early days has thus been well proved in practice, and if it were only a question of safety we should be content to leave things as they are. The cost of providing attendants has, however, risen very greatly in recent years, and in some cases as much as ten-fold, and furthermore there are growing difficulties in finding reliable men to act as gatekeepers, particularly at relief periods, as some recent accidents have shown. The only solution to these present-day problems is to take full advantage of modern technical developments, as is so often done in other spheres.

'Some years ago the railways began to consider the simple substitution of lifting barriers for the conventional swinging gates as a better engineering proposition . . . and an experimental installation has now been in use for some time at Warthill in the North Eastern Region, with the barriers

234

worked from an adjacent signal box and interlocked with the railway signals. . . .

'Only minor economies can result from the mere substitution of lifting barriers for swinging gates, but with lifting barriers, remote or automatic control without attendants at the barriers becomes practical technically, and the latter type of working has been developed extensively on the Continent and in the U.S.A. The British Transport Commission are therefore anxious to experiment on these lines for British Railways in order to save considerable expenditure, particularly at rural level crossings where the wages which have to be paid are altogether disproportionate to the amount of work a man has to do. It is the Minister's wish that the Commission should be encouraged in this direction.'

This letter reveals that cuts in working expenditure were among the principal objects of the exercise, though of course it was equally understood that any change in practice should not affect, in any way whatever, the safety precautions taken for the working of both railway and road traffic.

The working party returned convinced that automatic and remotely controlled systems might be employed at certain selected crossings after exhaustive tests, and they continued their report thus:

'We recognise the necessity for a fundamental change in outlook as to the purpose of protection at level crossings. The type of heavy wooden gate which has been in use for over 100 years was intended to be, and in fact was, a completely effective obstacle to the horse-drawn road vehicle. The situation has changed with the advent of the modern powered road vehicle which can easily break through such a gate, and its value, therefore, as an obstacle to vehicle movement when closed against the road lies primarily in its conspicuousness. This characteristic can be fully achieved with a barrier of suitable construction, especially when it is equipped with modern reflecting material. . . . The barrier can be of light construction, and as it is mechanically more efficient than the gate it can be operated more easily and more quickly. . . .

'We have not overlooked the safety of the pedestrian, although we feel that their attitude to the level crossing requires to be changed. The belief that pedestrians and particularly children must be afforded full protection against the dangers of the line is nowadays illogical. There are many level crossings where adults and children already have free access to the railway, *viz.* public level crossings with controlled gates but uncontrolled wickets, footpaths and accommodation and occupation crossings with wicket gates or stiles. Crossings of these types exist on the most important main lines and also on lines electrified with the third rail system. Furthermore, the dangers to which pedestrians are exposed on the roads are at least as great and certainly more frequent than those at level crossings.

'With the introduction of lifting barriers at level crossings, and in particular if automatic half-barriers are to be adopted, the principle must be recognised that it is the responsibility of the individual to protect himself from the hazards of the railway in the same way as from the hazards of the road....'

Before anything could be done however Parliamentary sanction had to be obtained to permit the use of automatic barriers instead of gated crossings, and a clause was accordingly inserted in the British Transport Commission Bill of 1957. The Bill was passed, and the first steps were taken to implement the authority duly provided. With characteristic British caution in approaching so revolutionary a development in railway practice the 'Provisional Requirements', published on May 1st, 1958, laid down the principle that automatic half-barrier crossings would be permitted only at crossings where the daily motor traffic (excluding motor bicycles) did not exceed 1,000 vehicles, and where the maximum speed of trains did not exceed 60 m.p.h. These requirements were far more restrictive than anything in practice on the continent of Europe and by the end of 1961 only two automatic crossings had been brought into use on British Railways. It is of interest to recall that the very first, installed in February 1961, at Spath was a little to the north of Uttoxeter, on the branch line that subsequently forks left for the

Churnet Valley, and right for Buxton. As the crow flies this pioneer installation is only eight miles from Hixon.

The conditions laid down in the 'Provisional Requirements' were in fact making things so restrictive as virtually to defeat the object of the new legislation, and as a result of visits to the U.S.A. and Canada by Colonel McMullen in 1961, and by another joint working party in 1963 led by Colonel Reed, the restrictions hitherto imposed were greatly eased—particularly in regard to the speed and frequency of trains. It was henceforth laid down that neither the speed nor the frequency of trains should be a limiting factor, provided,

(a) that the difference in time between the fastest and slowest train reaching the crossing after the warning should not be more than 40 sec., and

(b) that road traffic could clear readily between train movements. As a result of this relaxation no fewer than 207 crossings had been equipped by the time of the Hixon accident. It is interesting at this stage to study an analysis of equipment at all level crossings on British Railways at this same time, thus:

Crossings with signal protection:	
Crossings operated from a signal box	954
Crossings operated by a keeper with interlocked signals	453
	1,407
Crossings not protected by signals:	
Crossings operated by a keeper, no interlocking signals	514
Automatic crossings	207
Other crossings	297
	1,018

The general working of half barrier automatic crossings

must be known, in general terms, to a considerable number of motorists and other road users: but it is to be feared that many of these will not read the leaflets issued at the time each crossing so equipped was commissioned.

A tremendous amount of study and careful thought had been put into the drafting of the regulations for use of automatic half-barrier crossings, by the Ministry of Transport, both from the railway and the road users point of view. In November 1963, in particular, a copy of the Regulations and an Explanatory Note had been sent from the Home Office to the Chief Constable of Staffordshire, and in August 1966 the Revised Requirements, and Explanatory Note were similarly issued. The Public Enquiry revealed that neither the Chief Constable, nor any of his senior officers studied these requirements, and no one on the Police staff realised there was a hazard in the working of these half-barrier crossings.

The report of the Public Enquiry contains this trenchant paragraph:

'143. Further, leaflets relating to each new automatic crossing were sent to the County Police Headquarters by British Railways and sent to local police stations, but there was no suggestion that the police officers should study them. They were, like other publicity leaflets, put in the public part of the local police station for any member of the public to take, and a police officer would read one only if, in an idle moment, he glanced at the loose literature lying about. The British Railways' local publicity pamphlets had taken effect in the schools of the district for whom it was primarily intended but, in the police stations, it was mere flotsam.'

While the Ministry of Transport, in the departments concerned had been most diligent in drawing up the Regulations, there was another factor which had a vital bearing on the case. I quote a paragraph, 182, from the Report:

'At the opening of the Inquiry, Mr. Nigel Bridge, counsel for the Ministry of Transport, defining the attitude of the Ministry on this respect of the matter, said:

'. . . Before this accident the Ministry, as such, had never

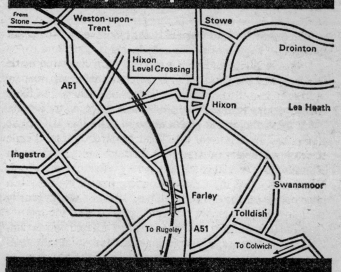

Fig. 16. Front cover of the Hixon pamphlet; the upper portion background was bright red.

specifically focused its attention upon the slow vehicle hazard. . . . Although it may well have been present to the mind of individual people in the Ministry, there is nothing to show it was present in the minds of individuals that half-barrier automatic crossings presented a hazard to slow-moving vehicles. Over the period of years during which these crossings have been developed, it does not appear, from the extensive researches undertaken by those instructing me, that this specific problem was ever raised in any Minute, in any Report or Memorandum, or in discussion between the various divisions of the Ministry which might have been concerned. If it had been, then it might have led, and very probably would have led, to the taking, before this accident, of the additional steps which, as I am going to tell you shortly, have been taken since the accident.'

The circumstances of the disaster at Hixon are briefly told. At 8.15 on the fatal morning the police at Stafford were advised that the load was ready for escort. And what a load it was! A huge transporter vehicle 148 ft. long, and owned by Robert Wynn and Sons Ltd., had been chartered by the English Electric Co. Ltd. to convey a transformer weighing 120 tons to a disused airfield. This is adjacent to the North Staffordshire Railway main line from Stoke to its junction with the London and North Western main line at Colwich. This was an abnormal load, and required a special order from the Ministry of Transport. Because of its abnormality, it required a special route, and a very circuitous one at that. Wynn's notified the County Council, British Railways and the police on the 29th December, 1967, of the impending journey, but it was not until the actual day of the trip that Police Headquarters was 'phoned to be advised that the load was ready to leave. Thus the constables providing the escort had very little notice of the journey or of the nature of the load. They had never been to Hixon before; neither had the driver of the transporter. This latter, Groves by name, asked J. H. Preston, Chief of Heavy Transport at English Electric, Stafford, the way to the disused airfield. He was told then when travelling along the A.51 road he should turn left, where guided by the police, go over the level crossing, and into the depot.

The 32-wheeled trailer, with its own steering cabin and impelled by a tractor at each end duly turned from the A.51 road and entered Station Road. One of the escorting constables told the driver to stop while he went ahead to find out the exact location of the English Electric depot on the disused airfield. The constable went over the level crossing, made his reconnaissance, and came back to tell Mr. Groves, the driver, 'this is the place'. He also told him of a hump in the road at the level crossing, and of the headroom restriction beneath the overhead electric wires. Then the cavalcade restarted. The police car went very slowly over the crossing followed, at 2 m.p.h. by the 'monstrous and complex equipage' . . . to quote the Report of the Public Enquiry. Its gross weight was no less than 162 tons, and it was manned by a crew of five. No one, neither crew nor police paused to consider whether the passage of a train might be imminent. No one was aware of the provision of a telephone at the crossing, whereby they could have asked the signalman if a train was due. They entered upon the crossing, and very slowly drew this terrible obstruction on to the main line.

No railway enthusiast needs to be told of the speeds attained by the London Midland electrically hauled express trains, and on January 6th, 1968, the 11.30 a.m. from Manchester to Euston was no exception. What the speed was when the driver sighted the obstruction can only be guessed, but the Report states that the actual collision took place at about 75 m.p.h. The results were ghastly enough in all conscience, but they might have been much worse. The total tare weight of the locomotive and the 12 coaches was 491 tons, and its terrific momentum cut the transporter clean in half, and hurled the 120-ton transformer out of the way. The locomotive, No. E 3009, though terribly damaged and with all three men in its cab killed, was scarcely deflected from its path and came to rest with its front about 300 ft. beyond the point of collision, and only slightly slewed from the straight. The way the coaching stock stood up to the impact, and extremely sudden stop was amazing. The leading van, and the three following coaches were all considerably smashed up; but the fifth and sixth coaches were no more than slightly jack-knifed and the remaining six remained more or less in line. That the casualty list in the train amounted to no more than 8 killed and 44 injured was astonishing in the circumstances, and provides a resounding tribute to the construction features of modern British rolling stock.

Little remains to be added. I can only quote certain paragraphs from the Report of the Public Enquiry, which put the matter in such clarity as to admit of no possible misconception:

'210. The real cause of the disaster was ignorance, born of lack of imagination and foresight at the sources where one would expect to find them. It is an odious task to criticise anyone unfavourably for having failed to foresee a danger, when many intelligent minds and experienced and talented people have conscientiously considered the same problem before the danger manifested itself, yet failed to appreciate it. The civil law of England tests negligence objectively upon the basis of the foresight of the "Reasonable man" (who in theory never suffers from an inexplicable oversight) but I think it is appropriate in this instance to adopt a more subjective approach lest able men of integrity be unfairly blamed for incompetence. A subjective judgment is, however, the more difficult to make, for it requires one to put oneself imaginatively in the place of the person to be judged at the time of the events.

'211. The actors on the scene of the accident in Station Road, Hixon, were mainly victims of shortcomings at more responsible levels. The essential facts which Mr. Groves and the police officers ought to have known was the need for the driver of an abnormal load always to use the telephone before attempting to cross the line. Without a telephone at Hixon, there would have been only the alternatives of asking the police to radio to police headquarters for advice, or of taking the vehicle across in the hope that British Railways had attended to the safety measures.'

'212. Mr. Groves did not know, and never had the means of knowing, that he might have only 24 seconds to get his enormous equipage over the railway; but he knew that half-barrier crossings were automatically operated by approaching trains, and he probably had read that they worked more rapidly than the traditional kind. His task required a great deal more thought and perception than driving a car. I have come to the conclusion that Mr. Groves did not think what he was doing when he negotiated the crossing. If he had thought about the matter when he realised that he was approaching a new automatic level-crossing, instead of basking in the shadow of the police escort he might have re-called that its operation was rapid and he would at least have paused to seek advice before launching his huge vehicle across the railway. A driver of such experience as he had of heavy haulage ought not to have risked, as he did, becoming immobilised across the railway for an indefinite time. More-over, he thought to have instructed his statutory attendant, Mr. Parsons, to look out for signs and notices and either he himself or Mr. Parsons ought to have observed and obeyed the Emergency Notice. On the other hand, he had not the foreknowledge that there might be a notice, other than a traffic sign, which governed his behaviour at the crossing.'

'215. The principal responsibility for Mr. Groves' failure to use the telephone to obtain permission to cross the rail-way immediately before the accident lies upon his em-ployers, Robert Wynn and Sons Ltd. The directors of that Company were aware of the introduction of automatic crossings into Britain, and ought to have been inquisitive to discover how the new automation affected their business. It is true that others, such as Pickfords Limited appear to have been no more inquisitive or perceptive than they, but Robert Wynn and Sons Ltd. had an advantage that no others, in the trade or even in the Ministry, had: in November 1966 the near-catastrophe at the level-crossing at Leominster had brought home to them the exceedingly short time which their large vehicles would have for traversing an automatic cross-ing and yet, though this had occurred in their own business they gave no real thought to the problem because they were annoyed by the tone of the letter received from British Railways. They gave no warning or information at all to their drivers, even of the foreseen risk of stalling, and continued to rely on their principle that their experienced drivers should be left to deal with all hazards of the road themselves, even though this was an invisible hazard which had taken the directors (themselves with long experience of the highways) by surprise. They ought to have made immediate enquiries, discovered the object of the telephone, and put a caution on all their special order and general order movement routes. In my opinion, the default of the directors of Robert Wynn and Sons Ltd. was the principal factor contributing to the disaster.'

In its concluding passages the Report has these paragraphs:

'222. I am satisfied that within the Ministry it was known from early in 1964 that there was a problem in regard to the use of automatic crossings by slow-moving vehicles, and that some time later it was appreciated that abnormal special order vehicles were the kind of vehicles which could cause such a problem. I do not accept that all officers of the Ministry were thinking only of agricultural vehicles; but, having thought of the problem, they did not clearly realise that it presented a grave danger. It was never discussed between the various departments not with British Railways and never as a special problem in the Railway Inspectorate. Mr. Holland, in charge of the Route Section, got nearest to the point when considering whether automatic crossings should be notified as cautions on special order routes, but established precedent dimmed the vision.

'223. It seems astonishing that, though so many talented and thoughtful men had the full facts in their minds, the essence of the matter did not occur to any of them. For that reason, it is most important to keep the problem in its proper perspective. There are 13,000,000 registered road vehicles in Britain but only a few abnormal indivisible loads: in 1967 there were 850 special order journeys, representing a vehicle mileage of 30,000 miles, whereas the total vehicle mileage of all road traffic is estimated at 100,000 million vehicle miles. Moreover, most special order vehicles, even of the length and weight of the transporter involved in the accident at Hixon, have a normal travelling speed of about 10 miles per hour, which would allow ample time for it to traverse the crossing before the arrival of a train. Most commercial vehicles nowadays travel at almost the speed of private motor cars; but assuming, for example, that a vehicle is travelling a crossing at only 14 miles per hour, and the lights begin to flash as it is crossing the stop line, it will not only have cleared the crossing but will be 150 yards away on the further side before the train arrives. Such were the considerations which the officers of the Ministry had in mind; no one directed his mind to the possibility of a vehicle moving at walking speed.'

'224. Despite such considerations, I think failure to appreciate the problem was due to a wrong approach in two ways. Firstly, the officers of the Ministry relied too much on statistics. For instance, the risk of a vehicle stalling on a crossing, rather than anywhere else on the 200,000 miles of roads in Britain, was accepted as very remote because it is statistically minute. But, of course, there are many reasons why vehicles may stall on crossings, and not elsewhere, such as panic on the part of the driver when bells suddenly ring, grounding, starting from the stop line in the wrong gear, etc. Likewise, most drivers slow down over level-crossings, especially if there are problems of clearance or where (unlike at Hixon) a heavy vehicle is going uphill.'

Then finally:

'230. When the Ministry and British Railways decided that the responsibility for safety at level-crossings should be transferred from the Railways to the public on the road, it behoved them to make sure that the public knew of that change and knew what they had to do. There can be no doubt that, in collaboration with the Railways, Mr. Scott-Malden and the officers of the Railway Inspectorate gave the most conscientious and careful thought to all questions of safety at these new level-crossings and it is, therefore, tragic that the proper way of dealing with and eliminating the comparatively infrequent hazard of the slow-moving abnormal vehicle escaped them. Such oversights may be inexplicable, but they are not unknown. Therein lay the origin of an accident which was both foreseeable and avoidable.'

It is indeed a poignant commentary upon the casual way in which innovations are regarded, both by the authorities concerned and by the general public that it seems to need a terrible accident to alert everyone to the full implications of that new facility. Just as the dangers of working with permissive block and non-automatic brakes were glossed over until there occurred the tragedy of Armagh, in 1889, so it was at Hixon. What Armagh did for the absolute block system, and for continuous automatic brakes, Hixon has done for the automatic half-barrier type of level crossing.

Appendix: A Note on the Railway Inspectorate

In the foregoing chapters reference is frequently made to the Inspecting Officers of the Board of Trade, and since 1921 of the Ministry of Transport, who have had the very difficult tasks of conducting enquiries into accidents and of ascertaining the precise cause of them. It has been, no less, their duty to recommend measures that would avoid such accidents in future. The qualities demanded of the Inspecting Officers are exceptional, combining those of penetrating enquiry, tact, humanity, and an all-round knowledge of railway engineering and operating practice. From the inception of the Inspectorate, in 1840, when Lt.-Col. Sir Frederick Smith was appointed as the first Inspector General of Railways, these officers have all been drawn from the Corps of Royal Engineers.

From the very nature of the tasks allotted to them these Inspecting Officers have included in their company some remarkable men, and apart from those like Lt.-Col. E. Druitt, who had the terrible job of conducting the enquiry into Quintinshill, or Lt.-Col. G. R. S. Wilson, who had that catastrophe of recent memory, Harrow, there were others who made a great contribution to the safe working of railways. In acknowledging my thanks to the present Chief Inspecting Officer, Col. D. McMullen, for his help in providing photographs of some of the more outstanding of his predecessors I would like also to add some notes about certain of the Inspecting Officers that lie a little outside the general theme of this book, if only to show what manner of men they were.

There was Col. W. Yolland, for example, who in one single action established a great principle in railway signalling safety precautions. Some interlocking had been asked for between the signals for a diverging route at Kentish Town Junction, North London Railway. The engineer concerned had designed a stirrup arrangement, whereby the branch line signal could not be lowered if the main line signal was already cleared. The converse also held true. This was demonstrated to the gallant Colonel, who agreed that it worked perfectly. Then he stepped forward, and carefully manoeuvred his foot into both stirrups, and lowered both signals simultaneously! In so doing he demonstrated the importance of providing against the unexpected, or the chance of a man, in the hurry of a moment, making some movement out of sequence.

Captain Douglas Galton was an Inspecting Officer for a relatively short time, 1850-1857; but subsequently he achieved a great reputation in connection with the development of continuous automatic brakes. Even with all the knowledge of braking that has been amassed since, the Galton-Westinghouse trials conducted in 1878 on the London Brighton and South Coast Railway, in collaboration with William Stroudley, and the papers that Galton afterwards read before the Institution of Mechanical Engineers remain classics of railway engineering practice and literature; for it was in those trials that it was first demonstrated that during a brake application the coefficient of friction between the wheels and the brake blocks varied with the speed of the train. It is this fact that forms the basic principle of some of the more recent developments in braking for very high speed trains.

Major-General C. S. Hutchinson, who conducted the enquiry into the Armagh disaster, in 1889, was the younger brother of Lieut. Hutchinson, R.E., who achieved distinction for his work in demolishing the Round Down cliff, by explosives, when Sir William Cubitt was building the South

Eastern Railway through the chalk cliffs between Folkestone and Dover. Following intense public anxiety after the fall of the first Tay Bridge, General Hutchinson had the task of carrying out quarterly inspections of the progress of the work in constructing the Forth Bridge, between 1882 and its opening in 1891. This was the only instance of the Board of Trade carrying out official inspections during the course of a railway constructional work, though in recent years informal visits have been paid to works such as the new Woodhead Tunnel, and the Victoria Line tube now in course of construction.

A remarkable instance of the prestige of the British railway inspectorate took place in 1936 when the Government of India invited the Chief Inspecting Officer of Railways, Lt.-Col. A. H. L. Mount (afterwards Sir Alan Mount) to become Chairman of a Committee of Enquiry into the standard Pacific locomotives of the Indian Railways, following the terrible accident on the East Indian Railway, at Bihta, in which over 100 people were killed.

But in my very pleasant contacts with the present Chief Inspecting Officer, and his colleagues, some interesting sidelights have been thrown upon other facets of the characters of these men. Some indeed played as hard as they worked. Lt.-Col. P. G. Von Donop, who held the older title of 'Inspector General of Railways' had the distinction of playing in the Royal Engineers team that won the Football Association Cup in 1875. Furthermore, in addition to winning the Cup that year the Royal Engineers' team reached the final in 1874, and the Captain of the side that year was Major Marindin who later, as Colonel Sir Francis Marindin, was Chief Inspecting Officer from 1895-1899. Marindin, who, as Brigade Major of the School of Military Engineering at the time, was undoubtedly behind the contemporary upsurge of Sapper Soccer; he was later President of the Football Association for many years. The 1874 team also included Von Donop and, to stretch the coincidence still further, it also included a Lt. Addison who later, as Lt.-Col.

G. W. Addison, was an Inspecting Officer, first alongside and then under Marindin from 1894-1899. Von Donop became an Inspecting Officer in 1899, and thus in that year the Railway Inspectorate included three men who had played together in the final of the F.A. Cup.

Index

252

If you would like a complete list of Arrow books
please send a postcard to
P.O. Box 29, Douglas, Isle of Man, Great Britain.